A
TYRANNY
FOR THE
GOOD
OF ITS
VICTIMS

A TYRANNY FOR THE GOOD OF ITS VICTIMS

*The Ugly Truth about
Stakeholder Capitalism*

ANDREW F. PUZDER

BOOKS

New York • London

First American edition published in 2024 by Encounter Books, an activity of Encounter for Culture and Education, Inc., a nonprofit, tax exempt corporation. Encounter Books website address: www.encounterbooks.com

Manufactured in the United States and printed on acid-free paper. The paper used in this publication meets the minimum requirements of ANSI/NISO Z39.48–1992 (R 1997) (*Permanence of Paper*).

FIRST AMERICAN EDITION

LIBRARY OF CONGRESS CATALOGING-IN-PUBLICATION DATA IS AVAILABLE

Information for this title can be found at the Library of Congress website under the following ISBN 9781641774154 and LCCN 2024045463.

TABLE OF

CONTENTS

This book is dedicated
to the memory of

Milton Friedman

1912–2006

*"Underlying most arguments against the free market is a lack
of belief in freedom itself."*[1]

FOREWORD

by Art Laffer

Andy Puzder, Andy Puzder—who is he?

Well, he's been a trial lawyer representing all sorts of people including the St. Louis police retirement system. He's an entrepreneur who managed a private equity takeover of a collapsing legendary fast-food chain—Carl's Jr.

As a professor at U.S.C. (the real one), I had been close to Carl Karcher, who started the Carl's Jr. quick-service restaurant company. In fact, Carl Karcher had asked me to be on his company's board of directors billions of years ago. At the time, it made no sense for me to do it, what with the Reagan ascendancy and my role in it. But I loved the chain, stopping twice every weekend at my favorite Carl's Jr. in Orange County off the 405 Freeway for my double bacon cheeseburger on my way back and forth between my home in Rolling Hills and weekend home in Rancho Santa Fe. Never, ever missed.

Later on, Andy inspired the greatest fast-food TV ad of all time—a gorgeous California surfer girl chomping down on a Carl's Jr. double bacon cheeseburger with that special sauce dripping down. We became great friends based on our shared worldview, which somehow emerged when he, as a lawyer for the plaintiffs, deposed me as an expert witness for the defense. That's weird enough, but it gets weirder. The case went to trial, and when I was on the witness stand, the judge very sternly admonished Andy, saying, "You aren't going to challenge Dr. Laffer's qualification in my court." Somewhat shaken, Andy politely explained that he had had no intention of doing so, and we proceeded. The judge was Stephen Limbaugh—Rush Limbaugh's cousin. I love retelling this story, especially when Andy is within earshot.

Since then, Andy and I have separately worked for the same causes—once sharing the scariest ride ever in his car up to Rancho del Cielo on Refugio Road. I also claim credit for his move to Nashville, Tennessee, from Southern California—taxes really do matter. Andy was a great supporter of my son-in-law's successful effort for the state senate in Michigan and my temporarily postponed attempt to reform Tennessee's property tax laws.

There was also the funniest damn thing I'd ever heard of, if it hadn't been so serious, when Andy's confirmation as secretary of labor was bogged down by silly accusations of plagiarism. They (and you know who I mean) said he had plagiarized—from me, no less—in his book. The same book where I had actually written the foreword. Huh?

Andy's book was great, Andy is great, and his practical knowledge of business, law, and economics is nothing short of amazing. His stories about how franchise owners develop equipment and procedures to replace minimum-wage workers when the minimum wage goes up are eye-popping. With higher minimum wages, franchise owners use higher-paid workers to replace those most in need of jobs. They develop hamburger-flipping machines, touchscreen menus for drive-throughs, and so on.

I remember vividly how it took only two months for grape farmers to develop grape-picking machines after Cesar Chavez unionized California's grape pickers. In all of these cases, the hammer fell hardest on the most vulnerable and those most in need of a job—minimum-wage workers—the less educated, minorities, and the poor.

Andy's research is an object lesson on what not to do, and he always points the way on what should be done. His concern is, and as long as I've known him always has been, the well-being and future of those trying to improve their lot in life. To Andy, the best form of welfare is a good high-paying job.

Read on, my friend. You'll just love this book written by a person who really knows of what he writes.

This book is an effort to make clear the threat that "stakeholder capitalism" and the ESG agenda pose to free-market capitalism and the democratic elements of our republican form of government. Andy refers to stakeholder capitalism as socialism in sheep's clothing and to ESG as the champagne-socialist agenda.

Andy lays out what the supposedly passive-investing Big Three—BlackRock, State Street (SSGA), and Vanguard—have done to advance the ESG agenda. He traces the rise of "the Resistance," a grassroots movement that opposes stakeholder capitalism and ESG—which is something Andy has been involved in from the start.

Based on President Reagan's theory that it's amazing what you can accomplish if you don't care who gets the credit, in chapters 7 and 8 Andy downplays his role in the rise of the Resistance. In Chapter 7, Andy describes how he was involved in an online debate on the subject in the summer of 2020 with Patrick Deneen from Notre Dame and published a *Wall Street Journal* op-ed "Biden's Assault on 'Shareholder Capitalism,'" about stakeholder capitalism that August based on what he had learned in that debate. Andy also drafted the State Fiduciary Duty legislation that ALEC and Heritage adopted as model legislation, versions of which a number of states have passed. Andy was way ahead of the pack in becoming vocal on this issue.

A central point of Andy's book is that one of the great market innovations of the last half-century has found itself co-opted by financial elites with a progressive political agenda in mind. In the old days, before index funds, stockholders voted on a company's governance matters. Today, given the ubiquity of index-fund investing, a significant portion of the owners of companies—the masses in 401(k)s, for example—own shares, in index funds, but rarely if ever vote those shares. The custodian of the shares, the investment intermediary, votes their shares at the company level.

What a world of witchcraft this separation of ownership from fiduciary duty invites. The Big Three, who are mere custodians, are acting like majority owners of the companies whose stocks they hold in trust for others. It has been the executives of the Big Three who have pressured companies to skimp on the quality of their products and operations in favor of poorly formulated diversity goals and tried to save the earth by harassing oil companies. The Trump administration did a very good opening job, as Andy relates, forcing stock custodians to remember that their first fiduciary responsibility resides in the performance of the assets of their clients.

A wonderful—if maddening—story is that of Silicon Valley Bank. For all the press the SVB failure got two years ago, Andy reveals what really went on. Andy rips the Band-Aid off that one. This fancy California bank got so enamored of diversity requirements for its board and staff that it forgot about risk-management and assessment officers—for its own balance sheet! The term structure of the bank's assets went upside down when interest rates rose. All it would have ever taken was Bank Management 101 for SVB to have a proper strategy on term structure. Surely SVB could have unwound its low-interest-paying asset position early (as innumerable other institutions did)—but SVB had devoted inordinate attention to ESG, as opposed to managing its own black-letter affairs. Who knew that diversity mania had felled SVB!

Andy warns us that even though ESG has been bopped on the head in the last year or two by public opinion—the mania for it seemed unstoppable five years ago—we should not for a second think that it has passed from the scene. It is busy reconfiguring itself in new garb, trying to fake its way back into the good graces of a public that has grown skeptical of it. Remain vigilant, Andy warns. Know that the separation of profit from corporate goals and strategy continues apace, and can only spell misfortune for the nation.

Andy praises the famous Angus Maddison "hockey stick" graph showing how much the world grew, in terms of economic output, once the Industrial Revolution hit in 1800. The increase was absolutely incredible, much greater than even the gigantic increase in population. This, Andy says, is what we risk in getting cute and unserious about profitability. The very prosperity of billions of people came from focusing on making profits in business to the exclusion of other more secondary concerns. He quotes Ben Franklin, worried that in the United States we have "a republic" only if we "can keep it." Our profound capacity to produce material well-being is threatened by the ESG onslaught. We are fortunate to have this seasoned executive and gripping writer illuminate our imperative task—to face down ESG in the name of ever greater prosperity for all.

INTRODUCTION

"The issue today is the same as it has been throughout all history, whether man shall be allowed to govern himself or be ruled by a small elite."

— attributed to Thomas Jefferson[1]

U p until a few years ago, few people had heard of stakeholder capitalism, "environmental, social and governance" investing, or its acronym "ESG." Even fewer understood that stakeholder capitalism is an economic system controlled by a small group of elites and that ESG is their social-justice, radical-environmentalist agenda. So before we really understood what they were doing, these elites were able to insidiously advance stakeholder capitalism and ESG to the point where they became pervasive and negative influences in our economy, our politics, and our lives.

In fairness, nothing in these phrases sounded any obvious warning bells. The Left is quite good at hiding what it is doing behind innocuous-sounding phrases. Even what they call themselves keeps changing once people realize what they actually support— Marxists, Communists, Socialists, Progressives, Globalists. The Left's names and tactics may change, but their objectives never do.

As with its collectivist predecessors, so-called "stakeholder capitalism" would empower a small group of elites to dictate our nation's social and political policy, all in the name of protecting the masses—because those elites do not trust us to make

1

decisions for ourselves, our nation, or our planet that are consistent with their values.

Stakeholder capitalism is socialism in sheep's clothing, an economic system based on collectivist ideology that these elites envision supplanting free-market capitalism—an economic system that has created the greatest wealth in human history, lifting billions of people out of poverty.

Rather than a free-market economy responsive to consumer demand, focused on individual opportunity, business success, and returns for investors, these elites prefer to focus on their social-justice, radical-environmentalist ESG agenda—purportedly to benefit an amorphous group of unidentified "stakeholders." These non-investor stakeholders are said to include a business's consumers, employees, suppliers, and the communities in which it does business; in reality, they are merely a proxy for society.

The ESG agenda attempts to turn elitist social-justice and radical-environmentalist goals into moral imperatives these elites have to impose on society for its own good, whether society wants them to or not. ESG is a ruse designed to mask an agenda only elites could afford, a champagne socialism that would devastate the world's poor and impoverish the working and middle classes globally.

Investment firms BlackRock, State Street, and Vanguard (the Big Three) have been at the forefront of this agenda. Each of them has accumulated massive shareholdings on behalf of its investor clients. Supposedly "passive" asset managers, they actively vote those shares to impose their collectivist ESG agenda on American businesses and, by proxy, on the American people.

Those shareholdings enable the Big Three to impose their will directly, avoiding the messiness and inconvenience of our democratic institutions and free-market economy—which respond to voters and consumers. It is so much easier to simply mandate compliance than to garner popular support—particularly because these elites know full well that the American people would reject their social-justice, radical-environmentalist agenda if it became visible. So for years they have cloaked their goals in the vague and malleable acronym ESG to conceal their intent.

INTRODUCTION

As people have come to understand what ESG represents, these elites have attempted to distance themselves from the acronym,[2] but not from the underlying "environmental, social and governance" agenda it represents. Their proposed replacement phrases include "sustainability," "rational sustainability," "decarbonization," and "transition (or trans) investing." As a substitute for increasingly suspect "stakeholder capitalism," they offer "conscientious capitalism."

Do not be fooled. No matter what phrases these financial elites eventually adopt, their agenda will remain the same—only the names will change. While they may no longer like the term "ESG" now that the collectivist cat is out of the bag, it is the appropriate acronym to identify their agenda precisely because people have come to understand what it actually means. Sunlight is an effective disinfectant, and for that reason I will use "ESG" on these pages.

At their core, stakeholder capitalism and the ESG agenda represent a rejection of our nation's founding principles. Shrouded in a thin veneer of post-modern morality and collective responsibility, they threaten our democracy, economic freedom, and individual liberty.

They threaten our democracy by creating a shortcut around the ballot box, allowing massive investment firms to implement collectivist ESG policies that lack popular support.

They threaten our economic freedom because the Big Three use their massive shareholdings to compel the CEOs of the companies in which they invest to put ESG's social-justice policies above their obligation to maximize shareholder returns.

And they threaten our individual liberty because they use our money to do it—primarily the monies that working- and middle-class Americans have invested in retirement savings, 401(k) plans, and pension funds.

As with their radical collectivist predecessors, the proponents of shareholder capitalism would diminish us as individuals and empower a group of elites to be our masters. But stakeholder capitalism and ESG differ from more classic forms of collectivism in two ways.

First, they empower financial as opposed to governmental elites—although the two often work together.

Second, they neither promise nor pretend to redistribute wealth for the benefit of workers or the poor. Their ESG agenda advances goals that are meaningful only to upper-crust elites who, no matter how much they damage the economy, will never have to worry about paying their bills at month's end.

In that sense, stakeholder capitalism and ESG are even worse than traditional socialism. At least they are more condescending. The purveyors of ESG—some of the richest people in this country—are using *your* money to advance *their* goals, which they know you do not support, in the smug confidence that you would support their agenda if only you were smart enough to make decisions for yourselves. Their goal is to simply override the will of the people, as they deem us incapable of governing ourselves.

The Threat to Our Democracy

Make no mistake, these elites intend to use their power to supersede the will of the people. BlackRock CEO Larry Fink has made it clear that he believes corporations, under the guidance of the Big Three, must implement ESG's social and political policies because our democratic institutions are incapable of making the right decisions—or of making them fast enough.

In a 2018 letter, Fink told America's CEOs that they must "respond to broader social issues," as opposed to concentrating on the success of their businesses, because "many governments are failing to prepare for the future."[3] His 2019 letter to CEOs reiterated the point, declaring that "some of the world's leading democracies have descended into wrenching political dysfunction" and asserting that American businesses needed to "address pressing social and economic issues" given "the failure of government to provide lasting solutions."[4] Fink simply does not believe our democracy is up to the job of governing. His solution is to bypass it.

Historical examples abound of aristocratic networks with a distrust of democracy and a preference for rule by the elites—or an elite.

But that is not how a republic works, and it certainly is not how our Republic works. As our Declaration of Independence states, government derives its "just powers from the consent of the governed."[5] Neither Fink, BlackRock, nor the Big Three have that consent.

For unelected elites to force businesses to implement policies that lack popular support strikes at the very heart of our representative democracy, undermining our right to determine policy as voters. No one voted them into office. Nor did their investors intend to empower these "passive" asset managers to actively impose their will on society. They assumed that power on their own initiative.

Popular lore has it that when Benjamin Franklin was walking out of the Constitutional Convention in 1787, a citizen approached and asked him what sort of government the delegates had created. His response was, "A republic, if you can keep it."[6] Stakeholder capitalism and its ESG agenda have made the question of whether we can keep it more relevant today than at any time since the Civil War.

The Threat to Our Economic Freedom

In addition to disenfranchising voters, stakeholder capitalism and the ESG agenda diminish the power of consumers to guide the economy. Economist Adam Smith, the founding father of free-market capitalism, called that power the "invisible hand"[7]—which is, essentially, consumer sentiment expressed by millions of people voting every day with every dollar they spend to determine which ideas, products, and companies will succeed and which will fail.

In this sense, free-market capitalism is a responsive form of economic democracy answerable to the people as consumers. Businesses succeed by making a profit. They make a profit by meeting their customers' needs. Their efforts to meet those needs guide the economy in the direction chosen by consumers—the people—not government or financial elites.

Of course, there are companies that enhance their profits by building social or political agendas into their brand. Ben & Jerry's and Patagonia are examples. But that is because they are providing what their customers want—social justice is a selling point for them. Fair enough. Those companies do not need the financial elites telling them how to appeal to their consumers and make a profit.

When profit is the goal, the people as consumers have the power. If they disapprove of a company's political or social views, they can stop doing business with it. If they approve, they can continue to purchase its products or services. Collectivist elites deplore this system, as it empowers consumers, depriving elites of the power to set economic policy themselves.

Economic and political elites have one common trait—an overwhelming confidence in their ability to set policies more effectively than the people those policies will affect. They have faith that their omniscience produces better outcomes than markets and their goals are more worthy than those of the plebian masses or their duly elected governments.

That is why stakeholder capitalism and ESG are such useful tools for financial elites. They can compel corporate America to do their political dirty work for them. They avoid the inconvenience of having to persuade consumers or voters and—since their financial coercion is less visible than government action—they believe they can avoid accountability for the financial damage their decisions will inflict.

Economic benefits inure to those with economic power. When the goal is profits, economic power lies with consumers, and businesses respond to their demands. The point of stakeholder capitalism is to reorient modern businesses so that they prioritize ESG's collectivist social and political goals over profits. To accomplish that reorientation, the elites at massive financial firms force businesses to prioritize social and political goals over consumer demand, diminishing consumers' economic power—and transferring that power to themselves.

Stakeholder capitalism and the ESG agenda are nothing more

than socialism in sheep's clothing and a champagne-social-justice agenda.

They Use Our Money to Do It

This reduced focus on profitability not only dilutes the power of consumers, it also reduces returns for the shareholders who, as Fink has acknowledged, are each business's "true owners."[8] In other words, there are costs in advancing an ESG agenda, and the financial firms who force it on their portfolio companies do not use their own money to pay those costs. Rather, the investors who trusted those firms to invest their monies prudently to maximize returns end up paying ESG's costs. Those costs are a social-agenda tax for which no one voted—and of which few are aware.

There is no doubt that diverting a business's focus from making a profit to addressing social policy diminishes its profitability. To state the patently obvious: *companies that focus on profits will be more profitable than companies that do not.* That may not be what you hear from stakeholder capitalists and ESG advocates, but it is unequivocally true.

As a former CEO, I can attest that it is hard enough to make a profit when you focus on it, let alone when elites are coercing you to substitute social justice and radical environmentalism for business performance. If the Big Three announce society is "demanding" that the companies in their funds pursue an agenda that "serve[s] a social purpose"[9]—to quote Fink—those companies will prioritize that agenda over profitability, diminishing their returns.

So how did this happen, and how can we stop it? Let us look at what empowered these financial elites to impose their social and political agenda on American businesses and, by proxy, on all of us, at the resulting attack on free-market capitalism, and at how America is resisting this latest collectivist assault.

Chapter 1

POWER TOO INTOXICATING TO RESIST

"The greater the power, the more dangerous the abuse."

—*Edmund Burke*[1]

The ESG agenda has come to permeate our financial markets to the point where it is all but impossible for investors to escape its devastating clutches. This was only possible because the rise of passive index investing inadvertently concentrated massive economic power in the hands of a few financial firms intent on co-opting free-market capitalism and replacing it with so-called stakeholder capitalism. Their efforts to implement ESG's social and political policy agenda has turned a half century of positive economic innovation on its head.

The increasing popularity of passive index investing has been perhaps the most important innovation in the financial markets over the past fifty years. It has reduced the risks and costs of investing while generally producing superior long-term returns. Passive index investing achieves these results by focusing on a portfolio of stocks chosen for their common attributes and calculated as an index rather than picking specific stocks for their individual potential to outperform the market.

An Unintended Consequence

Index investing started in the early 1970s and was focused on broad market indexes, which serve as proxies for the stock market—such as the S&P 500 and later the Russell 3000. It provided investors with the benefits of broadly diversified stock portfolios at extremely low cost, often one-tenth that of actively managed stock portfolios. Over the past thirty years, indexing has extended to sectors, factors, and even investment themes, taking advantage of the lower cost of passive strategies versus their active counterparts.

While incredibly successful, index investing had an unfortunate and unintended consequence. It turned certain passive-fund managers—primarily BlackRock, State Street, and Vanguard—into financial behemoths and empowered them to force political and cultural agendas on the companies in their portfolios. These managers gained the kind of power that normally only political leaders can exercise, and they could exercise it without a shred of democratic accountability. It would prove to be a power too intoxicating to resist.

Active versus Passive Investing

Index investing has changed both the way we invest and the expectations we have for those we trust to invest our monies for us.

Traditionally, investors relied on "active" financial managers, that is, stock pickers who strategize when to buy or sell the stocks they recommend. The financial manager makes recommendations based on research into factors that could affect a particular company's profitability, cash flow, value, and, therefore, its stock price. These factors may include the strength of the company's management, the demand for its products, and its profit margins, operating expenses, and debt load. Active managers continually monitor the companies they recommend to exploit profit opportunities and mitigate losses.

The amount of research required for each company is a limiting factor on the number of companies an active manager can evaluate or invest in. The process is both time-consuming and expensive. Investors bear the burden of those costs through the fees they pay.

Investors judge an active manager's performance on the basis of the returns the stocks that he picks generate, net of fees. As a result, the manager is extremely focused on having each individual company generate profits or cash flow that will increase its dividends or share price and the investors' returns. If the manager believes the company is performing in a way that diminishes its value, he may simply sell the company's shares.

With index—or "passive"—investing, rather than recommending investments in specific companies, the manager recommends investing in a group—or an index—of companies that represent a segment of the financial market based on shared attributes. The most common index-based investment products are mutual funds and exchange traded funds (ETFs), both of which I will refer to as "passive index funds."

Six popular indexes for such passive index funds are the S&P 500, Russell 3000—as well as its subsets the Russell 1000 and 2000—the Dow Jones Industrial Average (30 stocks), and the Nasdaq 100, each of which broadly tracks the stock market or some key component of it.

An index may also represent a particular segment of the financial market, such as energy or tech stocks, European stocks, small-cap value stocks, or nearly any other group you might imagine. The possibilities are virtually endless. According to a study by the Index Industry Association (the industry trade group for index professionals), there are over 3.7 million stock-market indexes globally.[2]

Passive investing is only as selective as the chosen index. Rather than evaluating, monitoring, and then buying or selling individual stocks, investors in an index-based product will buy or sell all the holdings in that index. The performance of any particular stock is less relevant, as the investor is betting on the performance of the entire index.

Unlike in the case of actively managed funds, the passive manager or investor is unable to sell any particular stock if it qualifies to be in the index. This eliminates the costs of tracking, evaluating, and then trading each individual stock. Thus passive index funds are a low-cost way to invest in a comprehensive portfolio of stocks representing the market in general or a specific market segment of the investor's choosing.

For example, the most popular index for passive index funds is the S&P 500—which includes five hundred of the largest publicly traded companies in the U.S., as measured by their market capitalization ("market cap")—the total value of their outstanding shares.

The premise behind investing in such an index is that five hundred of the largest U.S. companies will, on average, have good products or desirable services, good management teams and profit margins, reasonable operating expenses, manageable debt loads, and other attributes that landed them in the S&P 500 in the first place. They are, after all, among the very largest U.S. companies, and that did not happen by accident. So the likelihood that, as a group, they will produce positive returns over time is extremely high.

If any company in the S&P 500 should manage its business poorly, its market capitalization will likely decline. Because the S&P 500 is a weighted index, companies with higher market caps have more influence in the index. Weighting the companies in the index based on their market cap ensures that the index correlates with the overall market.

The more successful a stock is, the higher its weighting. So if companies underperform, their weight and influence in the index decline. If a company's market cap no longer meets the required threshold, S&P will remove it and another, better-performing company will enter the index. That is why it is difficult to outperform a market index like the S&P 500 over time—by construction, it consistently contains the most successful U.S. companies and is perhaps the best real-time reflection of the equity market. In S&P Global's own words, the S&P 500 is "considered to be a proxy of the U.S. equity market."[3]

Since inclusion and weighting in the S&P 500 index are based on a company's size, passive S&P 500 index-fund managers do not have to do time-consuming and expensive research into the prospects for each of the five hundred companies in the index. The firm offering such a product simply licenses the index from Standard and Poor's—which compiles and periodically updates it—and invests in line with the index's names and weights.

For all these reasons, passive index funds have two distinct advantages over actively managed accounts.

First, costs and therefore fees are low, as there is no need to research the potential profitability or monitor the progress of individual companies in the index—the investment product includes every company in the index, regardless of its profitability or potential.

Second, passive index funds generally produce superior net returns over time. Over the ten-year period ending June 2023, only one out of every four active funds outperformed the average of passive funds, according to the influential research and financial services firm Morningstar's Active/Passive Barometer.[4] The 2022 SPIVA Scorecard,[5] which has served as the de facto scorekeeper on actively versus passively managed funds since 2002, also found that the vast majority of passively managed funds outperformed actively managed funds over periods of ten years or more.

An Ironic Accumulation of Power

With benefits such as instant diversification at lower costs and generally superior returns, the percentage of investments held in passive index funds has grown exponentially. Passive index funds constituted only 21 percent of total assets managed by investment firms as recently as 2012.[6] By 2022, that percentage had surged to 45 percent.[7] In 2023, the assets in passive funds officially overtook those in active funds for the first time, according to Morningstar.[8]

Not surprisingly, the financial firms that market and manage passive index funds became massive in the process. The Big Three—BlackRock, State Street and Vanguard—are the dominant firms.

Formed in 1988, BlackRock is the largest of the Big Three and widely considered the group's leader. While assets under management (AUM) for all these firms will change over time—as their portfolios fluctuate in value and as clients come and go—BlackRock has around $9 trillion in AUM. Vanguard commenced business in 1975 and has about $8 trillion in AUM. State Street—the second-oldest bank in the United States—was founded in 1792 and has about $4 trillion in AUM.

Their combined AUM is about $21 trillion (about $65,000 per person in the U.S.), or an amount equivalent to over 80 percent of the annual gross domestic product (GDP) of the United States and an amount that exceeds the annual GDP for every country in the world but the United States and China.

Viewing the Big Three together makes some sense. They have extensive cross ownership. As a group, the Big Three directly own about 19 percent of BlackRock and 22 percent of State Street. Vanguard is not publicly traded, but it is BlackRock's and State Street's largest shareholder, in both cases followed by BlackRock. They each also own controlling interests in several other institutional stockholders that hold shares in the Big Three. After including those holdings, the Big Three cumulatively control—directly or indirectly—approximately 32 percent of BlackRock's and 42 percent of State Street's outstanding shares.[9]

This colossal three-headed Cerberus guards the gates of the low-cost passive-investment landscape. As such, the Big Three have massive and unprecedented financial power.

A 2017 study published by the Cambridge University Press found that collectively they "constitute the largest shareholder in 88% of the S&P 500 firms" and that they "utilize coordinated voting strategies" (although they do not vote their shares the same way 100 percent of the time).[10] This consolidation of corporate ownership and control is unlike anything the financial markets have seen since J. P. Morgan and J. D. Rockefeller controlled much of the financial sector in the early 1900s.

It is the most powerful financial-markets cartel in U.S. history.

BlackRock, the largest of the Big Three, is a dominant force in the U.S. public markets. The Securities and Exchange Commission (SEC) requires disclosure when an investor's ownership in publicly traded companies reaches 5 percent, the percentage at which an ownership interest is considered highly influential.[11] BlackRock alone has *at least* a 5 percent ownership stake in a stunning 97.5 percent of the companies in the S&P 500.[12]

While not all the assets the Big Three manage are invested in passive index funds, according to a June 2023 report by Morningstar Direct, the Big Three represent 43 percent ($10.3 trillion) of the U.S. funds market, with most of that capital ($8.9 trillion) invested in passive index funds.[13]

That kind of share ownership carries tremendous power. The Big Three may not beneficially own the shares—dividends and profits or losses accrue not to them but to the clients who have invested through them—however, the Big Three vote those shares. That gives them significant power over who sits on the boards of directors of virtually every major U.S. company—and over whether shareholder resolutions for those companies pass or fail.

This level of share ownership also provides the Big Three with tremendous influence even apart from actual proxy voting, as companies are reluctant to ignore or offend their largest shareholders. Given their massive shareholdings and associated proxy-voting power across an incredibly significant portion of the American corporate sector, when this triad of power speaks, corporate America has no choice but to listen. As the former CEO of a New York Stock Exchange–traded company, I can attest that when your largest shareholders speak, you listen—closely. You ignore them at your peril.

As a result, index investing has ironically enabled supposedly "passive" investing firms to very actively—if not aggressively—impose their will on American corporations. It may not have been intentional, but the Big Three have garnered an unprecedented level of power and influence over America's most important companies and the financial markets in general.

The great financial innovation of passive index investing was never supposed to entail power brokers co-opting their shareholders' rights with such a governance grab, enabling them to impose their will on American businesses. On the contrary, the notion of these firms actively dictating corporate strategy is at odds with the very nature of passive investing.

It is in the best interest of passive index-fund investors that each individual company in the index perform to the maximum of its potential, in order to produce the best index returns. The idea behind passive management is to invest in a diversified group of companies and let the management teams of those companies—who best understand their respective businesses—manage their businesses. The fund manager is supposed to sit back and let them perform. It is called passive investing for a reason.

Investment firms that sell passive index funds do not perform a deep dive on the individual metrics of the companies in which they invest. So even if passive investing included an element of active management, it is inconceivable that passive fund managers would know the right strategies or policies for each of the thousands of companies in the indexes they manage.

For example, when you invest in BlackRock's S&P 500 ETF (its most popular product), the idea is that you are investing in five hundred of the largest U.S. companies with competent CEOs who know best how to run their respective businesses. As an investor, it is in your best interest that as many companies as possible in that index are successful, producing the best consolidated results for the index.

You are invested in all of them, and you have five hundred of America's top CEOs striving to generate returns for you. You certainly do not expect BlackRock's CEO Larry Fink to use BlackRock's financial power to force companies to pursue social or political goals favoring particular companies and disadvantaging others.

Consider the impact of BlackRock (or the Big Three collectively) directing every S&P 500 CEO to operate and invest in a way that contributes to achieving net-zero carbon emissions by 2050, as Klaus Schwab and the World Economic Forum advocate. That might help some of the companies in the S&P 500, such as solar-panel manufacturers (including First Solar, Enphase Energy, and SolarEdge Technologies). But it would disadvantage every company in the S&P 500 that relies on inexpensive and reliable fossil fuels to enhance its profitability.

It would devastate S&P 500 oil companies such as Exxon, Chevron, and Marathon. What business sense is there in requiring oil companies to stop investing in oil—their most profitable product? How does this benefit BlackRock's investors, who are the true owners of these companies?

As an investor in an S&P 500 ETF, you own all five hundred companies, not just the solar-panel manufacturers. Such policies would inevitably reduce returns overall for the companies in which you have invested. In effect, BlackRock would be passively investing your money in a broad index of companies and then actively using its share-voting power and very tangible indirect influence to advance a political goal that diminishes the profitability of companies in that index, rather than letting markets and managers function for your benefit.

Or take, for example, a struggling company in need of knowledgeable directors. If the Big Three were to direct every company to have racially or sexually diverse boards, should this company add the most qualified members it can find, or limit itself to the most diverse? If the objective is for every company in the index to perform to its maximum financial potential, a company in need of expertise would add the most qualified board members, regardless of race or sex.

But if the directive from above is to achieve diversity, then the director nominees' true qualifications—and the company's best financial interests—are a lesser consideration. A policy requiring racial or sexual diversity would benefit companies having sufficient board expertise and disadvantage companies in need of added expertise.

It is in the best financial interest of passive index-fund investors to have each company in the index perform to the best of its ability.

In a free-market economy, companies do so by adopting policies that empower them to successfully compete with other companies and profit (within legal and regulatory boundaries). Consumers choose which companies succeed and which fail. Where it is appropriate to collectively require businesses to pursue goals unrelated to profitability, we have a political system with democratically elected representatives responsible for making such sweeping policy decisions.

Both our free-market economy and our representative democracy empower the people—directly as consumers or indirectly as voters—to make such decisions, not corporate elites sitting in BlackRock's, Vanguard's or State Street's corporate offices using other peoples' money to act as self-appointed political czars.

In the early years of passive investing, these firms engaged little with management, avoiding corporate decision-making and active participation on corporate-governance issues.[14] The idea was to invest passively, letting management teams and free markets do what they do best—maximize returns for investors. In this way passive managers would best fulfill their fiduciary duty to prioritize financial returns for their clients.

Around 2015, that began to change.

That year, a *Wall Street Journal* article noted that the Big Three "fund managers once known for quiet relationships with the companies in which they invest, say they are getting more assertive." BlackRock revised its voting guidelines, noting that it might oppose the re-election of corporate board members over issues including overly lengthy tenures, poor attendance, or a lack of diversity. A letter from Vanguard's CEO stated that corporate boards should be "substantially independent of management" and warned that it would not sit idly by on corporate-governance issues.[15]

A 2018 *New York Times* article noted the Big Three's movement from passive investors to shareholder activists. According to the *Times*, the Big Three had "traditionally been passive investors" that did "little to pressure the leaders of companies they invested in." Rather, "they were known for rubber stamping management's plans. It was active investors who sought to hold companies accountable—either by agitating for change or by selling their shares to express their displeasure." In 2014, BlackRock CEO Larry Fink had even "denounced 'activist' shareholders" stating, "'If you asked me if activism harms job creation, the answer is yes.'"[16]

But that was then. "Now," the 2018 article concluded, "he is changing his stripes."[17]

And change them he did—quickly and significantly. Once Fink understood the power he held, it would seem that employing it was simply too intoxicating to resist. Unfortunately, as the eighteenth-century statesman and philosopher Edmund Burke noted, "The greater the power, the more dangerous the abuse."[18]

Larry Fink's Sense of Purpose

Fink forcefully exercised his prodigious power in a 2018 open letter to America's CEOs.[19] In a single stroke, he sought to reorient the entire American private sector from its traditional focus on profits, shareholder returns, and value to advancing progressive social policy. Tellingly titled "A Sense of Purpose," Fink's letter was a stunning exercise of raw financial power designed to undermine the very foundations of free-market capitalism and breaking faith with his own clients, who had placed their money with BlackRock in the expectation that it would be passively invested for their benefit as shareholders.

The only thing scarier than Fink believing he had this power is how close he was to being right.

From 2012 to 2022, Fink issued an annual public letter to the CEOs of the thousands of companies in which BlackRock invests. At first, Fink's letters primarily discussed financial issues BlackRock was anticipating that CEOs might encounter in the coming year.

As every company has unique needs and business strategies designed to enhance its profitability, presumably each CEO would use this information to adjust operations in anticipation of problems or opportunities that might arise. Fink would later claim his letters were "never meant to be a political statement.... They were written to identify long-term issues to our long-term investors."[20]

Perhaps that was the original intent.

But Fink's 2018 letter was fundamentally different. With the confidence and hubris of someone who believes his power secure and his actions unassailably just, Fink directed America's CEOs to turn their businesses from engines of economic production to drivers of progressive social policy—an economic transformation of historic proportions executed on BlackRock's investors' backs and funded out of their retirement savings.

While Fink was clearly the self-appointed czar of this realignment, he claimed to be merely the messenger. According to Fink, "society" itself was increasingly "turning to the private sector and asking that companies respond to broader societal challenges," even "demanding that companies . . . serve a social purpose." Each company, he explained, "must not only deliver financial performance, but also show how it makes a positive contribution to society." He claimed that BlackRock's "clients" were also "asking you to demonstrate the leadership and clarity that will drive not only their own investment returns, but also the prosperity and security of their fellow citizens."[21]

Fink failed to note any source for his authority to declare society's will. We usually have elections for that sort of thing. Nor did he disclose why he believed BlackRock's clients were "asking" that the companies in which BlackRock invested pursue "the prosperity and security of their fellow citizens," as opposed to simply maximizing their returns.

Perhaps that was because, as Fink was certainly aware, a considerable number of BlackRock's clients were not demanding anything of the sort. Undoubtedly, many of them were conservatives or moderates who do not support the "social purpose[s]" Larry Fink espouses and would not vote for him if he were running for dogcatcher. These investors included numerous red-state governments that had invested hundreds of billions of dollars with Black-Rock through pension funds and other state accounts.

Nor did Fink consult BlackRock's more left-wing clients on

whether they wanted to risk their retirement investments to advance Fink's social vision for American life, even to the extent they agreed with it.

Finally, many other BlackRock clients—such as pension fund beneficiaries or 401(k) investors—were likely unaware of Fink's intent to use their monies to advance social goals. They were more likely just hoping to fund their retirements—and assumed Blackrock was maximizing their returns so they could do so, as was its fiduciary obligation. But ironically, they were unknowingly paying BlackRock to actively pursue an agenda that cut into the investment returns for which they thought they were paying.

BlackRock's Fiduciary Duty

The most significant obstacle Fink faced in his effort to reorient the private sector was the law governing fiduciary duties. A fiduciary is a person or entity that stands in a special relationship of trust, confidence, or responsibility empowering it to act on behalf of—and for the benefit of—others.[22] BlackRock has acknowledged that it is "an asset manager" and a fiduciary that owes its clients a "fiduciary duty"[23] requiring it "to prioritize [its] clients' financial interests above any commitments or pledges not required by law."[24]

As a passive fund manager, BlackRock traditionally satisfied this fiduciary duty by setting up a passive index fund, having its clients invest in that fund, and then allowing each company in the underlying index to succeed to the best of its individual ability, creating the greatest consolidated financial success for BlackRock's clients. Its role certainly was not to use its share-voting power to actively dictate collective strategic policies to all the companies in the index based on what BlackRock's management team deemed socially and politically desirable.

So how could a passive fund manager become an activist investor directing companies to respond to "broader social challenges" and still be acting consistent with its fiduciary duty to prioritize its clients' financial interests? To do so required a change or "transformation" of the fiduciary duty BlackRock admittedly owed its clients.

Lo and behold—according to Fink—"investors' increasing use of index funds [was] driving a transformation in BlackRock's fiduciary responsibility," making its "responsibility to engage and vote" the shares it held "more important than ever."[25] Fink felt no obligation to seek voter, legislative, or client approval for such a transformation, or even to consider what was best for the company or its funds' and clients' returns. He simply and unilaterally declared that BlackRock's fiduciary responsibilities had been—by something akin to an act of nature—transformed.

Why was it suddenly "more important than ever" (assuming it was ever important) that a passive fund manager actively "engage and vote its shares"? Well, Fink asserted that this "transformation" was necessary because, as a passive index-fund manager, if BlackRock disapproved of "a company's strategic direction" it was unable to "express its disapproval by selling the company's securities as long as that company remains in the relevant index."[26]

But wait a minute—passive-investment firms are not supposed to sell shares of individual companies. Investing in a group of companies and looking at the group's overall performance—rather than any individual company's performance—was literally the point of index investing.

It was not BlackRock's job to set collective direction for entire indexes of companies. It was up to the boards and management teams of each company to select the best strategy for that individual company. So of course BlackRock was unable to punish individual companies that were failing to adhere to BlackRock's preferred "strategic direction." Setting the strategic direction for an entire index of companies was never its right, nor the mandate from its client investors.

Ironically, Fink was claiming that the growth of index investing required a transformation of fiduciary responsibilities so *passive* fund managers, like BlackRock, could *actively* force the companies in which they *passively* invested to adopt non-economic strategies that responded to BlackRock's preferred social goals. *In other words, the success of passive investment funds meant that fund managers had to abandon passive investing.* The logic was circular, the irony was palpable, and the betrayal of BlackRock's clients was clear.

And, by the way, this activism clearly did not "prioritize" BlackRock's "clients' financial interests," as its fiduciary duty required. The key words in BlackRock's own definition of fiduciary duty are "clients," "prioritize" and "financial interests." Fink's problem was that instructing the companies in BlackRock's portfolio to serve "a social purpose" conflicted with BlackRock's obligation to prioritize its clients' "financial interests"—violating BlackRock's fiduciary duty, no matter what society was supposedly demanding.

Fink knew he needed a path around the strictures of BlackRock's fiduciary duty. So his letter linked and adopted two expansive, collectivist, and anti-shareholder doctrines—stakeholder capitalism and the ESG agenda.

Stakeholder Capitalism

With stakeholder capitalism, Fink sought to rationalize and expand the group entitled to BlackRock's fiduciary protections beyond BlackRock's clients to a broader group of "stakeholders."

Fink's letter acknowledged that its client investors were "the true owners," or shareholders, of the companies in which it invested. The problem was that properly prioritizing BlackRock's clients' financial interests was too restrictive. Logically, you cannot implement social change that may disadvantage your clients' financial interests as shareholders and simultaneously prioritize their financial interests. So, how does one wipe out—or transform—hundreds of years of common law and the vital foundation of business and society with a single letter?

Well, to do so, Fink first needed a broader group entitled to fiduciary protections. Shareholders would hold BlackRock and company CEOs accountable for generating profits, that is, a return on their investments. But with stakeholder capitalism, he could

expand the group entitled to fiduciary protections to an amorphous group of non-investors or "stakeholders"—who would hold
BlackRock and company CEOs accountable for nothing.

So he instructed those CEOs that, to show they were making "a
positive contribution to society," their "[c]ompanies must benefit
all their stakeholders," not just their shareholders (that is, Black-
Rock's own clients). In addition to shareholders, each company's
stakeholder group would now include "employees, customers, and
the communities in which they operate."[27] In other words, society
as a whole.

Benefitting a business's customers, employees, and communities is neither new nor remarkable. Had Fink's letter instructed these CEOs to prioritize their shareholders' financial interests
(that is, the profitability of the companies in which BlackRock invested their monies), while benefitting these other stakeholders,
his directive might have been consistent with BlackRock's fiduciary responsibility. The fact is that every business must benefit
these additional stakeholders if it is to stay in business—and make
a profit.

For example, all CEOs endeavor to benefit their business's customers (you would have to be an idiot not to). In a capitalist economy, the only way a business survives is by offering products or
services its customers want at prices they can afford. If you do not
do that, you will rapidly be out of business. If you do it well, you
may maximize the value and profitability of your business.

Intelligent CEOs also strive to benefit their business's employees, as employees are every business's most valuable asset. If you
do not take care of your employees, they will leave your company
and work for your competitors. That is especially true of your best
people, because they have the most options in the labor market.
Losing your best employees is a business death knell.

Finally, every CEO knows you need to have a good brand in the
communities in which you operate, or you will go out of business.
People rarely patronize businesses they dislike.

In each of these instances, benefiting additional stakeholders—
customers, employees, and communities—is simply good business

sense. It is a big part of what corporate management must do to make a profit for its shareholders. But the priority in doing so is to make a profit for your shareholders.

Fink missed the point that CEOs pursue these important secondary concerns to maximize their companies' values and best serve shareholders by producing investor returns—profits. His letter dismissed the notion that these CEOs would meet the needs of these so-called stakeholders as part and parcel of prioritizing their shareholders'—BlackRock's clients'—financial interests in the profitability of the companies in which they were investors. Rather, meeting the needs of "stakeholders" was the goal in and of itself.

Now free to decide what was in the best interests of these non-investor stakeholders, Fink needed to define the agenda for meeting their needs. ESG fit the bill nicely, enabling Fink to insist that BlackRock's portfolio companies prioritize social and political goals that he would set, rather than their businesses' financial success.

The Rise of ESG

To justify implementing an ESG agenda, Fink claimed that, in addition BlackRock's clients, his non-investor "stakeholders" (a.k.a. society in general) were also "demanding that companies exercise leadership on a broader range of issues." What issues were in such popular demand, and how should CEOs demonstrate that they were exercising the required leadership? Fink made that quite clear—"a company's ability to manage environmental, social, and governance matters demonstrates the leadership and good governance that is so essential to sustainable growth, which is why we are increasingly integrating these issues into our investment process."[28]

Of course, there is no accepted definition for what ESG's policy initiatives include, making it perfect for encompassing the "broader societal challenges" that Fink was unilaterally claiming society, BlackRock's clients, and now stakeholders were all demanding that the corporate sector address.

"Environmental, social, and governance"—it sounds so innocuous—if not moralistic. How bad could it be? Don't we all want to protect the environment, to assure that people are treated fairly and that corporations are properly governed? Of course we do. But at its core and in practice, ESG is little more than a ruse intended to conceal an aggressively collectivist agenda.

While no one knows the full extent of the ESG universe, we do know that ESG includes the core tenets of leftist activism. For example, the "E" in ESG represents the Left's highest priority—radical environmental policy to address climate change as a justification for transforming the world's economy and political structure. If ESG covered nothing else, for the Left, this sole goal would suffice.

But there are other issues that fall under the ESG rubric, including forced board diversity and workforce diversity, equity, and inclusion (DEI) policies (as opposed to merit-based, race- and sex-neutral policies), support for political entities such as Black Lives Matter, and pro-choice policies designed to evade the laws of pro-life states. The list of potential ESG issues is literally endless and always cloaked in a socialist commingling of postmodern morality and collective responsibility.

The key point with ESG is that it includes whatever the current guardians of collectivist ideology want it to include—and little, if anything, that prioritizes the fiscal interests of BlackRock's clients. In George Orwell's novel *1984*, a fictional totalitarian socialist government creates a controlled language called "Newspeak" with limited grammar and vocabulary. The point of Newspeak is to suppress the ability of people to think independently or abstractly, making it difficult to resist the ideological orthodoxy of the socialist collective. The words mean what the government says they mean.[29]

ESG fits nicely into the Newspeak lexicon.

Having explained the justification for transforming Black-Rock from a passive to an active investor, broadened to "stakeholders" (or society) the group whose interests America's CEOs were to serve, and employed ESG to expand the definition of what those interests were, Fink had essentially reinterpreted—or transformed—BlackRock's fiduciary duty to the point where it imposed no restrictions on BlackRock's ability to implement his version of society's will and force whatever policies it chose on America's corporate sector and its investors.

Whether Fink had successfully reimagined and transformed BlackRock's fiduciary duties, or simply explained how he was going to violate them, is part of the ongoing debate. But he clearly believed he had transformed them—in his own image.

To complete his desired reorientation of America's private sector, the only remaining question was how BlackRock would assure that America's CEOs were protecting the correct stakeholders and pursuing the approved ESG goals. In other words, how would it set America's social, political, and economic agenda? The answer was obviously to employ BlackRock's massive share-voting power and influence.

The New Sheriff in Town

Fink certainly was not shy about using BlackRock's power. In November of 2017, just two months before issuing his 2018 letter, Fink had said the quiet part aloud. In an interview on diversity hiring (part of the "S" in ESG), Fink stated that "[b]ehaviors are going to have to change, and this is one thing we are asking companies, you have to force behaviors, and at BlackRock, we are forcing behaviors."[30]

Think about that for a moment. Not American consumers or voters forcing behaviors. Not the CEOs of the companies in which BlackRock invests deciding what is in their respective companies' (and shareholders') best financial interests. Rather, BlackRock and financial elites at the Big Three such as Fink determining what social and political policies are best for our nation and then using their massive shareholder power to impose the preferred policies on the entire business landscape and, by proxy, on society in general.

No need for free markets or democracy. Fink would just do it himself. With BlackRock's substantial proxy-voting influence, he clearly had the power. The question was how best to deploy that power.

While proxy voting was the most obvious arrow in BlackRock's quiver, proxy contests were time-consuming and expensive. They were also very public and risked a backlash if investors and those who represented their interests objected to BlackRock's objectives. Better not to see how the collectivist sausage was made.

So Fink's letter declared that the "responsibilities" of passive fund managers—such as BlackRock—to be "active, engaged agents" went "beyond casting proxy votes at annual meetings." According to Fink, rather than companies "wasting time and money in proxy fights," the time had come for "a new model of shareholder engagement."[31]

He wrote that since 2011 BlackRock had been transforming its "practice from one predominantly focused on proxy voting towards an approach based on engagement with companies" and that "[t]he growth of indexing demands that we now take this function to a new level." The function he was referring to is what BlackRock's Newspeak calls "stewardship." Fink claimed stewardship would strengthen and deepen "communication between shareholders and the companies that they own."[32]

In practice, this so-called stewardship is more effective and insidious than proxy voting. Under the ever-present threat of an adverse proxy vote, stewardship is a way BlackRock can convey its ESG directives to management teams in C-suite conference rooms or on Zoom calls—and compel the desired conduct without either the shareholders or the public being aware of what BlackRock is doing.

Make no mistake, "investment stewardship" is where Black-Rock's real power resides. It is the "investment stewardship" team that votes the shares BlackRock holds—and the CEOs of the companies that BlackRock "stewards" know it.

So what happens in these stewardship meetings? Well, they are apparently all about ESG. According to BlackRock's Stewardship website, its "stewardship" and "investment" teams work together to provide corporate management with "insight on environmental, social, and governance (ESG) considerations."[33]

The goal is to include "the assessment and integration of environmental and social issues, within an investment context" and "hold directors accountable for their action or inaction."[34] Of course, the specifics of those assessments and the associated integration are not public. As such, there is no need to allow growth, profits, shareholders, dividends, value, cash flow, or returns to intrude on these important discussions.

Lest any CEOs thought they might slip under BlackRock's stewardship radar, Fink's letter informed them that BlackRock intended to "double the size of the investment stewardship team" to "help foster even more effective engagement with your company by building a framework for deeper, more frequent, and more productive conversations."[35]

Imagine their joy.

Fink's message could not have been any clearer. There was a new sheriff in town—and it was BlackRock.

Repudiating Milton Friedman

The media was quick to seize on Fink's letter as a rebuttal to Nobel Prize–winning economist Milton Friedman, an ardent defender of free-market capitalism and a perpetual thorn in the side of the socialist Left. The *New York Times* described Fink's letter as pitting Fink "against many of the companies that he's invested in, which hold the view that their only duty is to produce profits for their shareholders, an argument long espoused by economists like Milton Friedman."[36] Bloomberg asserted that Fink's letter had the effect of "kneecapping Friedman's dictum," upending "a half-century of business thought."[37]

They were correct—although they failed to note that the half century since Friedman's issued his "dictum" had been the most prosperous in human history.

Writing in the *New York Times* in 1970, Friedman famously stated that "there is one and only one social responsibility of business—to use its resources and engage in activities designed to increase its profits so long as it stays within the rules of the game, which is to say, engages in open and free competition without deception or fraud."[38]

According to Friedman, a corporate executive who claims that the problems society is facing "are too urgent to wait on the slow course of political processes" and that "the exercise of social responsibility by businessmen is a quicker and surer way to solve pressing current problems" is merely acknowledging that the proponents of the policies "in question have failed to persuade a majority of their fellow citizens to be of like mind and that they are seeking to attain by undemocratic procedures what they cannot attain by democratic procedures."[39]

It was as if Friedman saw Fink coming nearly half a century away.

Perhaps that's not surprising. Friedman was addressing collectivist ideology going back at least a century, of which Fink's letter would be just a later reincarnation. Friedman correctly perceived that those who would put "'social' ends," a "social conscience" or "whatever else may be the catchwords of the contemporary crop of reformers" over investors' returns—or profits—were "preaching pure and unadulterated socialism" and were "unwitting puppets of the intellectual forces that have been undermining the basis of a free society" for decades. He wrote that "the doctrine of 'social responsibility'. . . . does not differ in philosophy from the most explicitly collective doctrine."[40]

Rather than paid promoters of social policy, Friedman considered corporate executives to be employees "of the owners of the business" with "direct responsibility" to their employers and, as such, responsible for conducting "the business in accordance with their [employers'] desires," which are generally "to make as much money as possible while conforming to the basic rules of the society, both those embodied in law and those embodied in ethical custom." In other words, Friedman would prioritize the financial interests of the company's shareholders, as BlackRock's traditional fiduciary duties required—and as has been the law for centuries.[41]

Of course, Friedman was writing at a time before the Big Three had amassed such tremendous power. Fink's supporters have argued that firms such as BlackRock are now the owners of the businesses. But, as Fink's letters have repeatedly acknowledged, BlackRock's clients are "the true owners" of the companies in which BlackRock invests. Both BlackRock and the management teams of the companies in which it invests owe their fiduciary duties to those owners—BlackRock's investor clients—not to some amorphous group of unidentified "stakeholders."

For a great many of those clients, making a profit—or maximizing their returns—remains the desired goal, rather than accomplishing BlackRock's ESG policy agenda.

Friedman understood that in prioritizing business success company managers were benefiting everybody. Their shareholders would get a good return, their employees would get secure jobs and better compensation, the government would get more tax revenue, and the rest of society would benefit from the wealth that only free-market capitalism can produce.

Finally, it is worth noting that Friedman was writing about what he believed was best for a prosperous American economy. Unlike Fink, he was not issuing a mandate based on raw financial power. Nonetheless, Friedman's reasoning came to dominate one of the most productive and prosperous periods in history.

The Importance of Understanding Stakeholder Capitalism and ESG

The impact of Fink's diktat is unquestionable. In a single stroke, the world's largest passive-investment manager became the world's most powerful activist investor, driving leftist social and political policy under the guise of stakeholder capitalism and the ESG agenda. ESG has since come to guide decisions for virtually every major asset manager in this country (if not worldwide) and has become a pervasive influence in our economy and our lives.

But ESG is a ruse, an innocent-sounding acronym to conceal a collectivist agenda that dates back to Karl Marx's *Communist Manifesto*. It is a tool that allows financial elites to use the

American private sector as a way around what they view as the inconvenience and messiness of our representative democracy and our free-market economy. It is an unprecedented free pass to misappropriate investors' piggybanks for socialist ends.

The acronym "ESG" has come under attack and is already fading into the dustbin of collectivist misnomers and Newspeak. But only the Newspeak names will change. The social and political goals will not. So understanding the rise to prominence of stakeholder capitalism and ESG is the key to recognizing and preventing the Left's next innocuous-sounding acronym or phrase from concealing a collectivist threat to our freedom, our liberty, and our prosperity.

Chapter 2

CORPORATE GOVERNANCE

Question by Andrew Ross Sorkin at a Berkshire Hathaway shareholders meeting: "You've explicitly stated you do not consider diversity when hiring for leadership positions and board members. Does that need to change, and are we missing any investment opportunities as a result?

Answer from Warren Buffet, American businessman, investor, philanthropist, and Berkshire Hathaway CEO: "No."[1]

It is important to understand that stakeholder capitalism's most important advocates—the small group of individuals who run our biggest passive-investment firms—know full well that their ESG social-justice agenda is controversial, to say the least. So, to hide it, they use language that sounds innocuous, as if they were simply pushing their portfolio companies to follow sound and well-understood business practices.

The "G" in ESG

Take, for example, the "G" in ESG, which stands for governance. Corporate governance is a concept well known to everyone who has been involved in business at a high level. As traditionally understood, it means business practices that protect investors from self-dealing, mismanagement, and other illegal or fraudulent behavior by corporate insiders such as directors and managers. By that definition, no honest business executive objects to corporate-governance practices—such as management accountability, policy transparency, effective risk management, and an independent and qualified board of directors.

But that's not what ESG proponents mean by corporate-governance. The "G" in ESG should be a "D" because it stands for selecting corporate board members based on "diversity" rather than merit or value to the company. Worse yet, they value only the particular type of diversity that is most politically correct in the most progressive circles. In other words, the "G" in ESG demands that companies in which the Big Three invest choose directors who belong to identity groups that rank high in the intersectional pecking order, regardless of whether those board candidates have any business running large publicly held companies.

The "G" in ESG is social-policy engineering, not good corporate governance—in fact, it mandates bad corporate governance because it vastly increases the risk that the highest level of corporate management will be composed of people who lack the competence or experience to make the strategic decisions that can mean life or death for a business enterprise.

Silicon Valley Bank

Take the case of Silicon Valley Bank (SVB) which collapsed in 2023—the second-largest bank failure in U.S. history.[2]

The roots of SVB's demise date back to March of 2021, when the Biden Administration and a compliant Congress passed their first multi-trillion-dollar spending bill. Coming on the heels of a pandemic that had constrained supply chains, the injection of so much money into the economy signaled to anyone who understands economics, banking, or monetary policy that there was a real risk of inflation and higher interest rates.

You did not need a great understanding of economics to see the risk. You just needed to know that, as Milton Friedman taught, inflation occurs—prices increase—when too much money chases too few goods.

In February of 2021, Harvard economist Larry Summers—who had served as both President Clinton's secretary of the treasury and the head of President Obama's Council of Economic Advisers—warned in the *Washington Post* that President Biden's massive spending policies could "set off inflationary pressures of a kind we have not seen in a generation."[3] Other Democrat economists as well as Republican economists were also sounding inflation-risk alarm bells.[4]

To the surprise of no one outside the Biden administration, Summers was right, and inflation surged in mid-2021. Nor was anyone surprised when the Federal Reserve announced in March of 2022 that it would be raising interest rates to fight spiraling inflation and that it anticipated "ongoing increases."[5] The Fed's mandate includes price stability—it cannot allow runaway inflation, and its main tool in fighting inflation is to raise interest rates to a level that brings consumer demand under control.

There is danger for banking institutions in a scenario where inflation and interest rates are increasing quickly. If the bank has its assets tied up in long-term bonds that pay on average a low interest rate, and rates begin to rise, the value of the bank's bond portfolio will go down. That is easy to understand. Nobody wants to pay full price for bonds yielding 2 percent when, because the Fed has raised interest rates, they can easily get other bonds that are yielding 4 percent.

When a bank's investment portfolio goes down in value quickly and substantially, it raises the specter of insolvency; and when the bank's depositors (especially larger uninsured depositors) begin to suspect that the bank is insolvent, they tend to panic and begin to withdraw their deposits as quickly as possible.

There is a technical term for that in the financial community. It is called "a run on the bank." Anyone who has seen the Christmas movie *It's a Wonderful Life* will understand the concept.

The risk of a bank run is especially great if—as was the case with SVP—most of the bank's customers have deposits that greatly exceed the $250,000 limit insured by the federal government. If a run on such a bank were to happen, those depositors could potentially lose their money with no recourse, something that of course makes it much more likely that they would panic, start withdrawing their money, and trigger the very bank run that they fear. That describes the position SVP was in, because—as a direct result of its business strategy—it had an unusually high percentage of deposits that were far too big for FDIC protection.

Once the panic set in, SVB's investors and depositors pulled a gobsmacking $42 billion out of the bank in a single day. Within forty-eight hours, the bank failed.[6]

Again, this was an obvious risk once inflation began to rise, or at any rate once the Fed began raising interest rates in response to rising inflation. If SVB had reacted early or even had had a plan, there were obvious steps a bank can take to reduce the risk by what is called "hedging" against rising interest rates—for example, raising outside capital to supplement your deposits or purchasing interest rates swaps that may lower your rate of return but protect you from interest rate surges.

But SVB never recognized the risk and never took any of the obvious steps to reduce it. Why not, you might ask?

Well, for one thing, SVB did not have a chief risk officer for the nine months from April of 2022[7] into January of 2023.[8] It had a chief diversity and inclusion officer, but, alas, no chief risk officer. That is a hole any board of directors with banking-industry expertise would surely have recognized and insisted management fill—immediately.

But even apart from the lack of a chief risk officer, SVB's board and management team should have seen SVB's interest rate/liquidity risk. It was an obvious problem, the kind of problem every bank must consider and manage under even normal circumstances. This was particularly the case for a bank where balance-sheet risk was organic to its business strategy.

In fact, *over a year before its collapse*, SVB's Fed supervisors informed SVB that they had concerns about SVB's liquidity risk.[9] Obviously, that alone was an alarm bell requiring immediate attention, as a qualified risk manager or director with the appropriate level of banking expertise would have recognized.

The Fed literally told SVB that it was at serious risk.

After SVB's collapse, the Fed's vice-chair for supervision, Michael S. Barr, described the problems leading to SVB's collapse as "really basic"[10] and "a textbook case of mismanagement." Fed examiners had raised concerns about SVB as early as the end of 2021, and in May of 2022 they found that SVB had "ineffective board oversight" and "risk management weaknesses."[11] According to Barr, "[t]he examiners at the San Francisco Federal Reserve bank called those issues out . . . and those actions were not acted upon in a timely way."[12]

So, where was SVB's board of directors, the group responsible for overseeing SVB's management? Why did SVB suffer from "ineffective board oversight," as the Fed stated? How did SVB's board miss this "really basic" problem, particularly with alarm bells sounding? This was an epic corporate-governance misfire.

Critics later complained that the composition of SVB's board showed that the company had put "diversity"[13] and political associations[14] ahead of specific banking-industry expertise. They had a point.

SVB was overly concerned about board diversity—at least demographic diversity. In its 2022 proxy statement SVB boasted that its board was 45 percent female and had "other diversity" including one black member, one LGBTQ+ member, and two veterans.[15] Nothing wrong with that, so long as the board also had the high-level banking expertise needed to oversee management of a major bank. Unfortunately, it did not.

A *New York Post* article entitled "Obama Official, Hillary Donors, Improv Actor: Meet SVB's Board of Directors" reported that of SVB's twelve-member board, only one member had the necessary banking expertise. That sole director with "a career at the pinnacle of the banking world" was Thomas King, a former Barclays Investment Banking CEO.[16]

Unfortunately, he joined the board in September of 2022,[17] after the interest-rate ship had already left the port on its final voyage. That same month SVB's parent company disclosed a $15.9 billion balance-sheet loss on its long-term bond portfolio due to rising interest rates.[18] At the time SVB's total equity was $15.8 billion.[19]

But even if there had been time to address the problem after King joined SVB's board, the risk-management committee excluded him from membership, according to *Forbes*. That was despite his being SVB's "most qualified director" who "ostensibly ha[d] far greater substantive financial services experience" than the other committee members, "comprised of a Napa vineyard owner, a retired healthcare CIO, a former U.S. Treasury undersecretary, venture capital partners and consulting firm heads."[20]

As for the critics' concerns with political associations, SVB board members "donated to Obama, [Hillary] Clinton, President Joe Biden, and to local Democrat congressional reps including Pelosi—as well as political action committees for Senate Majority Leader Chuck Schumer (D-NY), and Sen. Mark Warner (D-VA), a longtime member of the powerful Senate Banking Committee," according to the *New York Post*.[21]

So why didn't SVB have greater banking expertise on its board? Why was it more concerned with the racial and gender diversity of its board (a social issue) than relevant banking industry expertise (an actual corporate-governance issue)? Why did it delay until after its interest rate/liquidity risks had all but destroyed the bank before bringing in a qualified director with a significant level of banking experience?

It is, of course, shareholders who elect directors. Surely the shareholders were pushing for actual good governance?

SVB and the Big Three

At the end of 2022, SVB's three largest shareholders were Vanguard, BlackRock, and State Street (in that order).[22] Combined, they owned an impressive 24 percent of SVB's outstanding shares—more than enough to have a major influence on SVB's board and management team.[23] So let us look at what the Big Three were publicly communicating about governance and board diversity prior to SVB's collapse.

As we have seen, when discussing diversity in a late 2017 interview, Larry Fink stated that "[b]ehaviors are going to have to change, and this is one thing we are asking companies, you have to force behaviors, and at BlackRock, we are forcing behaviors."[24] He then proceeded to prove that he meant it.

Fink's 2018 letter to CEOs—the one that informed them their companies would now need to "serve a social purpose"—made it clear that, as a part of that goal, BlackRock would "emphasize the importance of a diverse board" including "a diverse mix of genders, ethnicities, career experiences, and ways of thinking."[25] His 2019 letter to CEOs listed BlackRock's top "Investment Stewardship" priority for the year as "governance, including your company's approach to board diversity."[26]

Fink's 2020 letter left little doubt that BlackRock considered diversity important and was willing to use its proxy-voting power to enforce its diversity directives. According to Fink, "when a company is not effectively addressing a material issue, its directors should be held accountable."[27]

So BlackRock held them accountable, and in a big way.

In 2021, BlackRock voted against the re-election of 1,862 directors at 975 companies, based on a lack of board diversity.[28] That's right. BlackRock used its enormous proxy-voting power to attempt to force the election of corporate board members—the people who run our biggest companies—not based solely on merit, or what the candidate could add to the value of the company, but based on where they stood in the social-justice hierarchy of intersectional worth.

And it did so to almost a thousand of the biggest companies in America. I have had decades of experience at high levels of American business, and I cannot remember anything like it—outside of government directives. Larry Fink really wanted to send a message that he was running the show, and he knew that corporate America had no choice but to listen and submit.

Then he went even further. Having asserted its power, Black-Rock's "Investment Stewardship Policies Updates for 2022" went so far as to set diversity quotas for each company, stating that "in the U.S., we believe boards should aspire to 30% diversity of membership, and we encourage large companies" to have "at least two women and a director who identifies as a member of an underrepresented group."[29]

There was no quota for qualifications.

The good news, I suppose, is that SVB's board met BlackRock's diversity requirements. Then it collapsed.

And BlackRock was not alone in compelling board diversity. In its 2019 Annual Stewardship Report, SVB's largest shareholder, Vanguard, stated that it was "expanding" its focus to more explicitly urge boards to seek greater diversity across a wide range of personal (not professional) demographic characteristics, such as "gender, race, ethnicity, national origin, and age." It also asked boards to explain their views on diversity, to broaden their search for minority candidates, and 'to prioritize adding diverse voices.'"[30]

In 2021, Vanguard issued a report on "Voting Insights: Diversity-Related Proposals, January–June 2021." It stated that in the first half of 2021, Vanguard had "deepened" its "board diversity advocacy and engaged a greater number of companies on the topic, screening many of our largest holdings for a lack of gender diversity or a lack of racial or ethnic diversity."[31] There was no mention of any votes against directors based on a lack of professional qualifications.

While compared to BlackRock, Vanguard was a piker on voting against directors, the threat was there. It "ultimately voted against 173 directors at companies where [it] had concerns regarding the risks associated with the lack of progress or lack of a path forward to increase board diversity."[32]

State Street Global Advisors' 2022 "Guidance on Diversity Disclosures and Practices" similarly states that it expects "all companies in [its] portfolio to offer public disclosures" that "[a]rticulate efforts to achieve diverse representation at the board level (including race, ethnicity, and gender, at minimum),"[33] and that "[i]f a company in the S&P 500 . . . does not have at least one director from an underrepresented racial or ethnic community, we will vote against the Chair of the Nominating Committee."[34]

Beginning in the 2023 proxy season, SSGA announced that it "will expect companies" in certain "indices to have boards comprised of at least 30 percent women directors." If they fail to do so, SSGA "may vote against the Chair of the Nominating Committee or the board leader in the absence of a Nominating Committee, if necessary." In addition, for companies that fail "to meet this expectation for three consecutive years, SSGA "may vote against all incumbent members of the Nominating Committee or those persons deemed responsible for the nomination process."[35]

If those who vote your shares inform you that they are going to vote against your director nominees unless you meet their demands, you meet their demands. Their focus is your focus. When those shareholders have the Big Three's massive proxy-voting power, ignoring them is not a reasonable option, even if doing so would be in your company's best interests.

That is the danger of collectivist policies.

Is it a coincidence that, at a time when SVB clearly should have been focused on adding the board expertise it so desperately needed, its 2021 proxy statement proudly proclaimed that during 2020, SVB's "Governance Committee continued its focus on Board diversity" with a particular emphasis on "its commitment to expand the Board's racial and ethnic representation"? SVB promised that its "focus on overall diversity" would continue in 2021[36]—and apparently it did.

SVB's director nominees were all re-elected in 2021 and 2022. BlackRock,[37] Vanguard,[38] and SSGA[39] each voted in favor of all SVB board candidates. SVB's board met the Big Three's primary requirement—the requirements of the "G" (really the "D") in ESG. It was diverse.

In case you are wondering, at least one of the Big Three knew that SVB was in danger because of risk-management issues.

In early 2022, a full year before SVB's collapse, BlackRock's consulting arm warned SVB that its risk controls were "substantially below" those of its peers, according to the *Financial Times*. In fact, BlackRock's "risk control report gave the bank a 'gentleman's C,' finding that SVB lagged behind similar banks on 11 of 11 factors considered and was 'substantially below' them on 10 out of 11." It was another risk-management fire alarm that no one—not even BlackRock itself—heeded.[40]

Good governance indeed.

A year later, with SVB on the verge of collapse, BlackRock still included SVB in its ESG-based fund products.[41] Bloomberg reported, on the basis of disclosures between January and March of 2023, that BlackRock directly owned almost 380,000 SVB shares in its Article 8 ("green," as per the EU labeling regime) funds and non-EU ESG funds between January and March of 2023. That number, which did not include "BlackRock's indirect ESG exposure to SVB, represent[ed] just under $100 million, based on valuations at the times of filing."[42]

Why would BlackRock vote the SVB shares in its ESG products in favor of SVB's board nominees when it knew there were serious risk-management problems—a big "G" or corporate-governance issue? Hard to figure, until you understand that the "G" in ESG really stands for "D." BlackRock's major concern was not primarily corporate governance—it was diversity, and SVB gave BlackRock what it wanted. With its ESG-friendly, politically connected, racially and sexually diverse board, SVB was widely considered an ESG-compliant company—and that included the G.

In fact, at the time of SVB's collapse, MSCI ESG Research, an ESG-ratings service, scored SVB's parent company an "A," or above average on a scale that runs from AAA to CCC. In an effort to explain that rating following SVB's collapse, MSCI vice president Bentley Kaplan claimed that "E, S, G does not cover core financial risks. We're looking to assess financially-relevant environmental, social and governance factors, not financially-relevant financial factors."[43]

If that sounds like double-talk, that's because it is.

Apparently, Kaplan believes that governance does not include the most critical and fundamental factors in keeping a business from failing. Maybe someone should have reminded him that the

"G" in ESG stands for corporate governance, which most definitely does include "financially relevant financial factors" such as a qualified board and adequate risk management.

The bottom line is that SVB's board of directors unquestionably would have benefited from a greater depth of banking experience (an actual governance issue), even if the result had been reduced board diversity (a faux-governance issue). A board with an appropriate level of banking expertise surely would have recognized the "really basic" banking risks SVB's management team somehow missed—particularly given the Fed's warning that SVB had liquidity issues.

Lacking that expertise, SVB suffered the worst possible result for any company—it collapsed. Fortunately for SVB's depositors (and unfortunately for all other taxpayers), the federal government ended up insuring them all, notwithstanding the pre-existing limits on FDIC coverage. I guess SVB's political connections had some value.

The Impact of Forced Board Diversity

Of course, the effect of the "G" in ESG is not always so stunning. There are degrees of competence and incompetence. An ineffective board can reduce a company's profitability without bankrupting the business.

On the other hand, an effective board of directors can both obviously and subtly contribute to a company's success. Experienced board members are vital when it comes to big decisions, such as firing the CEO or choosing a new one, but there are a hundred smaller ways that a good board can help a business.

CEOs will often consult their board members outside of official meetings to get advice on difficult issues. Even something as subtle as a knowledgeable comment by a director at a board dinner can result in a management team taking a new and more advantageous approach or avoiding a pitfall. A director's ability to make such cogent comments is more dependent on experience and expertise than race or sex.

To repeat—it is hard enough to make a profit in business when that is what the business is trying to do. Similarly, it is hard enough to get good board members when getting good board members is the objective—that is, finding people who add real value to the enterprise. When companies are forced to prioritize anything else—including demographic diversity—the consequences may not be as bad as complete business failure, but it will hurt the business over time.

That is only common sense, and it has been confirmed by peer-reviewed research.

For example, a 2017 analysis by Wharton business-school professor Katherine Klein found that while there is "research conducted by consulting firms and financial institutions" showing that having women board members increases a company's profitability, such research "is not as rigorous as peer-reviewed academic research." She also found that "[r]igorous, peer-reviewed studies suggest that companies do not perform better when they have women on the board. Nor do they perform worse."[44]

Let us look at some other peer-reviewed research.

A 2009 analysis by University of Oxford professor Renée B. Adams and London School of Economics professor Daniel Ferreira titled "Women in the Boardroom and Their Impact on Governance and Performance" concluded that "the average effect of gender diversity on firm performance is negative. . . . Our results suggest that mandating gender quotas for directors can reduce firm value for well-governed firms."[45]

A 2021 working paper by Harvard University professor Jesse Fried for the European Corporate Governance Institute (ECGI) found that "the empirical evidence provides little support for the claim that gender or ethnic diversity in the boardroom increases shareholder value. In fact, rigorous scholarship—much of it by leading female economists—suggests that increasing board diversity can actually lead to lower share prices."[46]

In 2023 Alex Edmans of the London Business School, Caroline Flammer of Columbia University, and Simon Glosser of the Federal Reserve Board published a broader analysis of how DEI affected businesses, which found that "[n]ew ideas, and thus superior financial performance, stem from cognitive" diversity—rather than "purely demographic diversity"—and require "bringing a range of perspectives and backgrounds into an organization," including "gender, race, age, disability, religion, marital status, sexual orientation, experience, education, political views and socioeconomic background."[47]

However, even including this broader range of background and perspectives as well as elements of DEI, the authors found "no evidence of a link between DEI and firm-level stock returns when controlling for firm characteristics, and no alpha to DEI portfolios when controlling for risk."[48]

In other words, as the authors reported, there is no link between diversity and "future stock returns."[49] But future stock returns are the very point of investing as a fiduciary duty bound to prioritize the client's financial interests—as opposed to an activist investor trying advance a social or political agenda. Those future stock returns are what fund clients' retirements.

ESG advocates claim that diversity improves business performance on the basis of a series of reports by the consulting firm McKinsey that link executive diversity to superior performance. However, those reports have been criticized as lacking academic peer review, being deeply flawed for confusing correlation with causation, cherry-picking data, and conflicted—given McKinsey's goal of selling consulting services.[50]

A 2024 study by Texas A&M professor Jeremiah Green and University of North Carolina professor John Hand applied McKinsey's approach to companies in the S&P 500 index and found no "statistically significant relations between McKinsey's . . . measures of executive racial/ethnic diversity" and not only industry-adjusted EBIT margin but also "industry-adjusted sales growth, gross margin, return on assets, return on equity, and total shareholder return." In fact, "better firm financial performance causes firms to diversify the racial/ethnic composition of their executives, not the reverse."[51]

The study's abstract concludes that the authors "inability to quasi-replicate [McKinsey's] results suggests that despite the imprimatur given to McKinsey's studies, they should not be relied on to support the view that publicly traded U.S. firms can expect to deliver improved financial performance if they increase the racial/ethnic diversity of their executives."[52]

In November of 2023, BlackRock released its own study on diversity, entitled "Lifting Financial Performance by Investing in Women." It claimed that "linkages between workforce diversity and corporate performance" were "robust" and that firms with greater gender parity produced better financial returns.[53] It was not peer reviewed.

Professor and ESG proponent Alex Edmans of the London Business School decided to review it "to help readers understand what they can take away from the study." He concluded that "[u]nfortunately, the answer is: almost nothing." According to Professor Edmans, Blackrock's "study made fundamental errors," by "using dubious measures of financial performance (and switching between them, perhaps cherry-picking the ones that work), using dubious measures of gender diversity (and switching between them), and omitting basic controls."[54]

Perhaps the academic data demonstrating no financial benefits to racial or sexual diversity policies, combined with BlackRock's having advanced such diversity policies as a financial benefit for years, help explain why the results of BlackRock's study were neither surprising nor considered credible.

I was in business for a very long time, and I can confirm that there is nothing magically good or bad about a director's skin color, gender, or sexuality. The qualities of a good business leader run the gamut from honesty to energy to experience to insight to organizational skills, and those gifts can be found in professionals of every background and color.

Nonetheless, supporters of board diversity argue that a racially or sexually diverse board of directors can bring diverse backgrounds, viewpoints, and perspectives into board discussions.[55] But as the 2023 ECGI working paper found, cognitive diversity—the diversity that matters—requires differing viewpoints based on far more than race or sex, including characteristics such as such as religion, politics, and experience. As the U.S. Fifth Circuit Court of Appeals stated in *Hamilton v. Dallas County*, it is hard to justify a "vision of diversity [that] doesn't include diverse viewpoints, if equity doesn't encompass equality for people of faith, and if inclusion involves excluding politically unpopular beliefs."[56]

If bringing in differing backgrounds, viewpoints, and perspectives were really the goal, SVB obviously could have used some political diversity. Political diversity may not have been on the Big Three's list of diverse characteristics, but having a couple of qualified and fiscally conservative Republicans or independents on SVB's board might well have brought in some helpful and diverse viewpoints and perspectives—regardless of the directors' race or sex.

That is not something you will hear from ESG advocates because the point of a collectivist board diversity requirement is not really to bring in differing viewpoints. The point is to provide racial or sexual preferences or quotas to make up for past discrimination. That is corporate affirmative action—a social-justice issue this country has debated for decades—not a corporate-governance concern.

Is It Legal?

Forced board diversity may not even be legal after the Supreme Court's 2023 decision in *Students for Fair Admissions v. Harvard*[57]—holding that race-based affirmative-action programs in college admissions violate the Fourteenth Amendment's Equal Protection Clause.

To quote Chief Justice Roberts's majority opinion, "Eliminating racial discrimination means eliminating all of it. Accordingly, the Court has held that the Equal Protection Clause applies 'without regard to any differences of race, of color, or of nationality'—it is 'universal in [its] application. . . . the guarantee of equal protection cannot mean one thing when applied to one individual and something else when applied to a person of another color.'"[58]

Although the issue of corporate affirmative action was not before the Court, in his concurring opinion Justice Gorsuch pointed out that Title VII of the Civil Rights Act—which applies to private businesses—also bars discrimination in hiring "because of such individual's race, color, religion, sex, or national origin."[59] It is unlikely that the Court will give discrimination a different definition when a case involving a private-sector business reaches it.

The question is whether that is a risk the Big Three should be encouraging the companies in which they invest to take.

Not the Big Three's Job

Up to this point I have not discussed in any depth the merits of diversity as a business practice. It can be a thorny issue. On the one hand, companies should be and are concerned with how the public, and especially potential customers, view the company brand. We live in a multi-ethnic country, and people generally expect that a company's officers and employees will include people of all diverse backgrounds.

At the same time, no business is any better than its people, and the people who serve a business in any capacity need to be skilled at actually running it, so a company that makes any other consideration more important than business acumen may soon find itself in hot water—as SVB found out.

The point is that whether to go down the diversity road, and how to navigate that road once a business in on it, should be decisions that the business's managers make in response to the circumstances facing their company, and in light of whatever legal constraints are in force. The last people in the world who should be making those decisions are the elites at passive-investment firms, who do not possess the information required to effectively manage the companies in their portfolios and who are not elected to prescribe rules for those who do. They are not even the actual beneficiaries of the company's share returns.

The CEOs of the Big Three know that their ESG agenda is

illegitimate, which is why they are trying to impose it in the guise of corporate governance. They know that as passive investors, their responsibility is to set up an index fund and then allow the companies in it to run their individual businesses and make the decisions on what will best maximize their individual performance and, as a result, the entire index fund's performance. They also know that their fiduciary duty is to prioritize financial returns for their clients, not to compel all the companies in which they invest to adopt their preferred collectivist social goals.

When people invest in a passive index fund, their financial interests are best served by the management team of each company in the underlying index independently doing what is necessary for its business to optimally succeed. That was the intent of passive index investing. From a financial-returns perspective, each company's needs will differ.

But the purpose of the "G" in ESG is not to impose diversity because it is good corporate governance, or because it will improve future stock returns. The purpose is to make American companies dance to the Big Three's ESG policy tune, whether they want to or not.

While the Big Three have certainly amassed the power to force ESG social policies on America's corporate sector, exercising that power to advance collectivist board-diversity requirements is not only inconsistent with the duty to prioritize their clients' financial interests but a usurpation of the peoples' right to determine, through their elected representatives, the rules within which businesses must operate.

In other words, it is every socialist's goal.

Chapter 3

SOCIAL INJUSTICE

"Human beings are born with different capacities. If they are free, they are not equal. And if they are equal, they are not free."

—*attributed to Aleksandr Solzhenitsyn, Russian author and prominent Soviet dissident*[1]

"The point was to end discrimination, not replace it with different discrimination."

—*Elon Musk, American businessman and investor*[2]

Which brings us to the "S" or social element of ESG. According to S&P Global, "the central question behind the 'S' in ESG" is how a company manages "its relationships with its workforce, the societies in which it operates, and the political environment."[3] In his 2021 CEO letter, Larry Fink noted that "[q]uestions of racial justice, inequality, or community engagement are often classed as an "S" issue in ESG."[4]

That all sounds benign enough, but once again the Big Three are gaslighting—using innocuous language to hide policies that they know are repellant to most Americans. What they mean by "S" is DEI—"diversity, equity, and inclusion"—and DEI's primary focus is on its "E" or "equity" element. As Larry Fink has stated, when it comes to DEI, "90% of it is E."[5]

"Equity" sounds like the same thing as "equality," or equal treatment, but is in fact the exact opposite. Its intent is to compel businesses to favor certain individuals over others, not on the basis of their character or competence, but because of their race, gender, ethnicity, or sexual orientation. So, while "equity" may sound like "equality" at first blush, what it means in practice is the opposite of what people may assume.

Simply stated and to help sort this out—the "S" in ESG means DEI, "DEI" means equity, and "equity" means mandated discrimination. The purpose of this deceptive language is to hide what equity advocates such as the Big Three are really doing, because they know their agenda turns basic American principles on their head.

The equal treatment of every individual regardless of race, sex, religion, or ethnicity is unquestionably a core American value. In fact, as I noted above, our Constitution, federal law, and Supreme Court decisions prohibit discrimination based on an individual's "race, color, religion, sex, or national origin."

In his famous "I Have a Dream" speech, Dr. Martin Luther King said, "I have a dream that my four little children will one day live in a nation where they will not be judged by the color of their skin but by the content of their character."[6] That clear, articulate, and compelling sentence foreshadowed the passage of the Civil Rights Act of 1964. Its message has become a part of who we are as a nation.

Consistent with Dr. King's dream, the American people clearly support hiring and promotion based on merit rather than race. A PEW survey in 2019 found that while a majority—75 percent—of Americans value workplace diversity, a similar majority—74 percent—believe that only an applicant's qualifications should be considered in hiring and promotions, even if the result is less racial or ethnic diversity. Support for qualifications-based hiring over diversity hiring was strong across racial lines (78 percent for whites, 69 percent for Hispanics, and 54 percent for Blacks) and political affiliation (90 percent for Republicans and 62 percent for Democrats).[7]

A 2023 CRC Research poll similarly found that the vast majority of Americans believe U.S. businesses should hire executives based solely on merits, qualifications, and character. According to the poll, 87 percent support a merit-based approach, while only 8 percent support a race and gender quota system and 5 percent were unsure or refused to answer. Even among Democrats and self-identifying liberals, 80 percent supported merit-based hiring while only 12 percent supported a race- and gender-based quota system.[8]

Of course Americans support these ideas. They know that a person's worth resides in that person's individual humanity, not in sex or sexual orientation, not in "identity markers" such as gender, and certainly not in the amount of melanin in his or her skin.

My personal experience as a CEO was that hiring people based on merit—rather than non-job-related characteristics—resulted in a diverse team of qualified individuals. Any CEO will tell you that qualifications and merit are not dependent on race or sex. It is not only inaccurate to assume otherwise but also biased and demeaning to your employees.

Equal opportunity is not only the right choice morally but also a win for both employees and employers. If you hire on the basis of merit, your team will increasingly and ultimately be diverse. Your employees will know they got their jobs because of who they are, not what they are. Individuals who earn their success know they have benefited from personal performance and tend to continue their efforts to perform at an elevated level.

It is particularly important that employees know they have been hired or promoted on merit rather than non-job-related characteristics. Otherwise, they will never experience the dignity and self-respect that come from earning their success. As the Supreme Court quoted in *Students for Fair Admissions*, "One of the principal reasons race is treated as a forbidden classification is that it demeans the dignity and worth of a person to be judged by ancestry instead of by his or her own merit and essential qualities."[9]

Americans agree. A January 2024 Gallup survey asked respondents whether they "think the Supreme Court's ruling to end the use of race/ethnicity in admission decisions for colleges and universities was mostly a good thing or mostly a bad thing." Over two-thirds (68 percent) said "mostly a good thing." That included 63 percent of Hispanics, 63 percent of Asians (the principal victims of racial preferences), and 52 percent of Blacks.[10]

Were the Big Three encouraging companies to hire individuals based on qualifications and merit without regard to "race, color, religion, sex, or national origin," they would be acting consistent with our laws, our core values, and good business sense—as one would expect of any business.

But that is not what DEI is about, nor what the Big Three are pressuring companies to do.

Rather, under the guise of DEI, the Big Three pressure—or compel—companies to implement hiring, promotion, and cultural policies based on race, gender, sexual preferences, and "sexual minority" status. This social-justice view of race and gender equity promotes equal outcomes, which are the very opposite of equal opportunity.

Equal Opportunity versus Equal Outcomes

Because the terms are often mistakenly used interchangeably, it is important to understand the significant differences between "equality" (that is, equality of opportunity) and "equity" (or equality of outcomes).

To demonstrate that difference, so called "equity" advocates often use what has become an iconic image of three people of different heights trying to see a baseball game over a fence. They equate equal opportunity with everyone having a stool of equal height that enables only the taller two to see over the fence. The supposedly equitable—or equal-outcomes—solution is to give everyone a stool that is appropriate for his or her height so all three can see over the fence.[11]

But the issue is not whether we should help individuals who are disadvantaged. The issue is whether we should treat people as individuals at all, or if we should create a caste system that defines some classes or groups of people as more worthy than others based on characteristics that tell us little or nothing about the actual circumstances of their lives, including whether they have suffered any real disadvantage or faced any real obstacles that they need help to overcome.

Besides, watching a ballgame over a fence is a whole lot different from putting together a sports team those kids would find worth watching—in other words, running a successful sports business. The stool enables people to engage equally in doing something for which ability is irrelevant. We are talking about spectators, not players. Let us change sports and apply that analogy to players on a basketball team, where both height and ability matter.

Should we allow shorter players to stand on stools of differing heights near the basket to equitably offset the taller players' advantage? Should we install a second, lower basket for shorter players? Should quicker players wear heavier shoes to equitably offset the slower players' speed disadvantage? Should players who practice more be told to practice less to offset the disadvantage suffered by less motivated players?

Obviously, no—because the goal is to put together the best team, and, to do so, the rational approach is to give everyone an equal opportunity to perform and then select the people who perform best, regardless of non-job-related characteristics.

If you allowed shorter players to stand on stools, added a second, lower basket, made the faster players wear heavier shoes, or had your best players practice less, the more-qualified players would stop trying to perform to the best of their ability, as there would be equalizing offsets that made their efforts worthless.

The players with the most potential would never become the players they could have been, teams would not perform to the level they otherwise could, and few people would enjoy watching the games, with or without stools. The team—if not the sport—would go out of business.

Professional basketball would be ruined—just as the Big Three will ruin American business if they are able to fully enforce their ESG/DEI "equity" agenda.

Of course the characteristics relevant to DEI are not height, speed, or talent but race, gender, ethnicity, sexual orientation, or the avant-garde identity classes du jour. So if our basketball team were all male and mostly Black, should we add less qualified Hispanics and Asians or women and then cut more-qualified players from the team to achieve racial and gender equity?

Obviously—and I mean obviously—compelling a basketball team to include fewer qualified players would result in a team that was less competitive than if it included only qualified players, regardless of race or sex. The same holds true in the business context because businesses are a whole lot more like basketball teams than they are like spectators trying to see over a fence.

If you hire the best people you can get, you will have both a qualified and a diverse team. If your hiring decisions are based on race or sex rather than qualifications and merit, you will have a diverse team that is less qualified, diminishing your business's success. As a result, prioritizing DEI bona fides over effectively running the business will negatively affect your company's financial results—which are the results the Big Three are supposed to be prioritizing.

Incentives matter. If everyone is given an equal opportunity to perform to the best of his or her ability, the result will be superior performance, not only for individuals but also for the teams that employ them. The equity or equal-outcomes approach by definition produces mediocre results—at best.

I say "at best" because those who claim that equity can produce better-than-mediocre results assume that people who know they are not judged by their performance will nonetheless be inspired to perform to the best of their abilities. But the opposite is true.

Why should anyone do his or her best, or try to perform at the highest level, when the game is rigged to equalize outcomes? This is one of the primary reasons that equal-opportunity free-market economies produce abundance and prosperity while equity-based socialist economies, which limit the incentives for success, produce poverty and want.

Incentives matter. Ignoring them produces irrational results.

Nonetheless, the "equity" approach certainly has its supporters—for example, Vice President Kamala Harris. In a 2020 presidential campaign video titled "There's a Big Difference between Equality and Equity," Harris argued that two people with the same—or equal—opportunity but starting from different places would not end up at the same place, in contrast to "equitable treatment," which "means we all end up at the same place."[12]

Yes, she actually said that. Out loud.

As someone President Biden selected based on his commitment to nominate a woman as vice president and preferably a woman of color[13] (clearly DEI or equity criteria), she certainly benefited from the equal-outcomes approach. Whether she was qualified—let alone the most qualified person—for the job and what impact that could have on the business of effectively running America, I will leave to the job-approval polls and the electorate.

In any event, popular opinion overwhelmingly supports equal opportunity over equal outcomes. Despite what Larry Fink may believe, "society" is not "turning to the private sector and asking that companies" resolve the equality-versus-equity debate in favor of equity.

Even America's most prominent socialist, Senator Bernie Sanders, independent senator from Vermont, was unable to distinguish equality from equity when first asked which he preferred by talk-show host Bill Maher. But after Maher explained the difference as equality of opportunity versus equality of outcomes, Sanders said he preferred equality of opportunity.[14]

It was not a tough call.

As a study by the left-leaning Brookings Institution acknowledged, "Americans believe in opportunity. . . . They are far more interested in equal opportunity than in equal results."[15] Apparently that is true even for some socialists.

In *Price v. Valvoline*,[16] a discrimination case decided in December of 2023, Judge James Ho of the U.S. Fifth Circuit Court of

Appeals addressed the "the growing concern that diversity has increasingly become a code word for discrimination" in his concurring opinion, articulately stating, "It's no defense that a diversity policy may be well intended—and that it's designed, not to disfavor any particular group, but to favor other groups. That's because favoring one race necessarily means disfavoring those of another race—whether at a company or on a college campus."

In posts on X that started with "DEI must DIE," Elon Musk expressed what most Americans believe—"The point was to end discrimination, not replace it with different discrimination. 'Diversity, Equity and Inclusion' are propaganda words for racism, sexism and other -isms. This is just as morally wrong as any other racism and sexism. Changing the target class doesn't make it right!"[17] Those posts were heresy to DEI hypocrites.

Musk hit the mark when he said that this is at bottom a moral issue. "Equity" policies demean and divide people of all backgrounds; they destroy excellence and therefore have severely negative effects on economic opportunity and professional standards. But they are not wrong because they have evil consequences—they have evil consequences because they are wrong.

As a quotation attributed to Aleksandr Solzhenitsyn, a renowned Russian author and prominent Soviet dissident, puts it, "Human beings are born with different capacities. If they are free, they are not equal. And if they are equal, they are not free."[18]

DEI and the Big Three

This is not an academic discussion. While we debate this issue as a society, the Big Three's message to company directors and managers could not be clearer—a commitment to discriminatory DEI policies is the mandate, and companies will be held accountable for failing to advance it.

Let us start with BlackRock. As we have seen, in a November 2017 interview Fink stated that BlackRock would "force behaviors" on "gender or race," stating that "[b]ehaviors are going to have to change, and this is one thing we are asking companies, you have to force behaviors and at BlackRock, we are forcing behaviors."[19]

In that same interview, when asked how to speed up change on race and gender diversity, Fink made it clear that DEI requires that companies have a comprehensive plan to create a cultural shift toward a more DEI-focused workforce. According to Fink, "It has to be imbued in the culture of the firm. It has to be talked about, it has to be shown. Behaviors across the entire firm in every region have to be similar, and every citizen of the firm has to understand what [are] acceptable behaviors and what are unacceptable behaviors."[20]

A few months later, Fink's 2018 letter directing CEOs to "serve a social purpose" stated that "[c]ompanies must ask themselves" whether they are "working to create a diverse workforce."[21]

His 2019 CEO letter went further, reiterating that society was looking to businesses to address "gender and racial inequality."[22] In 2021, he commended compliant companies that had "responded to calls for racial equity" (notably, not racial equality). That letter also asked that "sustainability reports" reflect "long-term plans to improve diversity, equity and inclusion, as appropriate by region."[23]

Consistent with Fink's mandates, the mission of BlackRock's "Stewardship" team includes providing corporate management with "insight on environmental, social, and governance (ESG) considerations."[24] And, where it deems appropriate, it will "hold directors accountable for their action or inaction."[25]

The message could hardly be clearer—*You will comply!*

Again, BlackRock is not alone. Vanguard's "Investment Stewardship Insights" report for 2021 states that DEI "remain[s] a top engagement priority for Vanguard with our funds' portfolio companies" and that Vanguard's "oversight of strategy and disclosure of progress" on DEI, including "in the workforce is particularly acute for U.S. companies."[26]

The report called "for companies to proactively enhance disclosures of their commitments, strategy, and key risks related to DEI issues, along with the boards' process for overseeing these matters." Vanguard made it clear that it expected management to have "an ongoing process to identify, mitigate, and remediate company policies, practices, operations, and business cultures that may lead to inequities, including those related to gender, race, ethnicity, or other categories that include historically underrepresented groups."[27]

Of course, where Vanguard sees a lack of board oversight on DEI, it may "withhold support for the election of relevant directors in order to express [its] concern."[28]

Again, you will comply!

State Street Global Advisors has a website entitled "Guidance on Diversity Disclosures and Practices," which states that that "companies have a responsibility to effectively manage and disclose risks and opportunities related to diversity, equity, and inclusion, particularly regarding gender, race, and ethnicity." It considers this "a priority" for its stewardship team. SSGA encourages its "portfolio companies to consider providing disclosures about the full diversity of their organization" including "LGBTQ-identified individuals."[29]

If a company in SSGA's portfolio fails to make a commitment to align with the majority of its DEI "expectations" or if SSGA's "engagement" on DEI with a company "is not productive," SSGA "will most likely support proposals that would meaningfully advance diversity-related disclosures."[30]

In 2022, SSGA's "Stewardship team" reported "over 275 engagements with a variety of companies globally on the topic of diversity, equity, and inclusion" since August of 2020. It had "proactively reached out to 60 of the largest employers in [its] portfolio to have deeper conversations on human capital management and diversity, equity, and inclusion."[31] Its "goal [was] to increase our understanding of DEI best practices, monitor the state of DEI risk management at our investee companies, and drive greater adoption of our suggested disclosures across the market."[32]

DEI and the Big Three's Fiduciary Obligations

As perhaps the most powerful economic cartel in U.S. history, the Big Three may have the power to compel their portfolio companies to implement DEI, but they do not have the right. If you are a financial firm investing other peoples' money, your fiduciary obligation is to prioritize your clients' financial interests, not to implement policies designed to advance your CEO's social or political agenda—all the more so if you are a passive index investor.

Passive index investors such as the Big Three have been entrusted with other peoples' money to earn as big a return for them as is possible—and legal. These firms vindicate their trust, and satisfy their fiduciary duty, by allowing the management team for each individual company to perform to the best of its ability with a focus on profitability. Collectivist social policies—and especially policies like DEI, which typically undermine profitability—inhibit the ability of each company's management team to address the issues specific to its particular company, reducing its ability to maximize returns for investors.

As I noted in chapter 2, a 2023 European Corporate Governance Institute working paper found "no evidence of a link between DEI and firm-level stock returns when controlling for firm characteristics, and no alpha to DEI portfolios when controlling for risk."[33] Simply, "no link" between board, management, or workforce diversity and "future stock returns."[34] That seems like it should be important for organizations duty bound to prioritize their clients' financial interests.

Apart from the studies, it is common sense that companies that hire on merit will achieve the best business results over time. My experience has been that merit hiring will also typically produce a diverse workforce. No race and neither sex have a monopoly on merit. The only people who think otherwise are the elites of the world who, having lived in a bubble containing mostly people like themselves, seem to believe, whether they admit it or not, that nobody who is Black, brown, female, or gay is competent enough to succeed in business on his or her own. If they believed otherwise, merit-based hiring in this day and age would be a non-issue.

When the goal of a business is superior performance, it gives all applicants an equal opportunity and hires the best people without regard to characteristics that are irrelevant to their performance. In twenty-first-century America, the result will inevitably be diversity that is broad-based and natural rather than forced and resented.

It may not be diversity that meets the precise mathematical mandates or quotas of ESG or DEI advocates, but it will certainly not produce a lily-white male heterosexual workforce, because the qualities necessary for success in business (or life) are motivation, determination, intelligence, discipline, and leadership, and those qualities are found across all races, sexes, and backgrounds.

But equal opportunity and hiring based solely on qualifications, merit, and character are not what the Big Three are demanding. Rather, they are demanding that the companies in which they invest prioritize DEI regardless of the impact on any individual company's profitability or their own clients' financial interests.

These demands go well beyond hiring and require companies to imbed DEI throughout their corporate cultures. Not surprisingly, given the Big Three's overbearing commitment to DEI principles, companies are anxious to demonstrate their commitment to DEI's cultural and social goals to avoid threatened adverse proxy votes from the Big Three, who are likely their largest shareholders. So let us look at how policies designed to demonstrate a commitment to DEI could affect a company's financial results.

How a DEI-Focused Corporate Culture Can Affect Performance: Silicon Valley Bank and Boeing

Running a company successfully is extremely difficult even if that is your prime focus—and next to impossible when it is not. With DEI and the associated culture war invading boardrooms and C-suites, maintaining a focus on business success is increasingly difficult.

For SVB, not having a chief risk officer for nine critical months or a board with sufficiently qualified directors certainly contributed to its collapse, as we have seen. But beyond these obvious issues, SVB had a more insidious problem—management's focus on DEI.

There is no doubt that DEI was a pervasive factor in SVB's corporate culture. In a November 2021 document titled "Diversity, Equity & Inclusion," the bank touted its commitment to "increase diversity, equity and inclusion throughout our workforce."[35] SVB had DEI webinars where "panelists explore[d] ways to advance DE&I in the workplace."[36] Its 2022 ESG Report listed as a strategic initiative "Building a Culture of Diversity, Equity and Inclusion" and set percentage quotas for including women, Blacks, and Hispanics in senior leadership roles.[37]

SVB's DEI social goals permeated its corporate culture.

The message was clear, and SVB's employees heard it. When the *Financial Times* interviewed SVB employees following the bank's collapse, they expressed their belief that its management had been "inordinately focused on social issues" when they should have been focused on "properly hedging against its interest rate risk."[38] Apparently, it was that obvious.

One executive complained about a corporate culture where it felt like employees were "at work on a college campus," with "weekly internal 'TED talks' on social issues and classes on 'how to make sure you were not committing a microaggression.'" According to another employee, "there was an unseriousness to it" an "overemphasis on things that weren't important and not enough on things that are."[39]

These are comments any CEO would find disturbing. Yet upper management at SVB either never heard them (perhaps because employees felt uneasy expressing them) or failed to heed them. Even in retrospect, it is difficult to determine the extent to which the DEI "social justice" focus at SVB affected its performance. But for anyone who has ever run a large company, the risks should have been obvious—and terrifying. DEI here was more than just a distraction. It was destructive.

In retrospect, there must have been SVB executives who saw and understood the bank's obvious interest rate/liquidity risk. So, where were they, and why didn't they speak up? This is where the potential impact of a DEI-focused corporate culture is difficult to ignore.

To demonstrate the problem let us say, hypothetically, that a DEI—or forced diversity—hire with responsibility for a portion of the business failed to see an important business risk. With all the DEI webinars and classes on how to avoid "microaggressions," if a lower-level employee who was not in a favored group saw the danger, how likely is it that he would risk challenging that manager's competence by pointing out what he or she (or "they") were missing?

The DEI-hired manager might characterize such a challenge as a "microaggression" rather than constructive criticism. That concern could certainly discourage an employee from speaking up—making the risk that this problem would go unaddressed far greater.

For the employee who saw the problem, the safer course would have been to keep his or her mouth shut. Better to keep quiet than risk being labeled a racist, sexist, or homophobe.

When words mean something other than their accepted definitions, when a casual comment or constructive criticism can be interpreted as a microaggression, when you need classes to learn how to have a conversation with your co-workers, when people are hired on the basis of something other than merit—communications are stifled, employees become risk averse, problems go unaddressed, and opportunities are lost. When those policies are "imbued in the culture of the firm"—to quote Larry Fink—adverse consequences are all but unavoidable. A *macroaggression*, such as bankrupting the company, becomes a real possibility.

I am certainly not advocating that employees insult or verbally attack each other to make a point. Common sense and common courtesy can go a long way. But there are clear risks when corporate DEI policies displace commonsense, profit-focused business practices and create a fear of offense that can stifle employee communications essential to any business's success.

We will never know whether SVB would have pursued DEI goals as aggressively absent its largest shareholders—the Big Three—pressuring companies to pursue those goals. We will also never know for certain the extent to which SVB being "inordinately focused on social issues" led to its failure. But surely there were SVB executives and employees who understood the obvious interest rate/liquidity risks the bank faced. They either remained silent or were ignored—and the sixteenth-largest bank in America collapsed.

Unfortunately, these DEI risks have spread throughout the corporate community, permeating our economy in no small part because of the Big Three's encouragement. An online initiative called "CEO Action for Diversity and Inclusion" lists over twenty-five hundred CEOs who have pledged to promote DEI initiatives in their companies, including virtually every major American corporation.[40]

SVB's CEO was a signatory.[41]

Boeing is another example of a company where management diverted its focus from running a successful business to meeting DEI goals. Boeing describes itself as "a leading global aerospace company" that "develops, manufactures and services commercial airplanes, defense products and space systems. . . ."[42] A key—if not the key—to Boeing's historical success is that people considered the planes it designed and manufactured safe. Airlines will not buy commercial aircraft that travelers do not trust.

Unfortunately, Boeing's reputation for safety has taken several well-deserved hits in recent years, beginning with a 2018 crash of a Boeing 737 MAX 8 jet that claimed 189 lives, followed by a 2019 737 MAX 8 crash that claimed an additional 157 lives. In addition to the tragic loss of human life, hundreds of Boeing's planes were grounded for nearly two years, costing Boeing billions in financial losses and fines.

Concerns about Boeing's commitment to safety did not end in 2019. In 2020, on a Japan Airlines flight, a Boeing 777's engine failed in a "loud explosion." According to Aerotime Hub, "[t]he initial inspection revealed that the engine cover appeared to have come off during the flight.[43]

In 2021, the right-side engine of a Boeing 777 broke apart on a United Airlines flight near Denver, leading to the grounding of dozens of Boeing 777 aircraft worldwide.[44]

Obviously, job number one for Boeing's management team was to restore confidence in the safety of Boeing's planes. The company needed to let the world know that its corporate culture was centered on and dedicated to safety—and that message needed to reflect the real priorities of the company's operations.

If Boeing suffered further safety-related issues, or if the public perceived Boeing's corporate culture as focused on non-safety-related issues, the results could be disastrous for the business. While management made efforts to improve Boeing's safety-focused image, that certainly—perhaps strangely—was neither the sole focus of their message to consumers nor the primary goal Boeing's board set for management.

Boeing's largest shareholder is Vanguard, followed by Black-Rock. State Street is the fourth-largest shareholder.[45] Collectively, the Big Three held just shy of 20 percent of Boeing's shares. By 2020, their positions on DEI were well known to every CEO, including Boeing's.

So perhaps it is not surprising that, in 2020, Boeing "put in place an 'equity action plan' to raise the presence of under-represented groups in its workforce" and "established a Racial Equity Task Force"—according to an article in *Forbes*.[46]

The *Forbes* article, titled "Boeing Releases First-Ever Diversity Report, Moves to Bolster Inclusion Efforts," reported that in April of 2021 Boeing had issued its first assessment of workforce diversity in its 105-year history. According to Boeing CEO David Calhoun, the report showed Boeing was "on a par with the aerospace industry" and had "made advancements in some areas, but we are not where we want to be."[47]

Boeing's chief human-resources officer, Michael D'Ambrose, said that "the real goal is to change Boeing's culture because the research on how diversity and inclusion can improve a company's performance is 'compelling.'" One area of particular focus was "tracking the progress of LGBTQ+ employees within the company."[48]

According to *Forbes*, "The fact that Boeing pursued its diversity assessment in the midst of one of the worst years in the company's history presumably reflects the priority it assigns to becoming more inclusive."[49]

There is every reason to believe that is true.

According to Boeing's 2022 proxy statement, its 2021 management-incentive-compensation plan was based 100 percent on "Financial Performance" (so profitability) with a 15 percent kicker for "Product Safety | Employee Safety | Quality."[50] One could argue that product safety deserved its own category with a more significant percentage weighting to send the right message to Boeing's managers as well as its consumers and to actually increase the company's profitability—if not its chances of survival.

So maybe it was not a great idea to tell the public that Boeing's management was 100 percent incentivized to prioritize making money—with only 15 percent extra if they happened to find some time to focus on product safety—at a moment when people were starting to think that flying on a Boeing plane put their lives at risk. You would think an airline-manufacturing company would understand that when the reliability of its products was in question, an urgent emphasis on safety would be the best way to increase profitability.

But here is the really disturbing part—in 2022, Boeing changed its bonus plan. While a reduced 75 percent of management's incentive compensation would now be weighted towards profitability, Boeing was diluting the remaining 25 percent from where its focus should have been—on product safety, employee safety, and quality—by adding "Climate | Diversity, Equity & Inclusion."[51]

So, rather than increasing management focus on product safety, Boeing was including it in a grab bag of incentive-based goals that would now include both climate and DEI. Boeing acknowledged this change, stating that "[w]hile our 2021 design incorporated operational performance in the areas of product safety, employee safety and quality, for 2022 we will add two other focus areas critical to our long-range business plan: climate and diversity, equity and inclusion (DE&I)."[52]

At a time of broad-based public concern about Boeing's commitment to product safety—at a time its planes were literally falling out of the sky—Boeing's Compensation Committee placed its management team's focus primarily on profits while putting product safety and the quality of its products on the same level as climate change and DEI. The phrase "rearranging the deck chairs on the *Titanic*" comes to mind.

Just to be sure that people (and specifically that its DEI-supporting major shareholders) got the message, Boeing also issued a "Global Equity, Diversity & Inclusion 2023 Report," which stated that "in 2022, for the first time in our company's history, we tied incentive compensation to inclusion." According to the report, Boeing's goal for 2022 had been "to achieve diverse interview slates for at least 90% of manager and executive openings," and, the company boasted, it had exceeded the target, "with 92% of interview slates being diverse, resulting in 47% diverse hires." For 2023, Boeing "raised the bar and expect[ed that] at least 92.5% of those interview slates w[ould] be diverse."[53]

So Boeing not only admitted but bragged about hiring and promoting on the basis of identity rather than merit, at the very time when it was faced with rising and justified criticism over its ability to design and manufacture planes in which the public could feel safe risking their lives.

Perhaps it would have been more effective to state that Boeing was hiring the most qualified safety-focused personnel available—regardless of race, sex, or ethnicity—and that its bonus plan was based solely (or at the very least primarily) on product safety. But I guess hindsight is 20–20.

The following year, on January 5, 2024, a fuselage panel on a Boeing 737-9 Max blew out on an Alaska Airlines flight, causing the plane to depressurize and forcing the pilot to make an emergency landing. Luckily, no one was seated directly next to the panel that blew out. Following this incident, Alaska Airlines "decided to take the precautionary step of temporarily grounding [its] fleet of 65 Boeing 737-9 aircraft."

According to the *New York Post*, the National Transportation Safety Board said the Alaska Airlines incident "could have been caused by hardware intended to keep the fuselage panel secure that was never actually installed." United Airlines subsequently "found loose bolts and other 'installation issues' on some of its Boeing 737 MAX 9 jets that it inspected following the Alaska Airlines flight."[54]

The failure to attach necessary hardware and to tighten bolts seems like a pretty strong indication that the focus at Boeing should not have been ESG and DEI goals.

Elon Musk thought so. On January 10, 2024, he reposted a tweet on the reduced safety focus in Boeing's 2022 bonus plan and asked, "Do you want to fly in an airplane where they prioritized DEI hiring over your safety? That is actually happening." His post got 33.5 million views.[55]

He also said that "[m]erit should be the only reason for hiring, especially for jobs where your family's lives are at stake."[56] Despite criticism from DEI supporters on the Left, he subsequently added, "People will die due to DEI," citing an NBC news piece quoting Boeing's CEO as acknowledging Boeing had made "mistakes" with respect to the Alaska Airlines incident.[57]

The Left may not have liked it, but Musk was just stating what many Americans were already thinking, with some justification. A lot of them are travelers who like to enjoy incident-free flights— and arrive at their destinations alive. A March 2024 Morning Consult survey found that following the Alaska Airlines 737 Max 9 blowout, "[n]et trust in Boeing among U.S. adults [was] just 9 percentage points as of February, down 16 points since December" and that "[b]usiness and first class flyers lost the most trust in Boeing. . . . The company now has a net trust rating of 16 points among this group, a 26 point decrease from Q4 2023."[58]

And the hits kept coming. On March 4, 2024, an engine on a United Airlines Boeing 737 in flight from Houston to Fort Myers, Florida, caught fire shortly after takeoff. The pilot was able to return safely to Houston. An article in the *Dallas Express* titled "Is Boeing Prioritizing DEI over Safety?" stated that "[o]bservers of recent near-disasters in the airline industry are beginning to link the industry's troubles to efforts to implement diversity, equity, and inclusion initiatives in aviation companies' hiring practices rather than prioritizing safety."[59]

The Houston incident was apparently the straw that broke the DonkEI's back.

A March 7, 2024, *Wall Street Journal* article reported a change in Boeing's incentive-compensation plan. Titled "Boeing to Tie More of Employees' Incentive Pay to Safety," it reported a change in the incentive-compensation plan at Boeing's "commercial unit, its largest, where safety and quality metrics will now account for 60% of annual bonuses." As for "Boeing's other two units, defense and services, financial metrics will still determine 75% of bonuses. But quality and safety will be the only factors to determine the operational scores."[60] In other words, DEI and climate, thankfully, were out of the bonus formula—quality and safety were in.

Seriously, it was about time.

Whether Boeing can reverse its fortunes and restore its reputation for quality and safety, only time will tell. Increasing the quality and safety incentives for management will certainly help. But Boeing still claims online that it "aspire[s] to create the most equitable, diverse and inclusive company on earth."[61] Hopefully, it also aspires to design and manufacture the safest planes on earth. In either event, it appears that Boeing will continue its DEI hiring efforts.

While the repeated safety and quality incidents themselves are the primary source of Boeing's woes, its DEI directives and incentives have clearly contributed to the public perception that safety and quality have not been Boeing's primary focus. It is both the wrong policy and the wrong message.

It is difficult to ignore the extent to which DEI has contributed to the damage Boeing's reputation has suffered. It is also difficult to ignore the extent to which the Big Three's policies made it clear to the boards and CEOs of American corporations—including Boeing—that such DEI directives and incentives were required. But it is the company's shareholders—as well as its consumers, employees, suppliers, and the communities in which it does business—that will bear the financial burden.

It is important to understand that the stories I have related in this chapter are the tip of the iceberg—the most visible and immediately disastrous effects of the ESG movement and its DEI element. The actual damage is much greater. Under pressure from the Big Three, an enormous swath of American companies have been following policies that effectively sabotage the quality of their products, the competence of their management, and the profitability of their businesses.

And there you have stakeholder capitalism.

The Impact of DEI Differs by Company

As I noted above, there are times when a company's management might, for sound business reasons, want to visibly support a political cause and incorporate some aspects of the DEI agenda into the company's brand strategy. The most obvious case is when a company's customer base or target market tends to support progressive social or political causes. Think Nike, Starbucks, Ben & Jerry's, or Patagonia.

Let us look at Nike and its Colin Kaepernick ads. Kaepernick was never considered much of a football player, but he knelt during the national anthem before an NFL game to protest racial injustice and police brutality against people of color. In an interview with NFL Network's Steve Wyche, Kaepernick stated that "I am not going to stand up to show pride in a flag for a country that oppresses black people and people of color."[62]

His protest helped spark a debate on "social justice," and he became a controversial figure. So Nike used him in an ad.

After the ad ran there was backlash from people who objected to multi-millionaire athletes disrespecting our flag. Some people stopped purchasing Nike products, but the ad appealed to Nike's target youth market, and Nike's sales improved. The BBC ran an article headlined "Nike Sales Defy Kaepernick Ad Campaign Backlash."[63]

Discussing the Kaepernick ad, Nike CEO Mark Parker told financial analysts that it "resonated" with consumers, "driving a real uptick in traffic and engagement, both socially as well as commercially."[64] In other words, the ad campaign drove profits. That is not so much about promoting a culture of inclusivity as it is about making money with an ad that appeals to your target market. For Nike's management team, that was a good call.

By the way, my company did something similar, albeit in a different context. When I took over as CEO of CKE Restaurants, the company that owns the Carl's Jr. and Hardee's brands, we determined that our best target market would be hungry young men (eighteen- to thirty-four-year-old males) who account for a disproportionately significant percentage of burger sales. We asked ourselves how to get the attention of that market, and what resulted was a series of ads featuring scantily clad well-known models and actresses eating our products. We also had ads with male actors, but they garnered far less attention.

We received a lot of blowback from social groups (almost exclusively from the Right) complaining that the ads were inappropriate. But our sales and profits skyrocketed.

We were not trying to remake society, and we were not pursuing some political or social agenda. We just wanted to beat our competitors and make money, and we did. (It helped that we also improved our service and cleanliness, revamped our kitchens, and improved our supply chains so that we could produce the best hamburgers in the fast-food market. Your products must live up to your ads.) These ads were an important part of our success. It was plain old free-market capitalism, just like Nike's campaign.

In 2020, John Donahoe, who replaced Parker as Nike's CEO, told the *Wall Street Journal* that Nike would approach social activism "guided by what is good for our consumer, good for our athletes, good for our company."[65] It was a reasonable company-specific, profit-focused approach.

Nike's social-activist campaign increased both its DEI bona fides and its profits. But this approach does not make good financial sense for every company—which should be the Big Three's primary concern. That's why a collectivist approach is counterproductive.

On the contrary, social activism poses significant financial risks for companies with target markets that, like most markets, are focused on price and quality rather than progressive social or political causes. This is why decisions on such issues should be made by the management of the companies involved rather than by the Big Three pressuring companies to demonstrate their commitment to collectivist DEI social policies.

For example, support for the LGBTQIA community has become a prominent factor in demonstrating a corporate culture supportive of DEI norms.[66] As is noted above, SSGA encourages its "portfolio companies to consider providing disclosures about the full diversity of their organization" including "LGBTQ-identified individuals."[67]

One common industry measure for whether a company is DEI/LGBTQIA compliant is the Human Rights Campaign Foundation's (HRC) Corporate Equality Index (CEI), a "national benchmarking tool on corporate policies, practices and benefits pertinent to lesbian, gay, bisexual, transgender and queer employees" according to HRC's website.[68]

The CEI for 2023–2024 included 1,384 companies.[69] BlackRock and Vanguard were among the 545 companies that received perfect scores (as was Nike).[70] SSGA's website touts that it is "proud of receiving an 100% from the Human Rights Campaign's Corporate Equality Index."[71]

A perfect CEI score may be a plus for DEI purposes and even for your business if your customer base is progressive. But not so much for companies with a broader customer base and especially not for a company that has branded itself as producing products and entertainment families can enjoy without worrying about whether the content is age-appropriate or consistent with their values.

Let us take Disney as an example. With its theme parks and family-friendly movies, the Walt Disney Company has dominated the family-entertainment marketplace for decades. A key component—really the *sine quo non*—of its success was parental trust. It is no exaggeration to say that parents once trusted Disney with their children.

When my children were growing up, the observation, "It's OK for the kids to watch, it's a Disney movie," was a common parental refrain. The value of that phrase for Disney was incalculable. It was a huge competitive asset that Disney should never have put at risk.

So it seemed almost incomprehensible when Disney management went public with its opposition to a Florida parental-rights bill. People wondered why Disney was even taking a position on, let alone opposing, a Florida law barring classroom instruction on gender and sexuality before the fourth grade (when children are around the ripe old age of eight). It seemed inconsistent with everything Disney stood for, going back to the 1920s.

Then things got even worse, as the management explained that Disney was intentionally including woke sexual ideology in its content for children—regardless of their parents' values.

Disney executive producer Latoya Raveneau explained that her team had a "not-at-all-secret gay agenda" and was regularly "adding queerness" to children's programming with Disney's blessing, as the company was "going hard" to be supportive.[72]

So hard that Disney's general entertainment content president Karey Burke promised to make at least half the characters in the company's productions LGBTQIA and racial minorities by year's end.[73]

And if there were any remaining doubts about Disney's intent, its "diversity and inclusion manager" Vivian Ware proclaimed that Disney was eliminating any mention of "boys" and "girls" in its theme parks to create "that magical moment" for children who do not identify with traditional gender roles.[74]

Perhaps not surprisingly, Disney has received perfect CEI scores through 2022[75] and remains committed to both ESG[76] and DEI[77]—with a branding strategy disconnected from its target market and profitability. Some employees realized that these statements and policies would offend the traditional family segment of Disney's target market and spoke up, albeit anonymously.

In a 2022 open letter published online, these employees stated that Disney was "an increasingly uncomfortable place to work for those of us whose political and religious views are not explicitly progressive." They noted that "the tomorrow being reimagined doesn't seem to have much room for religious or political conservatives within the company." They warned that this "politicization" might make "our more conservative customers feel similarly unwanted."[78] Ya think?

While Disney did not seem to care, its customers and share-holders did. Disney's movies have recently underperformed at the box office.[79] According to *Forbes*, Disney lost about a billion dollars on just four "woke" movie flops in 2023, productions denounced by critics as pushing social agendas, storylines, and characters.[80]

And Disney's streaming operation, which is where kids watch these days, has shed tens of millions of subscribers worldwide (including losses in the U.S. and Canada).[81]

As a result, and according to Disney's financial disclosures, it has experienced a "decline in domestic advertising revenue . . . due to a decrease of 14% from fewer impressions, reflecting lower average viewership, partially offset by an increase of 7% from higher rates."[82] In other words, a double-digit drop in advertising revenue because people are not watching—partially offset by Disney charging advertisers more for reaching a smaller audience

Even Disney's theme-park business slowed. A July 2023 *Wall Street Journal* article titled "Disney World Hasn't Felt This Empty in Years" credited "Disney's recent price hikes and changes to park operations" for having "soured some families on visiting the Most Magical Place on Earth."[83]

Perhaps the higher prices and new features alienated consumers. Or perhaps something else was at play.

Turns out Disney's anonymous employees were right about certain customers not feeling wanted. After reports of Disney's plans to include queer ideology in content for children, a Trafalgar Group poll found that over 68 percent of respondents were less likely to do business with Disney—including 48 percent of Democrats. Overall, only 9 percent were more likely—including 14 percent of Democrats.[84]

In 2023, as part of a restructuring, through several rounds of layoffs, Disney announced it was parting ways with roughly seven thousand employees.[85]

The lesson here is simple—*do not offend your target market.* What Disney did was about as smart as if the producers of the old *Captain Kangaroo* kids' show had decided to feature a striptease in the opening credits.

I mentioned before that when I ran CKE Restaurants, we based a marketing campaign explicitly on the appeal of beautiful women who were—to put it bluntly—often scantily clad. That worked because our target market was young male adults. We would have had quite a different campaign if, like McDonald's, the customers we were targeting were families with young children. You must appeal to, not offend, your target market to be successful.

When management teams place social issues over appealing to (or at least not offending) their target markets, the consequences can be costly. That may sound obvious, but apparently it is not.

It was obvious to Disney's investors, though.

Disney's market cap was around $250 billion[86] when the controversy began in early March 2022.[87] By October, its market cap had declined to around $170 billion, a $80 billion or 32 percent drop. For comparison purposes, over this same period, the S&P 500 declined about 9 percent.[88] When the S&P went up in 2023, Disney continued to underperform. Its market cap, which had spent all of 2021 above $250 billion, spent nearly all of 2023 below $200 billion.[89]

By late 2023, the situation was so bad that Disney was compelled to admit that its DEI agenda had hurt the company and shareholders. In its annual SEC report for the fiscal year ending September 30, 2023, Disney acknowledged that its progressive social and political agenda might have alienated a segment of the population.[90]

Disney stated that "our revenues and profitability are adversely impacted when our entertainment offerings and products, as well as our methods to make our offerings and products available to consumers, do not achieve sufficient consumer acceptance." Disney then conceded that "consumers' perceptions of our position on matters of public interest, including our efforts to achieve certain of our environmental and social goals, often differ widely and present risks to our reputation and brands."[91]

Clear enough.

Sounds like a problem that good management with a profits focus could solve. Disney's consumers are making their position known, which is the hallmark of free-market capitalism—Adam

Smith's "invisible hand" in action. But the influence of financial elites who are determined to undermine consumer economic power to achieve their desired social goals—including DEI—remains an impediment.

Disney's largest shareholders are DEI stalwarts Vanguard, BlackRock, and SSGA, in that order. Collectively, as of May 7, 2024, they owned an impressive 19.05 percent of Disney's stock.[92] Those shares lost significant value because Disney decided to advance the ESG/DEI agenda despite the obvious potential to offend its target market and dilute demand for its products.

In an early 2024 proxy contest, hedge-fund icon Nelson Peltz attempted to elect two directors to Disney's board. Peltz stated in a March 2024 interview with the *Financial Times* that he did not want to fire Disney CEO Robert Iger. Rather he wanted "to help him."[93] Peltz criticized Disney for becoming too "woke." According to Peltz, "People go to watch a movie or a show to be entertained.... They don't go to get a message."

Peltz took particular aim at movies *The Marvels* and *Black Panther,* asking, "Why do I have to have a Marvel that's all women? Not that I have anything against women, but why do I have to do that? Why can't I have Marvels that are both? Why do I need an all-Black cast?"

Peltz lost the proxy contest. According to the *Wall Street Journal,* he "failed to win crucial support from the big index funds, Black-Rock, State Street and Vanguard, some of which had previously backed him" because he "turned off some of their top decision makers" in the *Financial Times* interview when he "questioned why 'woke' Disney made movies such as 'The Marvels' and 'Black Panther' with primarily female and Black casts, respectively."[94]

Apparently even questioning Disney's embrace of woke policies that were damaging its business was too much for the Big Three's decision makers. Politics and woke culture outweighed the best financial interests of Disney's investors. Again, it is difficult to say whether, absent support from its major shareholders, Disney would continue pursuing its destructive ESG and DEI goals in the face of consumer reaction. Disney CEO Robert Iger is an advocate for companies advancing progressive social goals despite the obvious financial risks. He might have pursued his DEI agenda even without pressure from the Big Three. But most CEOs would not, unless—as in Nike's case—they have a firm and well-documented belief that the market benefits outweigh the risk.

I have had personal experience with many top leaders of American business. It is safe to say that most of them would not deliberately risk destroying their company brands, alienating their customers, and sacrificing 32 percent of the value of their company's shares. They may not be as smart as they think they are, but they are not dumb enough to do that—unless they are coerced into it by financial firms that control a huge block of their stock and think they are entitled to force a social agenda down the throat of American business.

Disney is not alone in placing DEI goals over profitability. Target is another recent example. On May 17, 2023, Target CEO Brian Cornell described his support for his company's DEI initiatives, stating, "The things we've done from a DEI standpoint, it's adding value. It's helping us drive sales, it's building greater engagement with both our teams and our guests, and those are just the right things for our business today."[95]

Days later, a group of consumers declared a boycott, objecting to a line of June "Pride Month" pro-LGBTQ+ merchandise Target had introduced—including pride-themed children's items and baby onesies.[96] Facing a public-relations disaster, Target management took "emergency" action, "directing some managers and district senior directors to tamp down the Pride sections in their stores over fears of re-creating a 'Bud Light situation.'"[97] Target moved some LGBTQ+ items to less prominent parts of its stores and removed other merchandise including "tuck-friendly" (penis-concealing) swimwear.[98]

On May 17, Target's market cap was about $74 billion. Two weeks later, it was approximately $60 billion. By October, it was below $50 billion, a 32 percent decline.[99] Over this same period, the S&P 500 was flat.

Target's largest shareholders are Vanguard, State Street, and

BlackRock, in that order. Collectively, as of May 7, 2024, they owned an impressive 24.55 percent of Target's stock.[100]

Anheuser Busch InBev offers another example—the "Bud Light situation." Its controversial partnership with transgender activist Dylan Mulvaney—sending Mulvaney, a biological male, custom beer cans to mark "365 days of girlhood"—was a public-relations (and financial) fiasco. After more than two decades as America's top-selling beer, Bud Light lost the lead to the new American favorite—Modelo Especial—a month later.[101] The Bud Light brand may never recover.

AB's market cap was around $130 billion when the controversy began in early April of 2023. By October, it had dropped to about $106 billion, a $24 billion or 18 percent decline in five months.[102] Over this same period, the S&P 500 was flat.[103]

The lesson here is simple. If your company's target market consists of more than social progressives, "Go woke, go broke" might be a slogan worth keeping in mind. Your customers and shareholders will thank you.

The ESG "S" and the DEI "E"

Nobody should be fooled—and increasingly, Americans are not fooled—by the benign-sounding phrases the Big Three use to force their preferences on American business. There is nothing diverse, equitable, or inclusive about the DEI agenda—it is three lies in one acronym. It is a cover for racializing the hiring process and pushing racial and sexual equity and the queer/trans LGBTQIA+ agenda in the public square. Some select companies may profit from adopting some or all of the DEI agenda, but for most it is a recipe for losing market share and money. For some it is a recipe for disaster.

In fact, much like the efforts to abandon the ESG acronym now that people understand what it entails, there is an effort afoot to walk away from the DEI acronym—but not the harmful and discriminatory policies that underlie it. A May 2024 *Washington Post* article titled "DEI Is Getting a New Name. Can It Dump the Political Baggage?" states that "[a]mid growing legal, social and political backlash, American businesses, industry groups and employment professionals are quietly scrubbing DEI from public view—though not necessarily abandoning its practice."[104] Amid the public backlash, companies are "renaming diversity programs, overhauling internal DEI teams and [of course] working closely with lawyers."[105]

No matter how they rebrand DEI, the social-justice element in ESG will still refer to a progressive agenda that is neither broadly supported by society nor just. To the contrary, ESG's "S" encompasses fundamentally discriminatory DEI policies that can seriously, adversely, and demonstrably affect a company's financial performance.

By encouraging or bullying the companies in their portfolios to demonstrate their commitment to the DEI agenda—the "S" in ESG—despite the potential negative financial consequences for those companies, the Big Three are, as we have seen, failing to prioritize their clients' financial interests (which is their fiduciary duty) and usurping powers that properly lie with our democratic institutions and our free-market economy.

They may have the power, but that does not make what they have been doing legal, moral, popular with, or good for the American people—and most of the time, it is not profitable either.

Chapter 4

THE ENVIRONMENT, AS A TOOL

*"Climate change is the highest priority ESG issue
facing investors."*

—*The Principles for Responsible Investment's
Climate Change Website*[1]

E SG's "E" stands for the "environment," but it entails far more than responsible environmental stewardship. In reality, the "E" represents radical environmental policies the Left is employing to accomplish its highest priority—reordering the global financial system to empower a group of collectivist elites and to disenfranchise those they would rule. Environmental extremism is ESG's driving force, and it is not about science, climate, or the environment. It is about unelected elites exercising power over us. It is about control.

The "E" in ESG

For decades, environmental extremists have worked ceaselessly to create mass eco-anxiety, hammering on the message that climate change is real, human-caused, and an imminent threat to our planet. Despite this effort, the debate persists. Does climate change pose a critical threat to humanity requiring radical net-zero-carbon-emission goals despite their destructive consequences? Or is net-zero a luxury policy that would impoverish the middle and working classes while starving the poor worldwide to advance an unnecessary green agenda only wealthy elites can afford?

Skepticism in this "climate change" debate is understandable given the climate activists' narrative morphing from climate cooling to global warming to climate change; decades of supposedly "scientific" models and climate advocates (such as Al Gore and John Kerry) predicting "climate change" disasters that are consistently erroneous—repeatedly forecasting more climate change than actually occurs;[2] and claims that the science is settled when groups of credible scientists and other professionals consistently express vastly differing and opposing views.[3] It often seems that facts matter less than the scary story.

It is also difficult to take seriously global elites who claim human-caused carbon emissions threaten the very existence of life on Earth but nonetheless travel (even to climate-crisis events) in carbon dioxide–spewing private jets, yachts, and large gas-guzzling cars and buy expensive homes in coastal communities they claim will soon be submerged as polar ice melts, all while opposing the low-carbon-emissions natural-gas solution and the one viable zero-carbon-emissions baseload power source—nuclear energy.

So it is not surprising that Americans generally do not consider "climate change" a high-priority issue.

Much to the dismay of the *New York Times*,[4] a July 2022 *New York Times*/Siena College poll found that a mere 1 percent of voters "named climate change as the most important issue facing the country, far behind worries about inflation and the economy. Even among voters under 30, the group thought to be most energized by the issue, that figure was 3 percent." As a priority, it ranked seventeenth out of twenty-four issues.[5]

A July 2023 Quinnipiac poll found that a more generous 5 percent of voters considered climate change the most critical issue in the 2024 election. As a priority issue, it nonetheless ranked eighth out of eight.

Similarly, only 3 percent of respondents identified climate change as "the most pressing issue facing the United States right now" in a January 2024 CTUP/American Energy Alliance poll of battleground states (Georgia, Pennsylvania, Wisconsin, Arizona, Nevada, Michigan, Missouri, and Ohio). When the respondents were asked to identify the second-most-important issue, climate change did not even make the cut.[6]

So just how important is this issue? When asked how much they would "personally be willing to pay each year to address global warming," the median amount was ten dollars—or about the cost of a Hardee's Monster Burger combo—with "35% of all respondents/53% of Republicans/17% of Democrats" responding "zero."[7] Of course, if you live in a state like California, you are already likely to pay that $10 or more every time you fill your gas tank.

No wonder Larry Fink is so dissatisfied with how our democratic institutions are addressing the "climate change" issue that is so near and dear to him.

But the issue here is neither whether there is an imminent climate crisis nor which side is correct in the debate. Rather, the issue is how we as a society will respond to the issue. Even if a majority of Americans actually believed human-caused carbon in the atmosphere was creating a climate crisis requiring immediate net-zero-emissions policies (which does not appear to be the case), it nonetheless would be an issue properly addressed through our democratic institutions and our free-market economy—not by a small group of self-anointed financial elites.

There is a clear political division in this country between Republicans and Democrats on whether there is a climate crisis.

While the *New York Times*/Siena College poll found 3 percent of Democrats thought climate change was the most important issue facing the country, 0 percent of Republicans shared that belief.[8]

We are free to vote for whichever party we choose. Or, if you believe "climate change" is a critical issue that businesses should address, you can patronize companies that do so and boycott those that do not.

We live in a constitutional republic with a free-market economy, both of which empower the people. We do not live in a corporatocracy or a plutocracy controlled by financial elites—or at least I hope we do not. Our society is purposely structured around freedom and opportunity, not autocracy and control.

The Big Three derive their power from investing other people's money. As fiduciaries their sole duty is to prioritize their clients' financial interests, not to advance radical-environmental policies regardless of who agrees or disagrees with them. They have neither the sovereign power nor the popular mandate that would authorize them to force environmental extremism on either American businesses or society in general.

Nonetheless, that is what they have been doing.

Larry Fink's 2020 Letter to CEOs

BlackRock CEO Larry Fink's annual CEO letters reveal an unabashed crusader for the most radical environmental policies. With the enthusiasm of a religious convert, Fink's 2020 letter insisted in bold type, **"Every government, company and shareholder must confront climate change."**[9] Apparently light typeface was insufficient to make his point.

As both a warning and a command he wrote, again in bold type, **"Companies, investors, and governments must prepare for a significant reallocation of capital."** This was because a rapidly changing awareness of "climate change" was causing **"a fundamental reshaping of finance."** In fact, his entire letter was titled "A Fundamental Reshaping of Finance." He warned that "[i]n the near future—sooner than most anticipate—there will be a significant reallocation of capital."[10] You could almost hear him preaching, *The end is near!*

Consistent with that warning, Fink announced that going forward BlackRock would place sustainability at the center of its investment approach, portfolio construction, and risk management by, among other things, "exiting investments that present a high sustainability-related risk, such as thermal coal producers" and launching new sustainable index "products that screen fossil fuels."[11]

He made it clear that BlackRock considered "sustainable" index products the wave of the future. According to Fink, BlackRock's "investment conviction [was] that sustainability- and climate-integrated portfolios can provide better risk-adjusted returns to investors" and BlackRock believed "sustainable investing is the strongest foundation for client portfolios going forward." [12]

Fink warned the thousands of CEOs to whom he directed his letter that if their companies "do not respond to stakeholders" on "sustainability" they would "encounter growing skepticism from the markets, and in turn, a higher cost of capital." On the other hand, he claimed, companies that "champion transparency and demonstrate their responsiveness" on "sustainability" issues would "attract investment more effectively, including higher-quality, more patient capital."[13]

Fink was warning America's CEOs that, going forward, the assessments that investors would make concerning anticipated returns from investing in a particular company would increasingly depend upon how well that company was responding to "sustainability"—or climate-change—concerns. In other words, there would be greater demand (and investors would presumably be willing to pay higher prices) for the stock of companies that spent their shareholders' monies implementing radical environmental policies—such as net-zero carbon emissions.

Fink also gave notice that BlackRock was going to create new index products for companies that demonstrated such a commitment to sustainability, and that it believed such index products were the wave of the future. For CEOs running publicly traded companies, being included in a popular index can mean increased demand and higher stock prices. When the world's largest asset manager announces that it is going to "place sustainability at the center of its investment approach" and is setting up new sustainability indexes, it is in your company's and your shareholders' best interests to be included, if possible.

Of course, in passive index products (such as an S&P 500 index–based product) BlackRock was unable to ditch fossil-fuel stocks that otherwise qualified to be in the index—and about two-thirds of BlackRock managed assets sit in passive index products.[14] But it was advising CEOs that it intended to set up new ESG-based index products that would exclude non-ESG-compliant companies and that sustainability would be at the center of its investment approach for its actively managed accounts.

There is nothing wrong with issuing warnings, and BlackRock is free to set up whatever indexes it chooses. Nonetheless, it is important to keep in mind that Fink was writing his letters as the head of the world's largest investment firm and that the thousands of CEOs to whom Fink's letters were directed knew full well the risk of ignoring his warnings—even warnings couched as advice. And Fink's warning was clear—*Go woke or go broke.*

But Fink's letter went well beyond mere warnings. To make clear how seriously BlackRock took its "responsibility" and the importance Fink placed on playing a "meaningful role" on this issue, his letter pointed out that BlackRock was "a signatory to the UN's Principles for Responsible Investment" or the "PRI."[15] It was just one sentence buried in a lengthy letter, but the CEOs to whom Fink directed his letters knew full well what that reference entailed.

Founded in 2006, the PRI is a United Nations–supported international organization that bills itself as "the world's leading proponent of responsible investment." It works "to understand the investment implications of environmental, social and governance (ESG) factors" and "to support its international network of investor signatories in incorporating these factors into their investment and ownership decisions."[16]

A collectivist ESG organization if ever there was one. Black-Rock has been a signatory since 2008.[17]

All PRI signatories, including BlackRock, commit to implement six ESG-supporting principles, with the token condition that doing so is "consistent with [their] fiduciary responsibilities." Among other things, the signatories agree that they "will incorporate ESG issues into investment analysis and decision-making processes" and their "ownership policies and practices." They also commit to "seek appropriate disclosure on ESG issues by the entities in which [they] invest."[18]

Just so there is no question what is really going on here, PRI has a climate-change website that states unequivocally, "*Climate change is the highest priority ESG issue facing investors*" [emphasis mine].[19] To advance this priority, PRI supports radical net-zero-carbon-emission goals.[20]

As is noted above, PRI's "Six Principles" do have a caveat requiring that the signatories' actions be "consistent with [their] fiduciary responsibilities."[21] I called this statement token because in a 2019 report titled "Fiduciary Duty in the 21st Century," PRI sought to revise and rewrite the rules on fiduciary responsibility to specifically include advancing the ESG agenda. According to PRI, the report's purpose was "the integration of economic, social and governance (ESG) issues into investment practice and decision making" as a "standard part of the regulatory and legal requirements for institutional investors."[22]

So while advancing the "Six Principles" ESG goals appears to be limited by an asset manager's fiduciary responsibilities, PRI redefines such responsibilities to include advancing those very ESG goals—rendering any limitation meaningless. Advancing ESG goals obviously will be consistent with an asset manager's fiduciary responsibilities if those responsibilities are redefined to include advancing ESG goals. It is a simple tautology.

So addressing BlackRock's fiduciary responsibilities was now seemingly no problem for Larry Fink. Consistent with PRI's redefined concept of fiduciary responsibility, he simply redefined investment risk, declaring that "climate risk is investment risk."[23] In five simple words, Fink conflated addressing climate change and protecting the financial interests of BlackRock's clients—so that there was no bothersome need to even comment on the severe negative impact such collectivist policies could—would—have on companies in which BlackRock had invested its clients' monies.

Recall that when BlackRock functions as a passive index manager it is not BlackRock's job to balance investment risks, beyond deciding what indexes to set up and market. For example, with respect to BlackRock's S&P 500 index product, the investment risk is that those five hundred CEOs—who are all focused on maximizing returns—will not perform well. If BlackRock considers the risk of poor performance too great, it should not offer products based on the index.

But once BlackRock sets up such an index and people invest, the responsibility for dealing with the risks faced by businesses in the index lies with each individual company's management team, not BlackRock or Fink. Each company's management balancing those risks and striving for their own success and that of their shareholders is what passive investing is all about.

Of course, that would be inconsistent with Fink's all-encompassing view of BlackRock's role and how it should employ its massive proxy-voting power. Recall that in his 2018 letter Fink expressed frustration that, as a passive index-fund manager, when BlackRock disapproved of "a company's strategic direction" it was unable to "express its disapproval by selling the company's securities as long as that company remains in the relevant index."[24] In BlackRock's proxy-voting power, Fink found an outlet for that frustration. He would take it out on an offending company's directors. To quote a phrase, he would simply "fire the bastards."[25]

According to Fink, "when a company is not effectively addressing a material issue, its directors should be held accountable," and that is precisely what Fink intended to do. For the companies that failed to toe the line on climate change, Fink wrote—again in bold—that BlackRock **"will be increasingly disposed to vote against management and board directors when companies are not making sufficient progress on sustainability-related disclosures and the business practices and plans underlying them."**[26]

That statement went well beyond warnings that CEOs might

have difficulty raising capital or find their companies excluded from an index. It was a directive—adopt and disclose compliance with the environmental policies BlackRock approves, or we will find directors and managers who will.

Just to be sure no CEO believed this was an idle threat, Fink noted that in the previous year, "BlackRock voted against or withheld votes from an astounding 4,800 directors at 2,700 different companies."[27] Let those enormous numbers sink in for a minute—thousands of companies and thousands of directors. Unprecedented would be a gross understatement. This was an exercise of raw and absolute financial power, and Fink was bragging about it. If you were the CEO of one of the thousands of companies in which BlackRock invested, the message was clear—*Resistance is futile.*

To assure that he had covered all the means of compulsion, Fink also informed these CEOs that they could expect to hear his climate-change message directly, stating that BlackRock would "strengthen [its] commitment to sustainability and transparency in our investment stewardship activities."[28]

To sum it up, Fink's 2020 CEO letter informed thousands of CEOs that if they failed to adopt economy-crushing radical-environmental policies and fully disclose their compliance with those policies, they would experience increased costs of capital, be excluded from BlackRock's new sustainable-index products, and be subject to adverse proxy votes for their and their board's removal. And if that were unclear, they would be hearing about it in BlackRock's stewardship meetings.

A 2020 document from the BlackRock "Stewardship Team" titled "Our Approach to Sustainability" would later note that BlackRock had "identified 244 companies that [were] making insufficient progress integrating climate risk into their business models or disclosures." BlackRock "took voting action against 53, or 22%" and "put the remaining 191 companies 'on watch.' Those that do not make significant progress risk voting action against management in 2021." Exxon was one of the companies targeted by Blackrock.[29]

The pressure BlackRock was bringing to bear on America's corporate community was unequivocally immense.

Larry Fink's 2021 Letter to CEOs

As hard as it may be to believe, Fink upped the pressure in his 2021 CEO letter. While the letter's title was simply "Larry Fink's 2021 Letter to CEOs," the subtitles eliminated any mystery about its intent. They included "**A Tectonic Shift Accelerates**," "**The Opportunity of the Net Zero Transition**," and "**BlackRock's Net Zero Commitment**."[30]

Fink began with an "I told you so," claiming that the climate-change-inspired reallocation of capital he had predicted in his 2020 letter had "**accelerated even faster than I anticipated**." According to Fink, "the creation of sustainable index investments has enabled a massive acceleration of capital towards companies better prepared to address climate risk." According to Fink, even beyond ESG indexes, BlackRock was seeing that "companies with better ESG profiles are performing better than their peers, enjoying a 'sustainability premium.'"[31] Keep that phrase in mind.

Given Fink's role as head of the world's largest asset manager and his advocacy of these sustainable-index products as high-return propositions that were the wave of the future, hearing that investment dollars were gravitating to such funds was not a huge surprise. BlackRock was selling these "sustainable index investments" to its clients. As we shall see, the trend based on investing in companies focused on sustainability rather than profitability would soon fade, as would any supposed "sustainability premium," but for now the sustainability irons were in the fire—heating up demand for the stock of compliant companies.

As for "climate change," Fink's 2021 letter made it perfectly clear that BlackRock was "committed to supporting the goal of net zero greenhouse gas emissions by 2050 or sooner." He also made it clear that his mandate would apply to every company in Black-Rock's portfolio, declaring that "[t]here is no company whose business model won't be profoundly affected by the transition to a net zero economy."[32]

Lest any CEO believe he could put off adopting Fink's net-zero policy directives for a few years (or forever), Fink made it clear

90

that was not an option, stating that "we believe all companies—including BlackRock—must begin to address the transition to net zero today."[33] Talk about a collectivist statement!

To assure that companies were implementing BlackRock's desired policies, Fink stated that "**we are asking companies to disclose a plan for how their business model will be compatible with a net zero economy**" and to "**disclose how this plan is incorporated into your long-term strategy and reviewed by your board of directors.**"[34]

Apparently it was irrelevant whether such a strategy would affect the financial performance of the companies in which BlackRock invested on behalf of its clients—including oil companies in the S&P 500. Net-zero was a higher goal, of near religious significance, which Fink and BlackRock would collectively enforce across BlackRock's investment portfolios and indexes.

To assure compliance with his directives—that is, for every company to transition to net-zero immediately and tell BlackRock how it planned to do so—Fink reiterated that BlackRock would be "using stewardship to ensure that the companies our clients are invested in are both mitigating climate risk and considering the opportunities presented by the net zero transition."[35]

And then Larry Fink said the quiet part out loud.

What was the actual goal of all this climate-change, sustainability, net-zero activism? Where was it headed? What did its advocates expect to occur? If there were any doubt about the actual goal of environmental extremism, Fink's 2021 CEO letter cleared it up, declaring, "*It's important to recognize that net zero demands a transformation of the entire economy*" [emphasis mine].[36]

Well, of course it would, which is exactly why our democratic institutions and free-market economy are where we must address the issue—that is, institutions answerable to the people whom such a "transformation of our entire economy" would affect, rather than an exclusive group of ultra-wealthy financial elites convinced they know what is in our best interests better than we do—in short, a tyranny for the good of its victims.

This is the big reveal. Whether by transforming the focus of

American businesses from profits to social activism (and from shareholders to so called stakeholders), or by compelling companies to advance collectivist ESG dictates, the stakeholder capitalists' goal is and always has been "a transformation of the entire economy."

That is, a direct assault on free-market capitalism.

Using the power the Big Three derive from investing other peoples' money, Fink and his ilk intend to use climate as the vehicle to transform the "the entire economy" by transferring economic power from the people—who hold that power in free-market economies—to a group of financial elites who would run our lives for what they consider our own good.

It is not like he was keeping it a secret.

Rather than traditional shareholder- and profit-focused capitalism, Fink wrote that "we need companies to embrace a form of capitalism that recognizes and serves all their stakeholders,"[37] which, of course, is not capitalism at all. It is simply socialism in sheep's clothing. It is an economic system where individuals are supposedly motivated to invest money, take risks, and work to the maximum extent of their abilities not to improve their lives, but to achieve what a group of elites considers best for "society." It is dysfunctional, and the inevitable result of every effort to impose it has been poverty and want—unless you are a member of the elite ruling class. More on that later.

But let us take Fink at his word. He has stated that: (1) Black-Rock is "committed to supporting the goal of net zero greenhouse gas emissions by 2050 or sooner"; (2) every company will be "profoundly affected by the transition to a net zero economy"; (3) every company "must begin to address the transition to net zero today";[38] (4) BlackRock will enforce this net-zero goal by voting "against management and board directors when companies are not making sufficient progress";[39] and, (5) "net zero demands a transformation of the entire economy."[40]

Phew!

He should at least get credit for being direct. When a powerful individual tells you that he and his company support and intend to advance a policy that demands a complete transformation of the entire economy, it is best to take him seriously.

So how would Fink accomplish this massive transformation? Again, take him at his word, albeit in another context—"Behaviors are going to have to change, and this is one thing we are asking companies, you have to force behaviors, and at Blackrock, we are forcing behaviors."[41]

Of course, Fink and BlackRock have their allies. While not as vocal as Fink, Vanguard and State Street also have been net-zero advocates. In March of 2021, Vanguard and BlackRock joined the Net Zero Asset Managers initiative (NZAM),[42] an asset-manager coalition committed to "supporting the goal of net zero greenhouse gas emissions by 2050 or sooner."[43] That language may sound familiar. It appears verbatim in Fink's 2021 CEO letter.

Not to be left out, State Street joined NZAM in April of 2021.[44]

Beyond committing to support net-zero goals, NZAM members additionally commit to engage with "credit rating agencies, auditors, stock exchanges, proxy advisers, investment consultants, and data and service providers to ensure that products and services available to investors are consistent with the aim of achieving global net zero emissions by 2050 or sooner."[45] That is, they plan to turn the entire financial system inside out.

Apparently, it takes a village to transform an economy.

The Attack on Exxon

This brings us to another event that occurred in 2021. Exxon-Mobil, founded by John D. Rockefeller in 1882, is one of the world's largest publicly traded petroleum and petrochemical enterprises and America's largest energy producer. A powerful and influential company, it faced a challenge from a minor insurgent shareholder—an environmentalist hedge fund called Engine No.1 (E#1).

According to a *Wall Street Journal* interview, E#1 got its start at a 2019 family dinner when the son of hedge fund manager Christopher James "asked him how he could consider himself an environmentalist if he invested in energy companies." James "struggled with his explanation."[46]

In December of 2020, James founded E#1. Perhaps anticipating the need for powerful like-minded allies, E#1 hired Jennifer Grancio as its CEO. According to Forbes, she was "a founder and executive at BlackRock's iShares and BlackRock for nearly 20 years."[47]

While E#1's experienced management team would couch its goals in the language of improving financial performance and profits, E#1 was born in service of environmental extremism and committed to radical environmental goals. For example, shortly after its founding, E#1 released[48] a white paper explaining "[w]hy stopping climate change requires near elimination of conventional fossil fuels."[49] E#1's ultimate goals were always clear.

Ten days after its founding, E#1 went after Exxon. At the time (early COVID era), oil prices were extremely low (around $45 a barrel), negatively affecting Exxon's profits and share price. In a December 7, 2020, letter, E#1 wrote to Exxon's board, attributing the underperformance of Exxon's stock to "pursuit of [oil] production growth at the expense of returns and a lack of adaptability to changing industry dynamics, including higher production costs and growing long term demand uncertainty." It criticized Exxon for "dismiss[ing] carbon emissions targets as a 'beauty competition.'"[50]

In other words, with foresight rivaling British Prime Minister Neville Chamberlain's in the days leading up to World War II, E#1 claimed that increasing oil production capacity was a bad plan financially for Exxon. Of course, E#1's primary goal was never to improve the profitability of Exxon's high-return fossil-fuels business. It was to reduce that aspect of the business to a meaningless level—or end it—in favor of green-energy alternatives.

Exxon's management took the position that "oil and natural gas w[ould] continue to play a significant role for decades in meeting increasing energy demand of a growing and more prosperous global population."[51] Since it believed an energy transition was decades away and demand for oil would increase in the coming years, Exxon management stated that it would remain "focused on increasing long-term value for our shareholders by investing in our highest-return assets" which were, of course, oil- and natural-gas-producing assets.[52]

E#1 dismissed that reasoning, complaining that as "ExxonMobil continues to plan for long-term growth in oil and gas production (and thus increased overall emissions growth) for decades to come, this plan carries significant risk of further long-term shareholder value destruction"—"increased overall emissions growth" being the key phrase. It criticized Exxon for failing to acknowledge that the world achieving net-zero goals by 2050 would "likely cause an implosion in fossil fuel demand."[53] According to E#1, "it would be entirely economically rational for the world to act more quickly than many expect."[54]

Given that reasoning, E#1 advocated for Exxon to make a "significant investment in net-zero emissions energy sources and clean energy infrastructure," all as part of a plan "focused on accelerating rather than deferring the energy transition."[55]

Some might argue that a large and historically successful oil company, seeking to benefit its shareholders from a financial rather than a political perspective, would be well advised to enhance its production capabilities with the world increasingly dependent on oil. Some might even consider it unwise for such a company to support accelerating a speculative "energy transition" away from the very product that is its primary and highest-return source of revenue.

Management might reasonably believe that ramping up its oil-production capabilities would better position such a company for a host of likely, if not inevitable, global shocks. A whole range of dislocations in global energy could easily reduce the supply of oil available to billions of people who depend on that supply for their survival.

This is not to say that a company like Exxon should ignore alternative-energy sources or lines of business that could enhance profits over time. And in fact Exxon had not been ignoring those opportunities. Rather than making rapid and high-risk investments in undependable and expensive alternative-energy sources to achieve radical environmental goals, however, Exxon's management was moving cautiously and prudently in response to market demand, which was nowhere near as intense as the political demands of E#1 and the Big Three.

It was certainly reasonable for Exxon's management to conclude that increased oil-production capabilities would be in the best financial interests of an oil company and its shareholders. Speaking of "stakeholders," that capacity could benefit not only Exxon's shareholders, employees, suppliers, and communities but also U.S. and global consumers alike by keeping supply up and prices down in times of political or social unrest—as well as in times of peace and prosperity.

As an additional benefit, since many global energy producers are hostile powers willing to use oil as a tool to hold the world hostage, having a dependable U.S. domestic oil supply and export capacity is in the best interests of domestic and international security—this resiliency unambiguously benefits shareholders and stakeholders alike.

However, maximizing domestic U.S. oil production technology or capability would not advance a radical net-zero goal.

To advance that goal, E#1 nominated four independent director candidates it claimed had "successful and transformative energy experience" and could "help reposition" Exxon.[56] Exxon's management team opposed the environmentalist hedge-fund's director nominees. It argued that while Exxon should always look to alternative profit-enhancing energy sources and act both responsibly and within the law concerning the environment, it was primarily an oil company that should continue producing oil.[57]

Apparently, Exxon's management team viewed eliminating conventional fossil fuels as a problem for an oil company and its shareholders, not to mention that it would eviscerate the company's entire capital base.

I want to be clear that E#1 was acting within its rights. E#1 was not a passive manager that invested in Exxon as part of a wider index of companies. Unlike the Big Three, E#1 was an activist/impact-focused investor. It had purchased Exxon shares specifically with the intent to alter Exxon's business plan, and its investors/clients were well aware of its goals.

No matter how ill-advised, as an Exxon shareholder E#1 had every right to disagree with management and advocate for directors who would facilitate Exxon transitioning to a "net-zero emissions" business and to advance the "near elimination of conventional fossil fuels." It was wrong, but it had every right to be wrong.

Of course, with its minimal share ownership, E#1 had nowhere near enough votes to influence, let alone prevail in, a proxy contest. It needed support from likeminded net-zero advocates with more substantial holdings—and it just so happened there were some. In fact, all of this was occurring around the same time as Larry Fink's 2021 CEO letter demanding a "transformation of the entire economy" to achieve net-zero goals.

Three of Exxon's six largest shareholders were Vanguard (8.3 percent), BlackRock (6.6 percent), and State Street (5.7 percent), which collectively owned just over an influential 20 percent of Exxon's stock[58] and all of which, as we have seen, joined NZAM in March and April of 2021.

Aware of the Big Three's net-zero commitments, Fink's demand, and the need to address E#1's challenge, in April of 2021 Exxon issued a press release stating that it was "uniquely placed to help society meet its net zero ambitions, while capturing enormous future opportunities and delivering value for shareholders for many decades to come."[59] The release satisfied neither E#1 nor the Big Three.

Exxon's annual meeting and shareholder vote took place on May 26, 2021. Three of E#1's board candidates won board seats over management's objection. It was a devastating loss.

A *New York Times* article titled "Exxon's Board Defeat Signals the Rise of Social-Good Activists," stated that E#1's successful "battle to install three directors on the board of Exxon with the goal of pushing the energy giant to reduce its carbon footprint" would not "have had a chance" but for "the support of some of Exxon's biggest institutional investors."[60]

In particular, the *Times* noted that "BlackRock, Vanguard and State Street voted against Exxon's leadership and gave Engine No. 1 powerful support." Why? Well E#1 "convinced the mighty

BlackRock."[61] Given Fink's CEO letters and CEO Grancio's employment history, some might suspect that winning BlackRock's support was not a tremendously high bar.

BlackRock issued a statement explaining why it had voted for the three successful insurgent nominees. First, BlackRock noted that it had "a long history of multi-year, comprehensive engagements with Exxon on a wide range" of issues including "oversight of climate risk" and that over the previous year it had "engaged with the company twelve times."[62] That is a lot of "stewardship."

BlackRock then listed numerous actions that Exxon had taken to meet BlackRock's demand that it "enhance its climate commitments and disclosures." Nonetheless, despite its strongarm "stewardship" efforts, BlackRock believed "Exxon's energy transition strategy [had fallen] short of what is necessary to ensure the company's financial resilience in a low carbon economy." Like E#1, BlackRock was concerned about "the possibility that demand for fossil fuels may decline rapidly in the coming decades."[63]

As that statement demonstrates, BlackRock's net-zero advocacy presumes that a transition to a low-carbon economy is inevitable and that such a transition is around the corner, so to speak, rather than decades away—if it occurs at all. Exxon's management's strategic and real-world view on an evolving energy future was inconsistent with the collectivist narrative, so the omniscient elites rejected it and voted with E#1.

The fact is that at this point we still do not know whether there can or will be any meaningful net-zero transition, as global consumption of fossil fuels continues to rise, particularly outside the U.S. and Europe, despite climate activists' protestations to the contrary.

But, even if E#1 and BlackRock's belief about the inevitability of a net-zero economy turns out to be correct, certainly oil-company management teams in market-driven economies will see the evolving transition and position themselves to take advantage of it. Seeing an opportunity and seizing it before your competitors is a hallmark of success in a free-market-capitalist economy. In fact, it is one of the reasons free-market capitalism is the most successful economic system in human history. Everyone is always trying to best the competition.

Allowing that competition to play out is the essence of passive investing. Passive managers invest in an index of companies, knowing some will succeed more than others and some may even fail. Passive index investing avoids the risks of any particular company underperforming or failing by investing in every company in an index and allowing different approaches to play out and winners to emerge.

The problem with the Big Three collectively imposing their social-straitjacket approach to long- or short-term profitability on every company in an index is that investors lose the risk-reducing benefits of various companies employing a range of approaches to profitability.

Of course, Fink and BlackRock's response would be that climate change is a communal or existential crisis that demands an immediate and comprehensive response. That may or may not be the case, but even assuming it is, neither BlackRock nor the Big Three collectively are the entities that should be setting or enforcing the terms of that response—or the response to any other societal "crisis." As I have said, they lack both the sovereignty and the popular mandate.

The Big Three's sole responsibility is to prioritize their clients' financial interests. A passive manager satisfies that responsibility by allowing each CEO in each index to employ the business plans he or she believes will best result in the profitability of the company rather than by imposing collectivist policies—such as net-zero—on every company in an index.

What happened with Exxon is a good example of why the Big Three should not be making these kinds of social and political decisions for us. As it turns out, for U.S. and global consumers, international security, and Exxon's shareholders, forcing Exxon to reduce oil production and advance net-zero policies was unequivocally the wrong plan.

According to that June 2021 *New York Times* article, because of E#1's success, "climate activists declared a major triumph, and a blindsided Exxon was left to ponder its defeat."[64] Unfortunately, Exxon's management felt obligated to do more than ponder.

Four months later, in September, MarketWatch posted an article titled "Engine No. 1 Says Its New Representation on ExxonMobil's Board Has Already Scored a Win." It reported that E#1's CEO Jennifer Grancio had spoken at a Morningstar Investment Conference in Chicago and said that Exxon had "scaled back new long-term production targets." According to Grancio, Exxon was "keeping oil output at the lowest level in two decades in the years through 2025. That would be a 25% decline from forecasts before the pandemic started." She called it "a good kind of early win."[65]

As I said, E#1's actual goals were never in question.

In addition to scaled-back production targets, in January of 2022, Exxon—our nation's largest and most profitable oil company—disturbingly issued a press release titled, "ExxonMobil Announces Ambition for Net Zero Greenhouse Gas Emissions by 2050." According to the release, Exxon "is committed to playing a leading role in the energy transition" and to "helping society reach a lower-emissions future." The company claimed that its "business strategy is resilient when tested against a range of Paris-aligned net-zero scenarios."[66]

So, as absurd as it sounds, following the E#1 proxy vote victory, America's preeminent oil company adopted a policy intended to severely reduce—if not eliminate—demand for the high-return products that justify its existence.

Let that sink in for a moment.

That did not happen because we, the people, or our elected representatives want companies like Exxon to enact such self-destructive policies. If we did, there would be laws compelling them to do so.

It certainly did not happen because there is a lack of consumer demand for Exxon's products. On the contrary, demand for oil is and has been accelerating worldwide and is at historic highs.

It did not happen because Exxon's actual beneficial shareholders thought this was in the company's best financial interests—it clearly was not.

It did not happen because the Exxon shareholder base decided it wanted to place its bet (and capital) on Exxon as an alternative-energy leader.

It happened because a group of so-called "stakeholder capitalist"/ESG-supporting financial elites overrode both our representative democracy and our consumer-driven free-market economy to enforce their preferred radical-environmental policies. And they used our money to do it.

Unfortunately for the world, on February 24, 2022, Russia, having witnessed America's rushed and embarrassing withdrawal from Afghanistan and flush with cash from oil prices rising to over $90 a barrel as a result of increasing demand and reduced supply,[67] invaded Ukraine.

According to the U.S. Energy Information Administration, "On March 8, 2022," less than two weeks later, "the combination of Russia's invasion of Ukraine with low global crude oil inventories lifted the 2022 crude oil price to the highest inflation-adjusted price since 2014."[68] That price was over $120 per barrel. For the year, the spot price of oil would average $95 a barrel for WTI crude and $100 for Brent crude (the main benchmarks in oil pricing).

With increased pressure on oil supplies, Exxon went old school, focused on profits, and increased production (while taking some less significant actions to satisfy the Big Three's net-zero concerns); and its stock soared in value. That rise in valuation had nothing to do with Exxon's net-zero policies. Let us look at oil prices and Exxon's stock price.

On December 7, 2020, when E#1 sent its letter to Exxon's board, WTI oil was at $45.76 a barrel,[69] and Exxon's stock price closed at $40.90 per share.[70] By May 26, 2021, the date of Exxon's shareholders meeting, oil already had risen to $66.21,[71] and Exxon's stock price hit $58.94.[72] This rise was before E#1's much-touted proxy win.

On March 8, 2022, when oil hit $120 a barrel,[73] Exxon's stock closed at $87.78.[74]

In September of 2022, Yahoo Finance posted an article titled "Here's Why ExxonMobil (XOM) Stock Surges 74.3% in a Year" stating that "[t]he positive trajectory in oil prices is a boon for

ExxonMobil's upstream operations, as it holds a pipeline of key projects in the Permian, the most prolific basin in the United States."[75]

In retrospect, E#1's claims of an "early win" a year earlier based on Exxon reducing oil production targets was little more than a hollow political victory for the net-zero crowd, and a loss of valuable management time and focus for Exxon's shareholders.

On October 4, 2023, Bloomberg published an article titled "Exxon Sees $2.1 Billion Earnings Lift from Oil Prices, Refining Oil," which stated that "[r]ising crude prices accounted for a gain of about $1.1 billion over the previous quarter, while refining increased profits by about $1 billion."[76]

Maybe having an oil company focus on producing oil is not such a dreadful thing after all.

A few weeks later, Bloomberg reported that Exxon's board had approved a "$60 billion acquisition of Permian Basin behemoth Pioneer Natural Resources Co., a deal that will help raise Exxon's oil production to the highest in its 140-year history." Increasing its oil production capabilities with this acquisition was so obviously in Exxon's shareholders' best interests that all three of E#1's Exxon board members voted in favor of it.[77]

Oil began 2024 at $71.65 a barrel,[78] and Exxon's stock sat at $102.36 per share.[79]

In retrospect, from both financial and international-security perspectives, it is patently obvious that Exxon's management team was correct all along. Exxon should have been—and should be—focused on increasing production of its highest-return asset—oil—rather than adopting net-zero policies in pursuit of the "near elimination" of fossil fuels.

In other words, when it comes to the financial interests of Exxon's investors, Exxon's management approach was unequivocally correct. E#1 and the Big Three's anti-oil production approach was unequivocally incorrect. When and how to address any climate risk should have been left in the hands of Exxon's management team, not a collectivist passive-investing asset manager.

As for Fink's 2021 claim of a "sustainability premium," according to MarketWatch, of the eleven sectors in the S&P 500, "the energy sector was the only one to increase during 2022." Of the top ten best-performing stocks in the S&P 500, nine were energy company stocks. Exxon was the fourth-best-performing stock.[80]

Larry Fink's 2022 CEO letter, which came out in January of that year, was disingenuously titled "The Power of Capitalism."[81] Perhaps not surprisingly, it would be his last.

Chapter 5

THE WAR
ON PROFIT

"It's important to recognize that net zero demands a transformation of the entire economy."

—*Larry Fink, BlackRock CEO*[1]

I f there ever were any doubt that the ESG agenda is an attack on free-market capitalism, Larry Fink's 2021 CEO letter eliminated it by admitting that ESG's radical net-zero environmental policies demanded "a transformation of the entire economy." While the frankness of Fink's admission was surprising, his transformative goal was not.

In fact, it had been obvious since Fink's infamous 2018 letter directing CEOs to "serve a social purpose."[2] His ambition was, and always had been, to transform free-market capitalism, with its focus on profits and shareholder returns, into "stakeholder capitalism," where companies would prioritize the goals of the world's financial elites under the guise of benefiting non-investor stakeholders.

Just look at the title of Fink's 2019 CEO letter—"Purpose and Profit," with profit notably in second place.[3] That juxtaposition reflects the essential difference between free-market capitalism— the system that built the American economy into the greatest the world has ever known—and so-called stakeholder capitalism—a euphemism for transforming the American economy into a collectivist servant of the financial elites.

Profit Is the Purpose

Contrary to Fink's effort to separate them, in an actual capitalist economy, profit and purpose are synonymous. Profit is the purpose for which businesses exist. It is a direct byproduct of a free people's voluntary interactions to improve their lives and the incentive that motivates people to take the risks inherent in starting a business and then to dedicate the time and treasure required to make it succeed.

The profit motive is the notion, unique to free-market capitalism, that you can improve your life—you can profit—through your own efforts. And you improve not only your life but also the lives of other voluntary participants, such as your customers, employees, suppliers, and communities. Corporations expand that notion to groups of individuals working together to improve their lives and, incidentally, the lives of others. The profit motive is extremely powerful and has been the basis for the incredible historical success of free-market capitalism.

The greater the potential for profit, the greater the risks people are willing to take, the greater the investments they are willing to make, and the greater the resulting economic benefits. Diminishing the profit motive has the opposite effect—it reduces risk tolerance, stifles investment incentives, reduces or eliminates any financial benefits, and wipes out the real value that businesses create for all of society. Because collectivist/socialist economic systems lack or have a much-diminished profit motive, they consistently fail to create wealth—other than for the society's controlling elites.

So it was puzzling that Larry Fink, the CEO of an asset manager duty bound to prioritize its clients' financial interests, would so obviously attempt to separate purpose and profit—even putting the "purpose" cart before the "profits" horse. What is a business's purpose, if not to make a profit?

Well, according to Fink, a business's purpose is to prioritize the needs of a group of non-investor so-called "stakeholders" by pursuing ESG's social and political agenda—a collectivist agenda financial elites would set. He would put aside the benefits of free people interacting voluntarily to improve their lives and substitute involuntary interactions to achieve mandated social and political outcomes grounded in the knowledge of those who know better.

As I noted above, Fink clearly does not believe our democratic institutions can effectively accomplish that agenda. His 2019 CEO letter tellingly began by complaining that "some of the world's leading democracies have descended into wrenching political dysfunction," exacerbating "public frustration" with the current state of world affairs.[4] Luckily for that frustrated and incapable public, Fink had a solution.

He argued that businesses had to take up the social-policy cause because the world's wrenchingly dysfunctional democracies were failing to advance it. Where else could the public find salvation from a world failing to implement ESG's utopian social and political policies—such as net-zero and DEI—which Fink knew were in society's best interest?

So in 2019 he reiterated the theme of his 2018 letter, declaring that "[u]nnerved by fundamental economic changes and the failure of government to provide lasting solutions, society is increasingly looking to companies, both public and private, to address pressing social and economic issues." Of course the issues "society" was supposedly demanding businesses address ranged "from protecting the environment to retirement to gender and racial inequality, among others."[5]

Simply, ESG.

While Fink coyly claimed his focus on "purpose" in general was not an attempt to tell "companies what their purpose should be," his actions, and those of his allies, told a different story. Logically, collectively setting "purpose" for every company in an index also sets "purpose" for each of those companies—despite Fink's protestations to the contrary.

Fink and the Big Three troika were openly threatening to fire the directors and management teams of each and every company that failed to prioritize a diverse board, implement hiring policies based on discriminatory DEI principles, and both report and demonstrate progress on a net-zero climate change goal that—as Fink would admit in his 2021 letter—"demands a transformation of the entire economy."[6]

But what about the secondary part of his letter's title—"profits"—as an important "purpose" for starting and operating a business? Fink acknowledged that profits were "essential if a company is to effectively serve all of its stakeholders over time—not only shareholders, but also employees, customers, and communities."[7] It was an admission of the patently obvious—profitable businesses do benefit a broad range of individuals and entities. Unprofitable businesses benefit no one. But he also wrote that "[p]urpose is not the sole pursuit of profits but the animating force for achieving them."[8]

That was not a particularly cogent statement. I suspect that most people who have ever run a profitable business questioned whether Fink's vision of purpose—addressing "pressing social and economic issues" to benefit some unidentified non-investor stakeholders—was actually "the animating force" behind turning a profit? I did.

As I noted earlier, it is obvious that companies focused on profits will be more profitable than those that are not. When a group of elites (whether financial, government, or the two working together) reorient CEOs from focusing on success to advancing a collectivist social or political agenda, succeeding becomes difficult—if not impossible. This is why there are and have been no economically successful socialist economies. None.

But, as Fink noted, profitable businesses do benefit more than just their investors. In fact, profitable businesses benefit everyone on Fink's stakeholder list: customers, employees, suppliers, communities—and shareholders. However, businesses that are compelled to put collectivist social and political goals ahead of profitability, as Fink advocates, underperform, fail, and benefit no one.

So why make the patently absurd claim that addressing social/ non-profit-related goals is somehow the "animating force" behind making a profit? If Fink's goal was to put advancing the ESG agenda above achieving financial success, why not just say so? There are (failed) economies across the globe that put social and political purpose over profit, and the title of Fink's 2019 letter certainly indicated which of the two he considered most important.

BlackRock had the power to compel CEOs to prioritize ESG goals, particularly if doing so was a Big Three effort. In fact, the Big Three were already threatening to terminate board members and management teams that failed to toe the ESG line. Given what they were already doing, why even try to link advancing an ESG agenda with a business's profitability? Why not just admit that you have subjugated and subordinated profits to social activism and elitist-mandated outcomes?

Profit and Fiduciary Responsibility

The answer is that Fink had to link them. As BlackRock has acknowledged, its sole fiduciary duty is to prioritize its clients' financial interests—which are, of course, dependent on the performance and profitability of the companies in which it invests on their behalf. How could BlackRock satisfy its fiduciary duty to prioritize its clients' financial returns while simultaneously and actively directing the CEOs of the companies in which it "passively" invested to prioritize addressing ESG's "social and economic issues" over, above, and instead of profits?

Despite his effort to transform BlackRock's fiduciary duties in his 2018 CEO letter, Fink knew he needed a stronger explanation for why this transformation would benefit BlackRock's clients.

So with characteristic confidence supported by circular logic, in his 2019 CEO letter he simply asserted that addressing "social and economic issues"—or "purpose"—is actually "the animating force" that drives profits.[9] In other words, businesses will maximize profits not by focusing on maximizing profits but by prioritizing ESG's social and political goals. So, given Fink's logic, BlackRock would satisfy its fiduciary duty to investors by compelling the businesses in which it invested their money to pursue ESG goals—which is, of course, what it was already doing.

On a roll, so to speak, Fink went even further, claiming that "purpose"—that is, addressing "social and economic issues" to benefit non-investor stakeholders (his proxy for society)—was a business's "fundamental reason for being—what it does every day to create value for its stakeholders."[10] Note that he was talking about value for "stakeholders," the majority of whom were neither shareholders nor BlackRock's clients.

Stepping back for a moment—as Fink surely knows, the fundamental reason businesses exist is to make money. BlackRock invests its clients' monies in for-profit companies whose "fundamental reason for being" really is to make a profit and generate returns for investors—such as BlackRock's clients. In fact, BlackRock itself is in business to make money and sell its shares publicly to individuals who expect it to make money.

BlackRock's clients certainly do not expect it to invest their monies in charitable institutions or social-activist companies. BlackRock is and was primarily a low-fee/passive index manager tasked with prioritizing its clients' financial returns. Telling CEOs that addressing "social and economic issues" to benefit non-investor stakeholders would animate companies' profits and was their "fundamental reason for being" was a puerile effort to confuse social and political activism with profits—which is and was nonsense.

It is a sign of the bubble in which Fink operates that he evidently expected his clients and the public servants who protect them to accept his rationalizations quietly while he and the Big Three ignored or, at the very least "transformed," their fiduciary duties to their investors.

But to the surprise of no one outside that bubble, over the next couple of years Fink's effort to advance his ESG social and political goals by replacing free-market capitalism with stakeholder capitalism (which is not capitalism at all) came under increasing scrutiny and skepticism. Individuals, states, and other entities that had actually hired BlackRock to maximize the returns on their investments objected, wrote letters, passed legislation, and withdrew funds from BlackRock.

So, in his 2022 CEO letter, Fink again found it necessary to defend "stakeholder capitalism."

Corrupting Capitalism

Fink ironically (if not humorously) titled his 2022 (and last) CEO letter "The Power of Capitalism." He notably did not call it "The Power of Stakeholder Capitalism."[11]

Gone was the honest admission about a "transformation of the entire economy." Nor, according to Fink circa 2022, had the demands in his earlier letters been "about politics" or "a social or ideological agenda" or being "woke." Rather, he was simply reimagining stakeholder capitalism as "capitalism driven by mutually beneficial relationships between you and the employees, customers, suppliers, and communities your company relies on to *prosper*. This [he declared] is the power of capitalism."[12]

You would think the "power of capitalism" might also involve "mutually beneficial relationships" with a company's shareholders. But this time Fink failed to even include "shareholders" in his list of "stakeholders"—oops!

He did argue that a company must "**be valued by its full range of stakeholders in order to deliver long-term value for its shareholders**" and that "long-term profitability is the measure by which markets will ultimately determine your company's success."[13] At least he spoke about "value" for "shareholders." But what does "long-term profitability" really mean in the ESG context?

The phrase "long-term profitability" certainly sounds good and fiduciary-ish, and Fink often employs it. Of course, every business endeavors to be profitable in the long term—as well as in the short and medium terms. But when used in the ESG context, "long-term profitability" is simply another ruse. It is an effort to justify the pursuit of the ESG goals that a group of self-appointed financial elites believe may have some long-term social benefits—but that are unlikely to have actual financial benefits anytime soon, or ever.

For example, in some distant and hypothetical carbon-free future, it might be in an oil company's best interest to cease oil production and switch to production of carbon-free energy. Of course, that assumes ESG's net-zero-carbon-emissions agenda is the predetermined wave of the future—or even a reasonable view of the future—and that it will successfully transform "the entire economy." That is a huge and glaring assumption and certainly not one that is on the cusp of being realized—at least if voters and consumers have anything to say about it.

In the meantime, while the real world consumes 100 million barrels of oil per day and demand is accelerating,[14] there is a lot of money to be made in the oil business, as Exxon has been demonstrating in spades.

When BlackRock or the Big Three collectively vote the shares they hold in support of efforts to diminish the ability of oil companies to profit from the current global demand for oil—describing their actions as a focus on "long-term profitability"—they are really endeavoring to take the focus off of profitability, now and in the actual future, and put it on the "E" in ESG, in hopes that in some far-off, if not mythical, future the demand for oil will evaporate. Spoiler alert—it will not.

Of course, the very real possibility that this net-zero champagne-socialist goal would impoverish, starve, and immobilize millions of people and tank the global economy, diminishing the returns on just about every investment "long term," does not seem to factor into their view of "long-term profitability."

As for Fink's claim that a company must "**be valued by its full range of stakeholders in order to deliver long-term value for its shareholders,**" every businessperson is aware, as I have noted, that companies must have solid relationships with their customers, employees, suppliers, and communities to survive. That is not the issue.

Rather, the issue is whether the CEOs of passive-investment firms, who by rights should not be involved in the management of their portfolio companies at all, can force those companies to collectively substitute an ESG agenda for the pursuit of business success and shareholder returns—which is clearly what they have been doing. But the answer is "No" if their duty is really to prioritize their clients' financial interests.

Focusing on the social and political goals that financial elites believe are in the best interests of society—or of some non-investor "stakeholders"—is not an argument for maximizing shareholder returns or profits, either short- or long-term. At best, involuntary transactions and mandated strategies create value only accidentally.

As for Fink's new claim that stakeholder capitalism is not "woke" or political or "a social or ideological agenda," since 2018 he had been telling companies they needed to "serve a social purpose" because our political institutions were failing to do so effectively.[15] In 2019 he told them to "address pressing social and economic issues."[16] One need only read Fink's activist 2021 letter to understand that what he calls stakeholder capitalism is all about businesses "addressing" an ESG agenda, including a radical net-zero policy that he acknowledged "demands a transformation of the entire economy."[17]

That is about as "woke" a social agenda as you can get, at least outside of the sociology department at Harvard.

Without so much as an election, stakeholder capitalists would transfer political and economic power from voters and consumers to a group of self-appointed financial elites. Under the guise of benefiting non-investor stakeholders, they would empower those elites to impose on the economy their vision for what benefits society "long-term," without the annoying constraints imposed by the fiduciary duty to prioritize their clients' financial interests.

The result would be—may already be—an unconstrained and powerful financial cabal capable of imposing on America their vision of what is best for us. We are all the lumpenproletariat. The elites are the vanguard of a supposedly new and exciting future—that they will determine.

That is not "the power of capitalism," as Fink declared. It is the oppression of socialism.

The Actual Power of Capitalism

The actual power of capitalism lies in the profit motive, the most dynamic and positive economic force in human history. Capitalism is millions of individuals striving to—and with the freedom to—reap the benefits of their personal efforts. In that process they create the wealth that lifts society as a whole from poverty into affluence. In this profit-motivated system, businesses exist because individuals are willing to take the risks and put in the time and treasure required to make them successful. They exist to make a profit, not to advance any elitist notions of good social or political policy.

It is the profit motive that drives our engine of economic prosperity, lifting people out of poverty and creating the wealth that makes possible real charity for the helpless as well as opportunity and prosperity for those willing to take the risks and put in the effort. It encourages people to realize their full potential and spreads the benefits of their success to others in the form of jobs, wealth, and abundance—greatly reducing both poverty and human suffering.

Critics say that capitalism is based on avarice, but the opposite is true. In a true capitalist economy, you can only succeed—or profit—by satisfying the needs of others, that is by providing the goods or services people want at a price they can afford. Capitalism depends on the natural desire of people to better their lives, but it channels that natural desire into focusing on the needs of others. To be a successful free-market capitalist, you must shift your focus outward to the needs and wants of consumers. You only improve your life by satisfying their needs. That is a kind of altruism, not greed.

When I was the CEO of CKE Restaurants, we spent millions of dollars every year trying to determine exactly what consumers wanted and to let them know we had what they wanted at prices they wanted to pay. Under free-market capitalism, knowing your customers and offering them a superior product at an affordable price is the key to success. In fact, it is the key to survival.

Think about the thousands of producers who supply your local grocery store, shopping mall, and Amazon, all vying for your attention, trying to convince you they have the right products for you at the right price. Each of these products represents a business striving to meet your needs as the way to achieve its success. From Amazon and Anheuser-Busch to your local restaurant or gas station, every company is trying to sell products or services that people want at prices they can afford.

In this sense, capitalism is a form of economic democracy, where consumers vote with every dollar they spend, determining which businesses succeed and which fail. Businesses need consumers' votes for their success, and the competition for those votes puts consumers in charge of setting the economy's direction.

In any economic system, the benefits go to those with economic power. In a free-market capitalist economy, the people as consumers who engage in voluntary transactions have the power. The entire economy is focused on their needs. It is Adam Smith's "invisible hand" in action, determining what people need and shaping business practices to meet those needs at a reasonable price. In fact, meeting the needs of consumers—the people—is every successful entrepreneur's goal.

Henry Ford and Elon Musk both built cars for the common man and woman, not kings, queens, or nobility. Steve Jobs revolutionized personal computing for all of us, not government or corporate elites. Jeff Bezos became fabulously wealthy because he created the greatest distribution system in the history of the world. They each made or are making the world a better place one purchase at a time.

None of these individuals became wealthy because they stole from us. They all became tremendously wealthy because they provided us with tremendous benefits. From Bezos and Musk to the family that runs your local pizza or burger joint, in a free-market economy we benefit to the extent we benefit others.

As a result, throughout our history as a nation, self-made men and women, free from government interference, have forged ahead with innovative ideas and solutions that created jobs, wealth, and prosperity not only for themselves but for the entire nation. They improved their fortunes and, in the process, the lives of their fellow citizens and the human condition—one customer at a time and one paycheck at a time.

This is one of the reasons free markets always significantly outperform any system where a group of elites or so-called "experts" make decisions for the broader economy. No elites—not even the wise and public-spirited CEOs of passive-investment firms—can analyze the almost incomprehensible amount of data coming from millions of consumers acting to address their individual needs and wants every day across the globe. Nor do they have the creative and innovative skills essential to meeting those needs.

Add to that the fact that the elites are never as high-minded as they might seem. Once they get control—once they free themselves from the restraints of the market and the will of voters— their vision of what is good for society always seems to coincide with what is good for them. ESG is an example. It is designed to address the financial elites' priorities—to produce the kind of society where they are comfortable occupying the top strata of money and influence while feeling morally justified—and to ensure that others bear the costs of the society they envision.

These are the reasons socialism always fails and capitalism always succeeds. Collectivist economic systems—Marxism, communism, socialism, or stakeholder capitalism—are about control. They neither respond effectively to the needs of the people nor generate the economic energy and enthusiasm created by millions of free people motivated and striving to meet the needs of others as the way to improve their own lives.

Under free-market capitalism, everyone striving—and having the freedom—to profit by coming up with the next great product or service creates an incredible dynamic, an economic energy that results in creativity, innovation, widespread prosperity, and abundance.

That is the true power of capitalism, and its "animating force" is the profit motive.

Addressing Stakeholders without Elitist Dictates

While the focus of free-market capitalism is profits, it is important to understand how certain non-investors are also important to a business's profitability—even though they have no actual monetary stake in the business. Shareholder-focused capitalism already addresses the needs of the "stakeholders" about whom Fink appears to be so concerned.

As I noted earlier, businesses must meet the needs of their consumers. That is almost too obvious to need stating. They need a satisfied and enthusiastic workforce—also obvious. They must keep their suppliers happy so they will continue to get the products and services they need to run their business at acceptable prices—again, obvious. They must have a good reputation in the communities where they do business, as people generally do not patronize businesses they dislike—patently obvious. Of course, they must comply with applicable laws and regulations—and it helps if they have a reputation for lawfulness with government authorities.

Each of these so-called "stakeholders" must voluntarily buy from, work for, or supply the business if it is to succeed. If a business fails to keep any of them happy, it will underperform and ultimately fail, and anyone who has ever run a business knows it—because, again, it is obvious.

In other words, the profit motive already requires that businesses meet the needs of these non-investors—Larry Fink's so-called "stakeholders"—in order to make a profit. While meeting these non-investors' needs is not the business's "purpose," it is part of what each business needs to do to achieve its purpose—which is to make a profit.

The "animating force," to use Fink's words, for meeting the needs of these non-investors is not to arbitrarily advance social or political goals unrelated to business success. Rather, it is to make a profit. Contrary to Fink's notion, that does not work in reverse. The business's primary purpose cannot be to meet the needs of these non-investors.

Rather, businesses must balance the extent to which they benefit any particular group against the need to remain profitable. Failing to achieve that balance correctly—by either under- or over-responding to these non-investors—is a shortcut to the bankruptcy court.

For example, if you charge less for your products or services than they cost in order to benefit your customers, you will go out of business. If you increase your employees' pay and benefits above what your business's revenue can support, you will go out of business. If you over-order or over-pay your suppliers, you will go out of business. If you invest in your community beyond what your company can afford, you will go out of business. Every business must balance its expenses against its revenue so those expenses do not overwhelm its profits—or there will be no business, and no benefits for anyone.

To succeed, a business's purpose must always be profits, and that purpose must guide all meaningful business relationships and decisions. Fortunately, when businesses survive, this purpose benefits everyone.

Addressing Social Issues without Elitist Dictates

It may be in a business's best interests to occasionally take a position on a given social or political issue to increase consumer acceptance of its goods or services or to meet the demands of its target market. Recall the successful Nike/Colin Kaepernick ad campaign. Of course, it is important to understand that businesses are not the appropriate vehicles to advance such issues absent consumer support.

Recall the negative impact on Disney's, Target's, and Anheuser-Busch's brand images and financial results as a result of their ventures into the sexual-orientation and gender debates. Along with lower profits came reduced benefits for their laid-off employees and financially disadvantaged suppliers as well as fewer dollars to help their communities.

Each individual business must decide for itself whether to venture into a given social or political issue, because different businesses have different target markets and operate in different communities. Businesses with broad-based target markets (like Disney or Target) are generally best served by remaining neutral. But if consumer demand guides a business to address a given social or political issue, it should address the issue. That keeps a business's focus where it should be—on generating profits.

The danger lies in powerful financial elites employing businesses to advance their preferred social/political agenda regardless of the business' target market and how that market may react. These problems arise when financial elites seek to advance their goals using private-sector businesses as tools in order to avoid the inconvenience of having to gain the consent of either consumers or voters. It is much easier for the elites if, in their omnipotent wisdom, they can simply dictate to every business the policies they consider the masses too ill-informed to understand.

In short, collectivism.

Fink's 2019 letter claimed that a frustrated and unnerved "society" was "looking to companies, both public and private, to address pressing social and economic issues."[18] But that is a cop-out—a form of gaslighting. If there were a social consensus behind Fink's vision, it would have been enforced by consumer demand or through the electoral process. The best outcomes generally come about organically—not at the point of a gun or a threatening letter.

The truth is more nearly the opposite. Neither consumers nor voters want the ESG vision of a racialized society where everyone is judged by the color of his or her skin, and where energy is made increasingly scarce and expensive until only the very wealthy—the Finks of the world—can afford to heat their homes and drive their cars. In a free-market system, consumers are not restricted from voluntarily purchasing or pursuing any ESG product, idea, or outcome on their own. If they do not choose to do so, that tells businesses something.

That is why the Big Three must use unaccountable power to accomplish their ends. Once the mask comes off ESG, once people understand what the ESG movement is about, they reject it, and they certainly reject radically "transforming the economy" to achieve it.

The Collectivists' Critical Issue

Of course, when it comes to advancing ESG, transforming "the entire economy" based on radical environmental policies—primarily net-zero goals—is the central and overarching policy objective for these stakeholder capitalist elites. It is the one policy they find compelling enough to lever a massive realignment of our entire economy and society in order to create a power structure that prioritizes their influence and control. One need only read Larry Fink's letters (particularly his 2020[19] and 2021[20] CEO letters) to see that he is an environmental crusader with a near-religious fervor.

Net-zero is the issue of consequence for the world's financial elites. Control is the goal.

But, as we saw in chapter 4, climate change is not an issue of overarching significance for the vast majority of Americans (or even a notable minority)—certainly not an issue they consider important enough to justify "a transformation of the entire economy." If that were how Americans felt, they would express their desire at the voting booth and through their elected representatives. Our democratic institutions are the appropriate drivers for any transformation this overwhelmingly significant.

But Americans do not, either as voters or as consumers, consider climate change to be a problem requiring a realignment of that significance. Contrary to what Fink may believe, the problem is not that democracies are dysfunctional. The problem is that they are functioning as they should—just not as Larry Fink and his ilk believe they should.

Distinguishing Shareholder Capitalism from So-Called Stakeholder Capitalism

So, you may ask, if traditional profit-focused capitalism addresses the needs of Larry Fink's non-investor stakeholders and addresses popularly supported social issues, how does it differ from stakeholder capitalism? What is all the fuss about?

Here is the difference, and it is huge. To refer again to a quotation attributed to Thomas Jefferson, "The issue today is the same as it has been throughout all history, whether man shall be allowed to govern himself or be ruled by a small elite."[21]

In a free-market capitalist economy, businesses base their decisions on what will best improve their profitability—within the confines of law and custom. Consumer demand guides each business decision, and each company's success depends on how effectively it meets or anticipates that demand and benefits the participants. There is no central authority, no financial cabal, no group of self-appointed elites determining which policies businesses should collectively pursue and then forcing those policies down their—and by extension our—throats. Free-market capitalist economies are bottom-up consumer driven rather than top-down elitist driven.

And the elites—who believe they can run our lives better than we can—hate that.

Stakeholder capitalism supposedly prioritizes meeting the demands of so-called stakeholders—unidentified people who have no financial investment, or actual stake, in the business' success. But how do we know what their demands are without the market or the ballot box to guide us?

Well, in the stakeholder-capitalism world Fink envisions, we have a group of all-knowing financial elites with the power to tell us. Stakeholder capitalism would allow these financial elites to impose their policy preferences on the American corporate community, all in the name of what these elites tell us is required to meet what they claim are the demands of these non-investor stakeholders—their proxy for society.

121

When elites (government or financial) have the power to dictate policy, it is simply too intoxicating to resist.

When Passive Became Active

That the elites at passive-investment firms are advancing the collectivist notion of stakeholder capitalism is ironic, because the success of the passive-investment sector is itself a product of good old shareholder-focused free-market capitalism and the profit motive.

Millions of Americans have supported, individually or as part of their retirement funds, investing in the stock market without the costs that come with having to research individual companies or the risks that accompany betting on the success of any particular company. Passive-investment firms rose to meet that need by inexpensively and effectively diversifying those risks. This worked, and they prospered because the CEOs of their indexed companies all wanted to make their individual companies as profitable as possible—thereby creating the best consolidated financial results for a given index of companies.

But the creation and success of such an industry was not enough for Fink and his cronies. The success of their firms—which was only possible because of America's system of free-market shareholder-focused capitalism—resulted in the consolidation of unprecedented economic power in a small group of passive-investment firms. It was, truth be told, an accident; but it has resulted in a small group of very wealthy people who think that because they were successful beyond their wildest dreams, they now have the moral authority and economic power to actively impose a form of socialism on the rest of us.

In a world where these financial elites are duty bound to prioritize their clients' fiscal interests, they lack the authority to drive collective policy decisions at all, let alone policy decisions that will negatively affect the profitability of companies in their relevant indexes. In exercising a power they do not legitimately have—the power to manage and dictate policy to their portfolio companies—they are abdicating a real duty they do have—to maximize returns for the people who have trusted them with their investment dollars.

Is Stakeholder Capitalism Worth the Risks?

As I discuss in the next chapter, the last two hundred years has demonstrated unequivocally that free-market capitalism is the greatest economic system in human history. By energizing the profit motive, it has lifted billions of people out of poverty worldwide. It is literally about freedom, empowerment, and enrichment for all involved.

Stakeholder capitalism, on the other hand, is about control. It is not about creating wealth or reducing poverty. It is about implementing a champagne-socialist ESG agenda that would devastate the world's economy for all but the ultra-wealthy. Would the world truly be better off?

Before we transform the entire economy, let us consider what we would be sacrificing in exchange for allowing this group of elites to dictate our futures.

Chapter 6

AN ECONOMIC MIRACLE

"We don't dispute that the free market is the greatest producer of wealth in history—it has lifted billions of people out of poverty."

—President Barack Obama, Georgetown University, 2015[1]

As we consider stakeholder capitalism, keep in mind that the system it would displace—shareholder-focused free-market capitalism—is the only economic system that has ever enabled mass wealth creation sufficient to meaningfully alleviate both poverty and human suffering.

The publication in 1776 of Adam Smith's *The Wealth of Nations*—which explained how to create a modern capitalist economy and the benefits of doing so—set the stage for an historic surge in the world's wealth and an unprecedented plunge in global poverty. No other economic system has ever effectively reduced human suffering and elevated human flourishing—not one.

Despite claims that collectivist economic systems will elevate the interests of "society," "the people," or the "workers of the world," they have consistently failed. Rather than a more just and equitable society, collectivism produces only the inequity of oppression and the miserable equality of poverty—for all but the elites it empowers.

"The Most Important Graph in the World"

The graph below demonstrates the unprecedented impact of capitalism on human flourishing. It is based on data from Angus Maddison, a respected "world scholar on quantitative macroeconomic history, including the measurement and analysis of economic growth and development," who taught at the University of Groningen in the Netherlands. Following his death in April of 2010, a group of scholars launched the Maddison Project to continue his "work on measuring economic performance for different regions, time periods and subtopics."[2]

The graph below, which appears on the Our World in Data website, is based on Angus Maddison data.[3] It tracks the exponential growth rate of total world GDP—or the economic growth of the entire economy worldwide—for the period from the year 1 through 2021.[4] The result is obviously stunning.

TABLE 1

Global GDP Over the Long Run

Total output of the world economy. These historical estimates of GDP are adjusted for inflation.

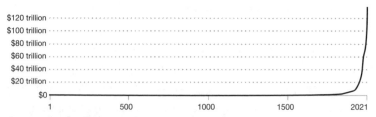

Data source: World Bank (2023); Maddison Project Database 2020 (Bolt and van Zanden, 2020); Maddison Database 2010 (Mlalddison, 2009)
Note: This data is expressed in international-$ at 2017 prices.
OurWorldInData.org/economic-growth | CC BY

From time immemorial through the early 1800s, the great mass of humanity lived in the depths of poverty—with starvation, homelessness, disease, and infant mortality the simple facts of truly short lives. When crop yields were good, people ate, and the population increased. When crop yields were poor, people died. A small group of feudal elites consolidated what little wealth there was by force and retained it through military superiority and oppression of a servile peasantry. Wealth neither grew nor was widely distributed.

Then, in the early 1800s, free-market capitalism arose, and an economic miracle occurred. GDP per capita—economic growth per person—*soared*, improving the lives of everyone reading this book, as well as your parents, grandparents, great-grandparents, and likely your great-great-grandparents. If we are able to hold back the forces behind collectivist threats—such as stakeholder capitalism—it will positively affect many generations yet to come.

And it happened in the blink of an eye historically.

I showed this graph to two of my sons when they were in their twenties, and they each asked whether this surge was a result of the Industrial Revolution rather than the rise of capitalism. It was a reasonable question. Looking at an earlier version of this chart, an article in the *Visual Capitalist* titled "2000 Years of Economic History in One Chart" made the same observation, stating that "innovations in technology and energy allowed the 'hockey stick' effect to come into play."[5]

But whether free-market capitalism or the Industrial Revolution came first is really a chicken-and-egg debate. Each furthered the other in an ever-expanding virtuous cycle that was surely the synergy of the millennium. Realizing the full benefits of industrialization required an economic system that encouraged foresight, initiative, investment, risk-taking, planning, and effort well beyond what the mercantilist economies of the pre-capitalist period allowed or could provide—"innovations in technology and energy" notwithstanding.

While many nations benefited from the Industrial Revolution, the nations that drove the exponential surge in GDP per capita had one thing in common—a profit-focused and consumer-driven free-market economy empowering individuals and motivating them to innovate, take risks, invest, and succeed.

The graph below makes the point. It breaks down the Angus Maddison data on increasing GDP per capita by regions of the world and shows the critical importance of free markets to that hockey-stick economic surge. An earlier version of it first appeared in *The Atlantic* in 2012.[6]

Jonathan Haidt, the Thomas Cooley Professor of Ethical Leadership at the New York University Stern School of Business,[7] nominated the original version for "the most important graph in the world."[8] I second that nomination.

TABLE 2

The World GDP Through 2022

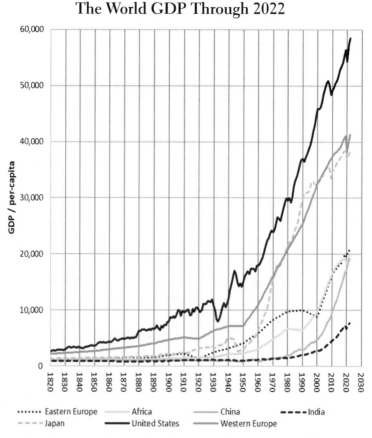

| ········ Eastern Europe | ——— Africa | ——— China | ▬ ▬ ▬ India |
| ▬ ▬ ▬ Japan | ▬▬▬ United States | ——— Western Europe | |

Source: The Maddison Project Database 2023
https://www.rug.nl/ggdc/historicaldevelopment/maddison/releases/maddison-project-database-2023

Haidt said that he loved "this graph because it shows us how capitalism changed the West and Japan in the blink of an eye, and it foretells a similar transformation in the rest of the world."[9] Let us hope he was right.

As this regional breakdown demonstrates, Western Europe's GDP per capita moved slightly above the rest of the world's in about 1500 with the rise of mercantilism. Western Europe dominated the world economy by taking advantage of both superior nautical capabilities and sophisticated financial institutions. But that increase is barely noticeable compared to the surge that begins around 1820 with the rise of free-market capitalism and industrialization.

The U.S. Leads the Way

This graph's most predominant feature is the rise of the indominable U.S. economy. That economic surge was powered by two events that took place in 1776—the American colonies' Declaration of Independence and the publication of Adam Smith's *The Wealth of Nations*. As Thomas Jefferson, the Declaration's drafter, later stated, "In political economy I think Smith's *Wealth of Nations* the best book extant."[10]

The surge itself followed ratification of the U.S. Constitution in 1788—creating an effective federal government and legal system that supported an economy now free from the British monarchy's taxes and trade restrictions. With a free-market capitalist economy powering an Industrial Revolution, America flourished.

In a little over a century, by 1899, the United States surged ahead of the United Kingdom and had the highest GDP per capita of any nation in the world.[11] To deny the importance of free-market capitalism to that surge is to deny reality.

Western Europe's and Japan's Economies Surge, but Later

The United Kingdom's GDP per capita grew with the Industrial Revolution, as did Western Europe's generally—although to a lesser extent.[12] But neither truly surged until the aftermath of World War II, with the defeat of the collectivist National *Socialist* German Workers Party (emphasis mine), a.k.a. the Nazis. With American influence and investment high and serving as a counter to the influence of the communist nations of Eastern Europe—primarily the Soviet Union—post–World War II Western Europe thrived. Technology and capitalism, girded by a framework of freedom, generated abundance. A report from Statista titled "Western Europe's post–WWII economies" calls it "the most prosperous period in European history."[13]

Germany's rise from defeat, devastation, and ruin following the war to become the world's third-largest economy was so impressive it became known as *Wirtschaftswunder* or "the German economic miracle"—and German economist Ludwig Erhard became known as its "father."[14]

West Germany's post-war Bizonal Economic Council elected Erhard the director of the Department for Economics, putting him in charge of economic policy. This "authorized him to go forward with his guiding princip[al] act, which stipulated the deregulation of the controlled economy and prices, while introducing the new Deutsche Mark currency."[15]

As a 1988 *Foundation for Economic Freedom* article titled "Origins of the German Economic Miracle" stated, "Erhard knew that only free market policies could get Germany back on its feet," so he introduced "sweeping free market reforms which gave economic freedom to over 80 million Germans and began West Germany's 30-year post-war economic miracle."[16]

In fact, the post–World War II era would become known as the "The Golden Age of Capitalism." According to the United Nation's Department of Economic and Social Affairs, this Golden Age of

Capitalism "spanned from the end of the Second World War in 1945 to the early 1970s" and was "a period of economic prosperity with the achievement of high and sustained levels of economic and productivity growth"[17]—as the regional-GDP-per-capita graph above reflects.

But it is Japan's post–World War II surge that most clearly demonstrates the importance of free-market capitalism to the world's hockey-stick-like growth in GDP per capita.

Japan began industrializing in the 1800s, boosted by the Meiji Restoration of 1868, which abolished Japan's feudal system. According to Stanford University's Program on International and Cross-Cultural Studies, the Meiji leaders adopted an economic system in which the government played "a significant role in determining what [was] produced and [it] allocate[d] capital through control of the financial system."[18]

The Meiji reformers rejected the free-market capitalist model "in which the market largely determines what products are produced, and banks and the stock market allocate capital" and adopted a system in which "[t]he legal framework [was] considered subservient to state interests and, most importantly, the economy [was] viewed as existing to serve the interests of the nation, not the individual."[19]

Nevertheless, the new system was certainly an improvement over feudalism, and Japan rapidly became Asia's leading industrialized nation. By the 1930s, Japan's industrial capacity was sufficient to wage World War II. Yet prior to World War II, Japan's GDP-per-capita increase was markedly inferior to that of both the U.S. and Western Europe and slightly below Eastern Europe's.

Then Japan experienced its own economic miracle, as its GDP per capita suddenly surged.

That surge followed General Douglas MacArthur's successful effort to dismantle Japan's wartime command-and-control economy and establish a free-market economy that encouraged competition and entrepreneurship. Almost immediately, for the first time in at least two thousand years, Japan's GDP per capita surged ahead of Western (for a time) and Eastern Europe, second only to the United States. Japan's average annual GDP growth rate would exceed that of both the U.S. and Western Europe for the period from 1950 to 1987.[20]

As was the case with Western Europe, had the Industrial Revolution *alone* been responsible for the global surge in GDP per capita, Japan would have surged well before the end of World War II. But it failed to surge until it had the right economic system. Absent free-market capitalism, Japan's state-centric pre-war economy failed to come anywhere near that nation's—and its peoples'—potential.

While the historic surge in GDP per capita was continuing in the U.S. and taking off in Western Europe and Japan during the Golden Age of Capitalism, GDP per capita in both Eastern Europe and China was meager, and growth was minimal. Not coincidentally, during this period Eastern Europe and China were home to the world's largest collectivist economies—the socialism of the Union of the Soviet *Socialist* Republics (emphasis mine) and the Peoples' Republic of China.

Eastern Europe and the Soviet Union

The Soviet Union's economic collapse in 1991 should have surprised no one. The real surprise should have been that it lasted as long as it did. From the outset, its collectivist economic system lacked both the incentives to motivate individual success and the capability to effectively manage a sophisticated modern economy. As a result, GDP per capita never improved to a level consistent with Russia's economic potential.

The die was cast when, under Joseph Stalin's quarter-century dictatorship, the Soviet Union implemented forced industrialization under a collectivist "command economy" in which the central government made all decisions on the production and distribution of goods and services. Government owned everything—or virtually everything—and government elites set policies for the entire economy. They measured success not by how well the economy performed, but by how well each industry, entity, or individual satisfied the government's policy goals, at least on paper.

Under this very "visible hand" of government, the Soviet hierarchy created a series of five-year plans from May 1929 to June 1941 setting targets for accelerating industrialization and economic development, employing centralized resources. With actual economic success subservient to meeting the government's five-year-plan goals, even obvious solutions to improve economic performance, efficiency, or productivity were ignored or punished, discouraging individual achievement, innovation, and work. The result was consistent and sustained shortages of essential goods, rationing, and millions of dead from starvation.

But the five-year plans were successful in transforming the Soviet Union from an agricultural economy to an industrialized economy capable of successfully waging war against the more economically advanced and industrialized German state in World War II—albeit with substantial U.S. support.

Thereafter, the Soviet Union engaged in a Cold War with the United States that also required significant industrial and military capabilities. Unfortunately, that was about all it could do. This command economy and five-year-plan strategy remained in place until the Soviet Union collapsed in 1991.

The Eastern European line on the regional graph above covers the entire history of the Soviet Union and reflects its failure to ever compete seriously with GDP per capita in Western Europe or the United States. Unfortunately for Soviet citizens, even the limited benefits of this command economy never reached them.

In 1950, Soviet GDP per capita sat at $2,834[21] compared with $4,594 in Western Europe[22] and $9,561 in the U.S.[23] By 1990, the Soviets' GDP per capita had increased to $6,871,[24] but was even further behind those of Western Europe at $15,988[25] and the U.S. at $23,214.[26]

In dollar terms, over this forty-year period, the Soviets' GDP per capita went from being $1,760 behind Western Europe and $6,727 behind the U.S. in 1950 to being $9,117 behind Western Europe and $16,343 behind the U.S. by 1990.

At that point, even the most ardent fans of the Soviet Union's collectivist economy knew it was over. Prominent holdouts included the U.S. academic community. For decades, this group authored books and lectured and gave each other awards and accolades, all for predicting that Soviet collectivism would eclipse American capitalism. According to a study in the *Journal of Economic Behavior and Organization,* "The collapse of the Soviet Union surprised many western students of economics in part because its economy had long been portrayed in textbooks as a viable alternative to democratic capitalism"[27]—although it really never was.

True believers to the end, many left-leaning economists almost inexplicably continued to hold, right up to the date of the Soviet Union's collapse, that a collectivist economy could outperform a free-market economy. One prominent example is renowned MIT economist Paul Samuelson, who in 1970 became the first American to receive the Nobel Prize in Economics and in 1996 received the National Medal of Science for his contributions to the field of economics.[28]

In 1948 he authored *Economics: An Introductory Analysis* which, through twenty editions, would become "the most widely used economics textbook ever published," according to the MIT Press.[29] Suffice it to say that many very well-educated and prominent economists got their basic training from Samuelson's textbook.

The 1961 or seventh edition contained a graphic projecting that Soviet GDP would surpass U.S. GDP as early as 1984, but not later than 1997. In subsequent editions, Samuelson maintained the notion that the Soviets would "bury" us economically (to quote former Soviet Premier Nikita Khrushchev), but simply moved the dates to adjust for an increasingly disappointing reality. By the 1980 edition, he had moved the date for Soviet economic dominance to between 2002 and 2012.[30] Of course, by then there was no Soviet Union.

Like many Keynesian economists, Samuelson was a collectivist at heart who made every effort to give the Soviet system preferential treatment, unsupported by reality. In fact, in the 1989 edition of his widely used textbook, literally on the verge of the Soviet's economic and political collapse, Samuelson and his co-author William Nordhaus wrote, "The Soviet economy is proof that, contrary to what many skeptics had earlier believed, a socialist command economy can function and even thrive."[31]

Shortly thereafter, the Soviet economy would prove exactly the opposite by collapsing. When you refuse to see the truth, it is highly likely that you will miss it, no matter how obvious.

Throughout the post-war period, the Soviet Union's collectivist economy, which dominated Eastern Europe, simply could not keep up with growth in the West. That was true at every point and in every year.

The Soviet Union was never a nation lacking in potential. The problem was its economic and political system. As former British prime minister Margaret Thatcher correctly stated, "Countries are not rich in proportion to their natural resources. If they were, Russia would now be the richest country in the world. . . . but they have not had an enterprise economy. . . ."[32] The Soviet system industrialized but failed to produce economic gains anywhere close to either Russia's potential or the gains in countries with free-market economies. As a result, the Soviet Union simply collapsed.

The global economy thrived in its absence.

The Heritage Foundation's "Index of Economic Freedom" has been measuring rising economic freedom and declining poverty every year since 1995, or shortly after the Soviet Union's collapse. The 2018 edition states that an "explosion of economic liberty" has produced "a massive worldwide reduction in poverty, disease and hunger"[33] and that "by a great many measures, the past two decades have been the most prosperous in the history of humankind." During that period, "the global economy has moved toward greater economic freedom, [and] world GDP has nearly doubled" lifting "hundreds of millions of people out of poverty and cutting the global poverty rate by two-thirds."[34]

From the Soviet Union's 1991 collapse through 2022, GDP per capita worldwide increased by 67 percent.[35]

China and Red Capitalism

China is a different story. Having seen what absolute collectivism did to the Soviets, China implemented free-market reforms after the death of Mao. The positive impact was undeniable.

While the regions chart above shows China's GDP per capita improving slightly during the Golden Age of Capitalism, through 2000 it remained well below that of even Eastern Europe. That is less impressive than you might expect from a country that would grow to have the world's second-largest economy (total GDP of $18 trillion in 2022), just behind the United States (total GDP of $25.5 trillion).[36]

Significantly, that growth was not a result of the Soviet-style collectivist command-and-control economy China had for decades under Communist Party Chairman Mao Zedong. On the contrary, China introduced free-market economic reforms shortly after Chairman Mao's death in 1976. This followed decades of economic failure under China's Soviet-style and Soviet-mentored economic system—which included Soviet-inspired five-year plans. The Chinese refer to their reformed economy as a "socialist open economy," or "socialism with Chinese characteristics," and colloquially as "red capitalism."

In a 2011 analysis, the U.S.-China Economic and Security Review Commission stated that since 1978 China's economy has undergone a significant transformation from a time "when private enterprise was frowned upon, capitalists were considered class enemies, and the economy was virtually closed to foreign trade and investment" to a time when more "market-oriented reforms have produced an economy that would have been unthinkable in the mid-1970s." By 2011, China had "a private sector" and "private entrepreneurs" who were even "allowed to join the Chinese Communist Party (CCP)."[37]

A 2019 report by the Congressional Research Service similarly found that "[p]rior to the initiation of economic reforms and trade liberalization nearly 40 years ago, China maintained policies that kept the economy very poor, stagnant, centrally controlled, vastly inefficient, and relatively isolated from the global economy." However, after "opening up to foreign trade and investment and implementing free-market reforms in 1979, China has been among the world's fastest-growing economies."[38]

Again, China's experience demonstrates that free-market reforms matter. Much like stakeholder capitalism, red capitalism definitely is not and never was real capitalism, but the regime's willingness to permit a degree of economic freedom and a profit motive, coupled with the dynamic energy of the Chinese people, resulted in an era of economic growth that has benefited hundreds of millions of people in China.

In 1960, eleven years after Mao founded the People's Republic of China, its GDP per capita was a pathetically low $90. By 1978, China's GDP per capita had risen only to $229.[39] These tragically sparse numbers were thanks to China's Soviet-style collectivist command economy in which "private enterprise was frowned upon" and "capitalists were considered class enemies."[40]

Between 1978, when China implemented its free-market reforms, and 2001 China's GDP per capita increased to $1,053. That is an impressive 360 percent growth rate between 1978 and 2001. But China's GDP per capita remained comparatively low, as the regions chart above reflects, because it started from such a low base. For comparison purposes, in 2001, U.S. GDP per capita was $37,134, the GDP per capita for the EU was at $17,198, and Japan hit $34,406.[41]

By 2022, China's GDP per capita had risen another 1100 percent, to $12,720.[42] That is a significant increase over twenty-one years, demonstrating the critical impact of China's free-market reforms in the decades following Mao's death. Nonetheless, at $12,720, China's 2022 GDP per capita remained far behind those of the U.S. ($76,330),[43] the European Union ($37,433),[44] and Japan ($34,017).[45] That is because China has a *red* capitalist economy, not a *real* free-market capitalist economy.

Despite significant GDP growth, in simple dollars China's GDP per capita went from being $36,081 behind the U.S. in 2001 to being $63,610 behind in 2022; from being $16,145 behind the EU in 2001 to being $24,713 behind in 2022; and from being $33,353 behind Japan in 2001 to still being $21,297 behind in 2022—despite Japan's economy stalling due to poor policy decisions by Japan's central bank.[46]

While China has made incredible progress over the past forty-five years thanks to its free-market reforms, it still has a long way to go if its people are to enjoy a standard of living comparable to that in Japan or Western Europe, let alone in the United States. That will require an energized free-market economy.

Unfortunately, China will probably never reach the living standards of its democratic competitors, because for the last fifteen years, and certainly since Xi Jinping assumed power, the Chinese Communist Party has not only failed to take further steps towards economic freedom; it has in important ways reversed course and stifled the dynamic impulses that are the hallmark of capitalist economies.

In 1759, Adam Smith wrote that government elites believe they "can arrange the different members of a great society with as much ease as the hand arranges the different pieces upon a chessboard" and fail to "consider that the pieces upon the chessboard have no other principle of motion besides that which the hand impresses upon them." But that never works because on "the great chessboard of human society, every single piece has a principle of motion of its own."[47] That principle is freedom, both economic and political.

China's problem is that autocratic rulers, including those in the CCP, know that at a certain point economic freedom leads inevitably to political freedom, or at least it leads to centers of power in society that are independent of state control.

In a fully developed free-market capitalist system, markets and businesses, not government, decide how to allocate capital. Individual citizens, not the state, decide where to invest their own money. A private financial sector is free to price risk into investment alternatives. An independent legal system is free to adjudicate and enforce property rights, regardless of the desires of political officials. Regulatory systems have some degree of certainty and legality; they are not generally tools by which rulers arbitrarily punish businesses that fail to cater to the whims of bureaucrats and party officials. Stock markets function freely, channeling money into productive enterprises and out of unproductive ones—the government does not get to intervene every time investors buy or sell in some manner that the rulers believe disserves the ends of the state.

Free-market capitalism—actual capitalism—cannot work the magic of economic growth unless businesses and individuals can pursue their own economic goals in their own way, free from arbitrary and lawless state control. And when push came to shove, that was something the Chinese Communist Party would not allow. The leaders of the CCP do not value freedom for its own sake. They care about capitalism only insofar as it produces wealth for the state to use, and when they had to choose between maintaining their control and enabling greater prosperity for the Chinese people, they chose control.

On January 5, 2013, Communist Party Chairman Xi Jinping delivered an important speech to members of the Chinese Communist Party's Central Committee. The speech was titled "Uphold and Develop Socialism with Chinese Characteristics."[48]

He spoke plainly, if somewhat inaccurately, stating, "First of all: *Socialism with Chinese Characteristics is socialism.* It is not any other 'ism.' . . . It was Marxism-Leninism and Mao Zedong Thought that guided the Chinese people out of that long night and established a New China; [it] is through socialism with Chinese characteristics that China has developed so quickly." He concluded his speech with a rejection of free-market capitalism, stating that "capitalism is bound to die out and socialism is bound to win." That sounded much like American academics and Soviet propagandists (but I repeat myself) prior to the Soviet Union's collapse. To make sure people knew Xi meant it, the Communist Party took the unusual step of republishing his speech in 2019.[49]

Following Xi's speech, China has pursued policies that reversed many of its free-market reforms and reasserted the heavy hand of government over the businesses and entrepreneurs responsible for China's economic improvements and expansion.

A majority of China's economy is concentrated in government hands through State Owned Enterprises (SOEs). According to the Stanford Center on China's Economy and Institutions, China has "363,000 firms [that] are 100% state-owned, 629,000 firms [that] are 30% state-owned, and nearly 867,000 firms [that] have at least some state ownership."[50]

Like all nationalized or government-controlled enterprises, they are highly inefficient and shot through with cronyism. They are grossly misallocating billions in capital and dragging China's economy down, yet the CCP refuses to break them up and sell them off. In fact, the Party's answer to the inefficiency of the SOEs has been to consolidate them further and to take numerous steps to increase the influence of the Party over the businesses that remain nominally private.[51]

Effectively, no large company in China today is private. Every business leader watches the various pronouncements from Beijing and tries to adapt his company to the priorities of the CCP. He knows that his company is at the service of the Chinese state. What the Party demands—even what it suggests or encourages—it gets.

Xi's zealous "anti-corruption" campaign has been so comprehensive that it is discouraging individuals from initiating valuable or profitable new projects out of fear of being deemed corrupt. Those policies are damaging investor confidence in a sweeping array of targeted sectors—"finance, energy, pharmaceutical and infrastructure"—where, according to Xi, "power is concentrated, capital is intensive and resources are rich."[52] Similarly, Xi's so-called anti-espionage policies are so broad they have effectively muzzled consultants who normally advise foreign businesses looking to invest in China.[53]

The impact of Xi's policies goes well beyond foreign investment. According to a November 2023 CNN article titled "Detained, Missing or under Investigation: Business Leaders in China Face an 'Aggressive' Crackdown," "more than a dozen top [Chinese] executives from sectors including technology, finance and real estate have gone missing, faced detention, or been subjected to corruption probes." Why? Well because Xi's Communist Party is intensifying "a regulatory crackdown on companies and strength-en[ing] its control of the economy."[54]

Those investigations and disappearances have vast economic impacts. "Even international consulting firms have been caught up in the sweep" as they face "rising risks, including the possibility of police raids and detentions of staff, in the world's second largest economy."[55]

As a result, in 2023 "China reported its smallest annual foreign direct investment since the 1990s." According to the *Financial Times*, direct foreign investment in China declined 82 percent from 2022 to 2023, to the lowest annual amount since 1993. Hardly a surprise, given China's cracking "down on foreign consultancies over the past year amid concerns that international businesses sharing sensitive information to clients could pose a national security threat."[56]

If you are a businessperson in China, rather than focusing on how to achieve financial success, your biggest concern is that you might be the next executive to disappear. In fact, meaningful success—or profitability—will make you a target.

Remember Jack Ma, once the richest man in China whose business empire included Alibaba, the Amazon of China, and Ant Group, the world's largest fintech company? *Forbes* magazine described him as "an entrepreneur, an innovator, and charismatic spokesman for Success in the New China."[57] In 2020, he gave a speech "critical of the Chinese financial industry establishment"—and then he was disappeared for about three months. He is now retired and reportedly living in Tokyo.[58]

To quote Jack Ma, "Among the richest men in China, few have good endings."[59] If you are an aspiring Chinese entrepreneur, this is not encouraging—unless you plan to leave the country.

As a result, China's economic growth is stalling out. China is now facing a massive property crisis,[60] tremendous overcapacity in key industries,[61] declining population producing a demographic nightmare,[62] high youth unemployment,[63] weak consumer spending,[64] high local government debt,[65] weakening of international demand,[66] and increased international tensions.[67]

But at least the CCP has more control.

Even Beijing knows that China's economy is in trouble; its response has been to clamp down even tighter. An August 2023 *Financial Times* article entitled "Chinese Economists Told Not to be Negative as Rebound Falters" told the story. It stated that "Chinese authorities are putting pressure on prominent local economists to avoid discussing negative trends such as deflation, as concerns mount about Beijing's ability to boost a flagging recovery in the world's second-biggest economy."[68]

According to a December 2023 International Monetary Fund article, "The underpinnings of China's growth seem fragile from historical and analytical perspectives" with "some analysts say[ing] the day of reckoning has finally arrived." There is a possibility that "China's economy is headed for a crash similar to those experienced by other high-flying Asian economies—such as Malaysia and Thailand." One major problem is that "[r]econciling the government's two contradictory impulses—more freedom for markets but with a heavy hand of government intervention to maintain 'stability and order'—poses difficult challenges."[69]

Not surprisingly, China's stock market is crashing. A 2024 article in *Forbes* titled "China's $7 Trillion Crash Masks the Really Bad News," stated that "[e]conomists are struggling to put China's epic $7 trillion stock crash in perspective" but that the best reflection of its "size and scope may be that, since 2021, the market has lost the combined gross domestic product of Japan and France."[70]

But "the war that Xi Jinping's inner circle seems to be waging [is] against bad news itself." According to the *Forbes* article, "the state security ministry has reportedly made clear Beijing is on the lookout for those disseminating negative views on China's economic and market prospects" with a "chilling warning not to 'denigrate China's economy' via 'false narratives'" which "is Mao Zedong, not Adam Smith."

How bad is it? Well, a 2024 *Financial Times* article reports, "China's state-owned enterprises have begun setting up in-house reserve military units, a legacy of the Mao Zedong era, in a sign of authorities' increasing concern about social and political instability amid the country's economic slowdown, according to analysts."[71]

These challenges to economic freedoms matter. Speaking in a 2024 CNBC interview, JP Morgan CEO Jamie Dimon observed that "anyone who is looking to invest in [China] has to be a little worried . . . the risk/reward changed dramatically."[72]

Despite Chairman Xi's effort to enshrine "Marxism-Leninism and Mao Zedong," it was China's free-market reforms, not Mao's Marxism, that were responsible for its post-1978 economic ascent. Absent those reforms, the inevitable result for China would have been a Soviet-style economic collapse like that of its former Communist mentor. Mao's collectivist economy simply could not have survived.

The problem with the Soviet economy and the pre-1978 Maoist Chinese economy was always the underlying collectivism, which failed to incentivize individual achievement and incorrectly assumed a small group of elites alone could make effective decisions for a complex modern economy. The Soviets were unable to reform their collectivist system, and it collapsed. The Chinese reformed theirs for a while, and they were rewarded with remarkable success—but that success cannot survive as China abandons the reforms that enabled it and reintroduces the policies that were stifling it. With or without "Chinese characteristics," collectivist economic systems simply do not work.

Unfortunately, we cannot expect that China's economic troubles will cause it to become less aggressive in foreign affairs, or more lawful in its international economic relations. The opposite is more probably true. As discontent over the economy grows, the CCP will likely attempt to focus popular dissatisfaction outwards, against its neighbors. And it certainly will not slow its efforts to gain wealth by flouting its trade commitments and using its economic leverage to capture markets or corrupt local elites in the global South. Nor can we expect it to stop stealing technology others have created.

But foreign affairs are beyond the scope of this book.

In any event, whether in the United States, Western Europe, Japan, or China, history makes it clear that the phenomenal global surge in economic growth per person over the past two hundred–plus years occurred because of free-market capitalism's effectiveness. No other system or event can explain this economic miracle.

If we keep markets free and open, profits will drive broad-based abundance, global economies will grow, and that surge will continue. Should we revert to collectivism—whether through authoritarian socialism or its close cousin, stakeholder capitalism—that prosperity will recede as quickly as it arose.

Did This Surge in Wealth Actually Benefit the Poor?

Of course, the next question is whether the historic surge in GDP per capita benefited the poor. Free-market capitalism unquestionably created incredible wealth, but did it reduce human suffering, or did the rich just get richer? If the great mass of society benefited, we should find a lower percentage of the world's population living in poverty today than in the early 1800s and a direct relationship between that reduction and increased GDP per capita. As you might suspect, there is an undeniable correlation.

While deep poverty was the widely accepted human condition for millennia, in the age of free-market capitalism it has become increasingly a thing of the past. As even President Barrack Obama stated at Georgetown University in 2015, "We don't dispute that the free market is the greatest producer of wealth in history—it has lifted billions of people out of poverty."[73] Truer words were never spoken.

Up to 1820, most of the world lived in extreme poverty. The chart below appeared in a 2016 Our World in Data article titled "The Short History of Global Living Conditions and Why It Matters That We Know It" by economist and Oxford professor Max Roser.[74] Professor Roser updated the article in 2024. The chart shows the percentage of the world's population living in "extreme poverty"—or less than $1.90 per day—from 1820 to 2018. According to Professor Roser "The United Nations focus [is] on 'extreme poverty', an extremely low poverty line that has the purpose to draw attention to the very poorest people in the world."[75]

So how did the very poorest people in the world fare over the past two hundred years? Did they benefit from the surge in GDP per capita? Well, there were certainly fewer of them in 2018 than in 1820.

Professor Roser's chart shows estimates of global poverty over this two-hundred-year period, first published by historian Michail Moatsos. These figures consider "non-monetary forms of income"—which are important for poor families, as many are subsistence-level farmers living largely on the food they produce. They also consider differing price levels in different countries and adjust for inflation over time. The data is in international dollars, with one international dollar having the same purchasing power as one U.S. dollar in 2011.[76]

TABLE 3

Extreme Poverty in the World

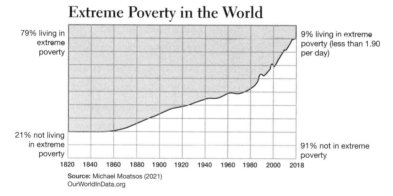

Source: Michael Moatsos (2021)
OurWorldInData.org

As this chart shows, 79 percent of the world's population was living in extreme poverty in 1820. As difficult as it is to imagine today, eight of every ten people were living on less than $1.90 a day. By 2018, that number had declined to under 9 percent, which is fewer than one out of ten—a single-digit percentage for the first time in history.[77]

To put that in some perspective, in 1820 the world population was just over 1 billion people[78] and, according to the Moatsos data, 795 million of them lived in extreme poverty.[79] By 2018, the world's population was almost 8 billion,[80] and 634 million were living in extreme poverty.[81] So the population living in extreme poverty declined, both as a percentage and numerically—despite an eight-fold increase in the world's population. If the percentage living in extreme poverty had stayed the same as it was in 1820 (79 percent), by 2018 over 6 billion people would have been living in poverty.

While 2019 is the most recent year for which we have the data, the World Bank has estimated that, but for the COVID-19 pandemic, the number of people living in extreme poverty would have declined to 581 million by 2022. But because of the pandemic, that number is likely closer to 657 million and could be as high as 677 million.[82] In any event, it is between 8 and 9 percent, despite a worldwide pandemic stifling economic growth.

As Professor Roser points out, "every single day since 1990 . . . on average, there were 130,000 fewer people in extreme poverty than in the previous day" and "no matter what poverty line you choose, the share of people below that poverty line has declined globally."[83] This is a second economic miracle—and it was dependent on the first. Free-market capitalism kept billions of stakeholders out of poverty.

The next graph shows the correlation between growth in GDP per capita and the decline in extreme poverty. It sets forth the Angus Maddison data, going back to 1820, soon after capitalism began its rise, and compares it to the Moatsos data on extreme poverty, also going back to 1820 and through 2018.[84]

TABLE 4

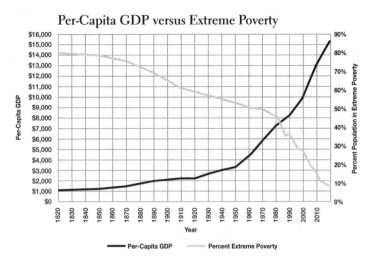

Per-Capita GDP versus Extreme Poverty

While we have two quite different data sets on this graph, they move relatively in tandem. As GDP per capita increased, the percentage (and number) of people living in extreme poverty decreased. In fact, it dropped like a rock. This graph confirms President Obama's admission that "the free market is the greatest producer of wealth in history" and that "it has lifted billions of people out of poverty." According to Professor Roser, "That is a huge achievement. For me, as a researcher who focuses on growth and inequality, it may be humanity's biggest achievement of all in the last two centuries."[85]

A Rising Economic Tide That Lifted All Boats

Absent growth in GDP per capita—increased wealth creation—any growth in the world's population would have resulted in less wealth available per person, and a concurrent increase in extreme poverty—the disastrous outcome predicted by Thomas Malthus. But that is not what happened. Quite the opposite—while the population increased eight-fold, the percentage of people living in extreme poverty massively decreased, by over 70 percentage points.

That occurred because free-market capitalism elevated the human condition by enabling economic growth. With the limited growth that existed in the pre-capitalist world, the only way people could improve their condition was by getting more of the wealth that already existed. It was a world where wealth was a zero-sum game. The poor could only get richer if the rich got poorer. Class warfare was inevitable, unless those with wealth also had the power to suppress dissent.

Capitalism changed that.

That is the power of capitalism. The power to grow the economic pie for everyone. President Kennedy said it best—"A rising tide lifts all boats." He was arguing for tax cuts, which he believed would generate economic growth that would benefit everyone—the poor, the working class, the middle class, and the upper class. Class warfare was neither necessary nor desirable.[86]

Kennedy believed that wealth creation was not a zero-sum game in which the poor only get richer when the rich get poorer. He believed—he knew—everyone could get richer. History has shown that he was correct. Capitalism grows our economic pie so that everyone can get a bigger piece. Collectivist economic systems are often justified with claims that they will redistribute wealth more fairly—but what they produce are smaller shares of a smaller pie, at least for everyone unconnected to the political authorities who control the economy.

A Far Better Life

The benefits for the world's poor have extended beyond a simple reduction in poverty. In fact, the range of benefits has been truly spectacular. As the additional charts on the next page from Professor Roser's article demonstrate, since the rise of capitalism, infant mortality has decreased while basic education, literacy, vaccination rates, and freedom have all increased.[87]

The numbers are stunning.

In 1820, 43 percent of children died before the age of five. By 2021, that number was 4 percent.[88]

Educational opportunities also dramatically increased. In 1820, only 17 percent of people worldwide had at least a basic education, and a mere 12 percent could read. By 2019, 86 percent had a basic education or more, and 87 percent could read.[89]

Political freedom also expanded. In 1820, fewer than 1 percent of people lived in a democracy. By 2015, that number was up to 54 percent.[90] The percentage was boosted by the fall of the Soviet Union, but the share living in democracies has failed to increase over the past thirty years, held down primarily by those still living in China.

As Adam Smith aptly stated in *The Wealth of Nations*, "No society can surely be flourishing and happy, of which the far greater part of the members are poor and miserable."[91] Since 1820, hunger, poverty, illiteracy, and child mortality have all declined

TABLE 5

The World as 100 People
Over the Last Two Centuries

Poverty

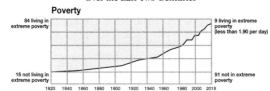

84 living in extreme poverty — 9 living in extreme poverty (less than 1.90 per day)

16 not living in extreme poverty — 91 not in extreme poverty

1820 1840 1860 1880 1900 1920 1940 1960 1980 2000 2018

Literacy

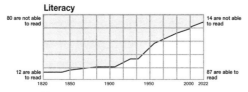

80 are not able to read — 14 are not able to read

12 are able to read — 87 are able to read

1820 1850 1900 1950 2000 2022

Democracy

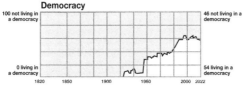

100 not living in a democracy — 46 not living in a democracy

0 living in a democracy — 54 living in a democracy

1820 1850 1900 1960 2000 2022

Basic Education

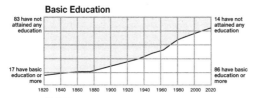

83 have not attained any education — 14 have not attained any education

17 have basic education or more — 86 have basic education or more

1820 1840 1860 1880 1900 1920 1940 1960 1980 2000 2020

Child Mortality

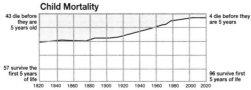

43 die before they are 5 years old — 4 die before they are 5 years

57 survive the first 5 years of life — 96 survive first 5 years of ife

1820 1840 1860 1880 1900 1920 1940 1960 1980 2000 2020

Vaccination (against diptheria, whooping cough & tetanus)

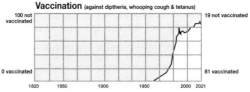

100 not vaccinated — 19 not vaccinated

0 vaccinated — 81 vaccinated

1820 1850 1900 1950 2000 2021

This visualization is from my article: "The Short History of Global Living Conditions and Why It Matters that We Know it".

Data Source:
Poverty: Michalis Moatsos (2021). (All measured in international $ to adjust for inflation and price differences between countries)
Education: Wittgenstein Center (2023), World Bank (2023), van Zanden, J. et al. (2014).
Literacy: Zanden, J. et al (2014) and UNESCO.
Democracy: regime classification by Skaaning et al. (own calculation of global population share)
Vaccination: WHO (Global data are available for 1980 to 2017 – the DPT3 vaccination was licenced in 1949) (Vaccination refers to children (ages 12–23 months) in each year and not the entire population)
Child mortality: up to 1960 own calculations based on Gapminder: UN-IGME thereafter

The world population increased more than 7-fold over these 2 centuries
8.1 Billion
1.1 Billion 1.7 Billion
1820 1900 2024

A visualization from OurWorldInData.org
The online publication that presents the research and data to make progress against the world's largest problems.
Licensed under CC-BY-SA by the author Max Roser.

significantly, despite a massive eight-fold increase in the world's population. More people, less poverty, less hunger, and fewer babies dying and, as a result, far fewer people either poor, miserable, or uneducated.

That is what economic freedom—capitalism—does. This is how businesses in a real free-market capitalist system "serve a social purpose," to quote Larry Fink. Capitalism does this better than any other system ever devised, and that certainly includes so-called stakeholder capitalism. It must bother the stakeholder-capitalist/World Economic Forum crowd greatly that free-market capitalism, with no one at the helm, improves the human condition so much more than any system guided by omniscient elites. This helps explain why they shroud their goals in misleading labels and acronyms and promote them based on fear and prejudice.

The point here is simple—with the dramatic increase in GDP per capita since 1820, the poor unequivocally saw significant benefits. Life was and is dramatically better for them, and better for almost everyone else as well, including for those who, like Larry Fink, are now attempting to undermine the very system from which they have so handsomely profited.

There Is Still More to Do

Going from seventy-nine people out of every hundred living in extreme poverty to eight or nine is an incredible improvement, but even eight is still too high. If we are going to reduce that number further, we need to acknowledge what drove that spectacular decline over the past two hundred years, rather than listening to collectivist elites who are doing everything in their extensive power to rewrite economic history.

The simple truth is that over the past two hundred–plus years, the world has experienced a massive increase in wealth, accompanied by precipitous declines in both extreme poverty and infant mortality, all while the share of people who are healthy, literate, educated, and living in freedom has increased to levels once unimaginable.

Perhaps most amazingly, this all occurred despite an eight-fold increase in the world's population, proving that wealth is not a fixed commodity but can grow, allowing people to thrive and flourish.

This miraculous improvement in the human condition was unequivocally due to the emergence of free-market capitalism—and it can and should continue. Free-market capitalism works because of the incredible economic energy generated by individuals free to focus on improving their lives through their personal efforts—in other words, from profit. It is the profit motive—the fact that we all have the freedom and the opportunity to better our lives—that drives this great engine of economic prosperity, reducing both poverty and human suffering.

What sane person would want to abandon that system?

The advocates of stakeholder capitalism, by their own admission, would transform our entire economy. Like their collectivist predecessors, they want a system they control, where businesses cater to their social and political agenda rather than the needs of their customers and investors, never mind the ambitions of their employees to prosper by doing honest work for a profitable company. Continued progress and abundance in a free society are most assuredly *not* their goals.

Make no mistake—what Larry Fink and the other stakeholder capitalists seek is the same in fact, if not in form, as the economic systems that trapped humanity in poverty and want for thousands of years. To achieve their goal, they demean profit as the goal of business, posture as the avatars of an elevated morality, and take advantage of their outsized presence in the public square to gaslight the public with their morbid fear-based agenda.

Fortunately, in this country we have a strong attachment to freedom and a healthy latent distrust for the pretensions of financial elites. Most Americans do not appreciate being lied to, especially about their financial affairs. As a result, and as you might expect, the resistance to stakeholder capitalism and its ESG agenda is growing. We might even style it the Resistance.

Chapter 7

THE

RESISTANCE

"Where there is power, there is resistance."

—Michel Foucault, historian and philosopher[1]

I n retrospect, it seems shocking that the ESG "Resistance" movement took so long to coalesce, given the clarity of Larry Fink's 2018 CEO letter and its open attack on free-market capitalism, a system that has not only lifted billions of people out of poverty and misery but also made many others rich, including Larry Fink himself. Add to that the actions the Big Three have since taken to promote their ESG agenda, and a Resistance was inevitable, if slow to arise.

In fairness, people initially found it difficult to believe that American businesses would actually set aside the profit motive to pursue social and political goals dictated by a group of obscure financial elites. Why would anyone think American businesses would reject over two hundred years of unprecedented economic success to elevate a collectivist agenda by which they would hurt themselves? Were we really going to kill the goose that laid the golden eggs? I know I was skeptical. Maybe in Europe, or South America, or China, but surely not in America.

Nor was my level of concern aroused by the growing influence of Klaus Schwab, the German-born founder and CEO of the

World Economic Forum (WEF), which holds annual events in the Alpine ski-resort town of Davos, Switzerland, where ultra-rich and moralistic elites decide which of their luxury beliefs they intend to inflict on an unsuspecting public next.

Klaus Schwab has opined that a technologically driven revolution would "lift humanity into a new collective and moral consciousness."[2] As Schwab was obviously aware, imposing a tyranny for the good of its victims requires broad acceptance of tyrannical beliefs as moral imperatives. Since 2020, he has been calling for a "Great Reset" to replace free-market capitalism globally with his collectivist creation—"stakeholder capitalism."[3] In a June 2019 editorial titled "What Kind of Capitalism Do We Want?," Schwab said that "stakeholder capitalism" was "a model [he had] first proposed a half-century ago" that "positions private corporations as trustees of society, and is clearly the best response to today's social and environmental challenges." He advanced—and took some credit for—the collectivist concepts that Fink had laid out in his 2018 and 2019 letters.[4] Schwab's effort to remake capitalism into a system mirroring European socialism should all along have raised more concern than it did. His proposal to transform modern corporations from entities focused on meeting the needs of consumers to the "trustees"—or literally the caretakers—of society was hardly subtle.[5]

But Schwab just seemed too extreme—too European—to have a meaningful impact outside of the WEF's elitist/globalist/collectivist bubble.

It is true that, for years, a large network of progressive activist groups in the U.S. had been filing hundreds of craftily worded shareholder resolutions to advance leftist causes, alter corporate behavior, and drive public policy. They were quite successful, despite David-versus-Goliath-like opposition from conservative groups such as the National Center for Public Policy Research and Justin Danhof, long the director of its Free Enterprise Project (FEP).

But this initial shareholder activism was generally seen as specific to certain issues rather than a concerted effort to bring about a European-inspired social and economic transformation. So it was difficult to get the word out on the importance of opposing it. The need for an organized and effective resistance too often fell on deaf ears. As a result, what would become known as "woke" language began working its way into a vast number of corporate purpose statements on issues such as the environment, "equity," and so-called social justice.

Yet even with our corporate culture obviously drifting leftward, Schwab's vision for a collectivist "stakeholder capitalist" future long seemed too extreme for America, where our entrepreneurial spirit runs strong, the right to choose our leaders is enshrined in our founding documents, and our liberties are endowed by our Creator. But Schwab's 2019 editorial was emboldened by shocking news that should have made the defenders of our free-market system realize we were facing a crisis.

The Wake-Up Call

On August 19, 2019, the notion that such a transformation could not happen here took a body blow. On that date, the Business Roundtable (BRT), an influential group of 181 CEOs of major U.S. companies, signed a "Statement on the Purpose of a Corporation," embracing stakeholder capitalism.[6]

Since 1978, the BRT had periodically issued "Principles of Corporate Governance" that "endorsed principles of shareholder primacy" under which "corporations exist principally to serve shareholders" as Milton Friedman had opined.

Like Fink's 2018 CEO letter, BRT's 2019 "Statement" endeavored to change all that. Its signatories agreed to move from shareholder primacy to stakeholder primacy. Of course, the stakeholders (in addition to the shareholders) were the same as those named in Fink's 2018 letter and Schwab's editorial—consumers, employees, suppliers, and communities. The BRT also referenced the shareholders' "long-term" interests.

According to Alex Gorsky, Chairman of the Board and CEO of Johnson & Johnson and chair of the BRT's Corporate Governance Committee, this move "affirm[ed] the essential role corporations can play in improving our society when CEOs are truly committed to meeting the needs of all stakeholders."[7] In an interview, an elated Gorsky said that while preparing the statement, "There were times when I felt like Thomas Jefferson."[8]

Jefferson surely rolled over in his grave.

Of course, the *New York Times* loved it, claiming that the BRT had broken "with decades of long-held corporate orthodoxy" in "an explicit rebuke" of Milton Friedman. It credited the usual suspects, including "BlackRock's Larry Fink" who in the previous year "had begun calling on companies to be more responsible" and Klaus Schwab, noting that in that same year at Davos, "the discussions often centered on how businesses could help solve thorny global problems."[9]

The BRT's Statement also had its critics.

For example, the Council of Institutional Investors (CII) issued a response criticizing the BRT for "placing shareholders last and referencing shareholders simply as providers of capital rather than as owners." According to the CII, the BRT Statement undercut "notions of managerial accountability to shareholders" while failing to make management accountable "to any other stakeholder group."[10]

The CII acknowledged the obvious importance of stakeholders, stating that "it is critical to respect stakeholders," and recognize "stakeholder contributions to" long-term goals. Nonetheless, it argued that "[t]o achieve long-term shareholder value," businesses must also "have clear accountability to company owners." Otherwise "[a]ccountability to everyone means accountability to no one."[11]

Well, of course it does.

In retrospect, the whole point of Fink supporting stakeholder capitalism was to transfer the fiduciary responsibility CEOs owed "company owners"—who would hold them accountable for returns—and transfer it to an amorphous group of anonymous non-owners—who would hold them accountable for nothing.

As for addressing broader social issues, the CII response said that "[i]t is government, not companies, that should shoulder the responsibility of defining and addressing societal objectives with limited or no connection to long-term shareholder value."[12]

The CII hit the nail on the head. We do, after all, have a republic.

In any event, like many business leaders (including me), CII believed that investors—that is, actual shareholders—would defend their own interests and stop the stakeholder-capitalist movement. CII noted that "[s]hareholders have a very particular role in allocating (and re-allocating) equity capital"—meaning they invest where they believe they will get the best returns as owners. This makes "company managers vulnerable to changes in company valuation that can be rapid, as investors reassess company prospects."[13]

In other words, if your company focuses on social issues rather than profits, your business will underperform, your shareholders will sell their shares, and the value of your company will decline. Under normal circumstances, that kind of thing would constrain CEOs because, as I can attest, business leaders do not want to crater the value of their company's stock. So the CII concluded that "nothing in the BRT statement will change this real-world dynamic of public equity markets."[14]

The CII's point was that the BRT's stakeholder capitalists simply lacked the power to accomplish such a transformation because investors would stop them by divesting from companies that put social and political issues over profits and, as a result, underperformed. It made sense.

Unfortunately, the CII was missing a critical point—actual shareholders were no longer the main actors driving the "real-world dynamic of public equity markets" and "allocating (and re-allocating) equity capital" based on financial performance, as the CII believed. Rather, the passive index-investing Big Three were driving the private-equity markets—and already using their massive proxy-voting power to impose a collectivist ESG agenda on the American business community.

Recall Larry Fink's 2020 CEO letter, asserting that "when a company is not effectively addressing a material issue, its directors should be held accountable" and bragging that in 2019—the very year in which the BRT issued its "Statement"—BlackRock had "voted against or withheld votes from 4,800 directors at 2,700 different companies."[15]

As we have seen, Fink's message was unequivocal—BlackRock was going to "hold board members accountable." Just in case any CEOs missed his point, Fink's letter stated in bold type that "**we will be increasingly disposed to vote against management and board directors when companies are not making sufficient progress on sustainability-related disclosures and the business practices and plans underlying them.**"[16]

So while CII and others may have underestimated the Big Three's activist determination, rest assured the CEOs on the Business Roundtable did not. They got the message loud and clear—from Fink's increasingly aggressive CEO letters, from BlackRock's shareholder activism on director nominees, and, undoubtedly, from the so-called "stewardship" meetings BlackRock had with these CEOs and their management teams personally.

It may have been a coincidence that the BRT issued its stakeholder-capitalism concession in a year when BlackRock alone "voted against or withheld votes from 4,800 directors at 2,700 different companies"—but I seriously doubt it.

BlackRock, State Street, and Vanguard were (and are) the largest shareholders in virtually every company that signed the BRT's Statement. For example, with respect to Gorsky's company, Johnson & Johnson, the largest shareholders are Vanguard (9.5 percent), BlackRock (7.9 percent), and State Street (5.6 percent).[17]

There were certainly some CEOs who understood and opposed the stakeholder-capitalism agenda, but even they would have wanted to at least appear supportive of their largest shareholders' dictates.

In any event, the themes of Fink's letters, Schwab's editorial, and the BRT's "Statement" were consistent—businesses exist to meet the collectivist needs of non-investor stakeholders (a proxy for society) by advancing a moralistic ESG agenda set by a small group of financial elites. CEOs could either get on board or find themselves ousted by newly elected ESG-sympathetic directors.

Contrary to the CII's assumption, this was not a simple problem of CEOs heading down a misguided collectivist path that shareholders could correct by selling their shares. In reality, the financial firms supposedly representing those shareholders—but no longer tethered to their best financial interests—were the CEOs' guides. They, not the actual owners or the markets, were the CEOs' new masters.

That is stakeholder capitalism in a nutshell.

Now What?

Even after the BRT's shocking "Statement," it was not certain that business leaders were serious about adopting stakeholder capitalism. Some observers thought the BRT's Statement was an effort to mollify leftist activists who had been harassing CEOs and corporate boards for years. The notion that the BRT's Statement was a misguided effort to assuage activists made sense at the time. Since addressing the needs of so-called "stakeholders" was something that effective businesses do in the normal course of running a profitable company anyway, it did not appear that much would change. In hindsight, those of us who believed that were simply wrong.

As for the Big Three, they are primarily passive fund managers that invest in an index of companies and then (should) allow the CEOs of those companies to do their jobs and drive investor returns. As the low-cost/high-return alternative to investments in individual stocks, the Big Three had a good thing going. Would they really jeopardize that to pursue leftist activism? It was reasonable to believe they were not really serious.

A few people saw the potential threat. Justin Danhof, who had been on the front lines in this fight, warned at the time that the BRT's Statement would only exacerbate the problem. He wrote that while it was "possible that the folks at the Roundtable are attempting to assuage activist investors and socialist politicians with their statement, the exact opposite is likely to occur." He believed that the "Statement" was likely to energize progressive activists, creating an even bigger problem.[18]

For me, things began to come clear about a year later. In June of 2020, Oren Cass, an acquaintance from the Romney campaign economic team, called me to ask if I would defend free-market capitalism's shareholder focus in a written online debate on the obligations of business. Taking the position that corporations should serve a social purpose would be Patrick J. Deneen, a highly regarded author and professor at the University of Notre Dame.

Oren had started a new think tank called American Compass. According to its website, American Compass was "developing the conservative economic agenda to supplant blind faith in free markets with a focus on workers, their families and communities, and the national interest."[19] Oren and I have some disagreements but were (and still are) friendly.

I agreed to the debate—and it was eye-opening.

Titled "The Corporate Obligations Debate," it received a positive response and is available online.[20] I may be biased, but I thought Patrick and I did a good job flushing out the issues from both sides. It became clear during our exchange that Patrick, who is certainly a knowledgeable and well-informed man, actually believes that stakeholder capitalism is a transformative force that could—and should—supplant free-market capitalism, despite our values as a nation, our history, and the potential negative impact on global prosperity.

A less well-informed man who shared those stakeholder capitalist beliefs was presidential candidate Joe Biden. In a July 2020 campaign speech, Biden said that "it's way past time we put an end to the era of shareholder capitalism. The idea [that] the only responsibility a corporation has is with shareholders, that's simply not true, it's an absolute farce."[21]

A grasp of our nation's history and economy have never been Biden strong points.

Fresh from "The Corporate Obligations Debate," I wrote a *Wall Street Journal* opinion piece titled "Biden's Assault on 'Shareholder Capitalism,'" explaining that what Biden called shareholder capitalism had "created the greatest period of prosperity in human history" and that "[w]hen you strike at its ability to encourage investment and profit, you strike at the good it [has] done for [all] stakeholders."[22] I do not believe that Biden read it—or that it would have mattered if he had.

Over the following year, it became increasingly obvious that left-wing shareholder activists were not the real problem. There had been collectivist threats to free-market capitalism going back to Karl Marx and the publication of the first volume of *Das Kapital* in 1867.[23] They always ended in failure, misery, and poverty—for all but the governing elites.

Replacing the "society" aspect of socialism with a "stakeholders" collective was merely a change in nomenclature. Collectivism would remain a terrible idea no matter what the Left called it, and Americans have long understood what it would cost them. From the five Socialist Party presidential campaigns by union leader Eugene Debs between 1900 and 1920 through "democratic socialist" Vermont senator Bernie Sanders's efforts in 2016 and 2020, the American electorate had always resoundingly rejected collectivism whenever it appeared on the ballot—at least when its appearance was obvious.

But that result was dependent on the electorate being in charge.

Progressive activists and socialist politicians were not the driving force behind changes brewing in the business world. That driving force was the Big Three, who had been empowered by the success of passive index investing to exercise unprecedented control over the American business sector. They were using that power to transform stakeholder capitalism from a misguided and misnamed collectivist concept into a force that threatened our democracy, our economic freedom, and our individual liberty.

By 2021, the cat was out of the bag.

Larry Fink's 2021 CEO letter made it clear that there was a radical effort afoot demanding "a transformation of our entire economy." In May of that year, Exxon's proxy contest loss to the environmentalist hedge fund Engine No. 1—backed by the Big Three—eliminated any question about whether stakeholder capitalists had the power to accomplish that transformation. With the BRT on board and President Biden in office, such a terrible transformation was beginning to feel inevitable.

Others were coming to the same or similar conclusions. Recognizing a threat is only the first step in addressing it. The next step for the nascent ESG Resistance was creating public awareness. At first, that was a struggle. ESG is not exactly a sexy-sounding topic.

Author and political analyst Stephen Soukup's book *The Dictatorship of Woke Capital: How Political Correctness Captured Big Business* was an excellent and early effort to point out the dangers.[24] It was published shortly after Fink's 2021 letter and presented the intellectual case against ESG, woke capital, and anti-democratic efforts to undermine free-market capitalism.

The *Wall Street Journal* named Soukup's book one of the best political books of 2021, describing it as "an exceptionally useful presentation of the intellectual origins and present-day lunacies of woke capitalism." According to the *Journal*, the "most enlightening parts of the book" dealt with "multibillion-dollar asset-management companies such as BlackRock and State Street" whose leaders "embrace a variety of radical ideologies—broadly known as 'sustainability' and ESG . . . and routinely use their massive financial leverage to push publicly traded companies to alter their policies according to progressive political ideals."[25]

If you were involved or interested in ESG at the time, Soukup's book was a must read (and is still a very worthwhile read). But people in general were reluctant to listen. If I mentioned ESG in a speech, I could see everyone's eyes glaze over. When I was invited to speak at events and offered ESG as a topic, the general reaction was—*Can you please talk about the economy, Biden, capitalism, politics, or anything else?*

I was certainly not alone. To get the word out, a lot of people, often risking their careers, reputations, and credibility, had to stand up and point out the threat in language everyone could understand. It would take an entire chapter to list everyone who contributed to the growth and momentum of the ESG Resistance movement. I mention some in the following pages and endeavor to list many others in the Acknowledgements section of this book. It is an impressive group of individuals, with whom I am proud to be associated, and many of whom have become friends.

For purposes of this chapter, I will focus on the three primary legislative and regulatory efforts to curtail the ESG/stakeholder capitalism threat—the fight over the Trump-era ERISA regulation, enforcing the Texas boycott legislation, and passage of state fiduciary duty bills.

1. THE TRUMP-ERA ERISA RULE

In 2019, stakeholder capitalism's supporters were moving ahead like the German Panzer divisions invading Poland in 1939 and meeting little effective resistance. The Trump Administration's Department of Labor (DOL) under Labor Secretary Eugene Scalia attempted to change that. Secretary Scalia published a proposed rule in June of 2020 that would be the first major offensive against stakeholder capitalism and ESG investing. That such a rule was necessary at all was indicative of just how bad the situation had become.

Scalia proposed this rule under the Employee Retirement Security Act (ERISA),[26] which Congress had passed in 1974 "to address public concern that funds of private pension plans were being mismanaged and abused." DOL is tasked with enforcing Title I of the law, which contains the rules governing fiduciary conduct.[27]

ERISA's fiduciary duty provisions are clear—private-pension-fund fiduciaries must act "solely in the interest of participants and beneficiaries and for the exclusive purpose of providing benefits" and paying plan expenses.[28] That sentence would have made sense without the words "solely" and "exclusively," but Congress included them to make it crystal clear to whom fiduciaries owe their duty and their loyalty. It is not to an amorphous group of stakeholders. While this should have been patently obvious, it was good to have it enshrined in law.

Secretary Scalia's proposed rule "remind[ed] plan providers that it is unlawful to sacrifice returns, or accept additional risk, through investments intended to promote a social or political end," as he explained in a *Wall Street Journal* opinion piece titled "Retirees' Security Trumps Other Social Goals."[29] In other words, no matter what Larry Fink claimed "society" was "demanding," it was inconsistent with fiduciary responsibilities to invest in order to "serve a social purpose"[30]—as opposed to "solely" and "exclusively" serving the financial interests of pension-fund beneficiaries.

Scalia wrote that the proposed rule would govern how "private pension plans should be managed in light of the push to consider the environment, social factors and corporate governance, or ESG, when making investment decisions."[31] He noted studies showing that "when investments are made to further a particular environmental or social cause, returns unsurprisingly suffer" and pointed out that under ERISA[32] "investment decisions must be based solely on whether they enhance retirement savings, regardless of the fiduciary's personal preferences."[33]

In fact, Scalia noted that "it is unlawful to sacrifice returns, or accept additional risk, through investments intended to promote a social or political end."[34] In other words, "investors' increasing use of index funds" was not "driving a transformation of BlackRock's fiduciary responsibility" as Fink's 2018 letter claimed.[35] At least not under ERISA, a federal law with crystal-clear language. Scalia believed that law meant what it said.

As for stakeholder capitalism, Scalia noted that "ESG investing often marches under the same banner as 'stakeholder capitalism,' which maintains that corporations owe obligations to a range of constituencies, not only their shareholders." But under ERISA, "[a] fiduciary's duty is to retirees alone, because under Erisa one 'social' goal trumps all others—retirement security for American workers."[36]

A good point well made.

DOL published the final rule, titled "Financial Factors in Selecting Plan Investments," in November of 2020. Rather than targeting ESG specifically, the final rule took a broader approach, providing that ERISA requires plan fiduciaries to focus only on pecuniary factors—that is, only on factors that have a financial rather than a social or political impact.[37]

It was a smart approach. Stakeholder capitalists would eventually try to discard the ESG acronym, once people figured out what it really meant. Scalia wisely kept the focus on a fiduciary's duty to act "solely" for pension fund beneficiaries and "exclusively" in their best financial interests—as ERISA provided.[38]

Under the final rule, fiduciaries could consider any factor—including ESG factors—as long as the sole focus remained maximizing returns for the funds' participants and beneficiaries, as opposed to advancing a social or political cause.[39] That was an important aspect of the Trump-era rule.

The final rule took effect on January 12, 2021.[40] President Biden was inaugurated eight days later. His administration declined to enforce it, which was hardly a surprise. First, as we have seen, Biden had come out the previous year, during his presidential campaign, opposing shareholder capitalism.

Beyond that, the Trump-era rule would have significantly affected BlackRock—and BlackRock alumni permeated the Biden Administration.

A July 2021 article appearing on Nicolette Investment Management's website noted that former BlackRock investment executive Brian Deese was serving on Biden's National Economic Council. The former chief of staff to BlackRock's chief executive Larry Fink, Adewale Adeyemo, was deputy secretary at the Treasury Department. Michael Pyle, who had formerly been the global chief investment strategist at BlackRock, was the chief economic advisor to Vice President Harris. Deese, Adeyemo, and Pyle had all also served in the Obama administration.[41]

So, to no one's surprise, about a year after Biden took office, his DOL rescinded the Trump-era rule and adopted a rule[42] that it claimed was necessary because the Trump rule had a "chilling effect" on consideration of "environmental, social and governance factors in investments."[43]

Well, yes, it did, but only because ESG explicitly does not maximize returns for retirees, as ERISA unequivocally requires. If the Trump-era rule chilled investing intended to accomplish social or political goals—and it did—it was doing exactly what Congress intended and what ERISA clearly stated.

But the Scalia rule did not even mention "environmental, social and governance factors." It required only that fiduciaries adhere to the goal of maximizing returns. Under that rule, a fiduciary could consider anything relevant to the investment's "pecuniary" or financial performance, including ESG considerations where they were related to financial returns, but could not invest for the purpose of advancing such social or political considerations rather than the financial interests of the fund's beneficiaries—as was ERISA's clear intent.

The stark difference between the Scalia rule and the Biden rule is apparent if we compare how each might apply to a fiduciary's investment decisions.

Say, for example, that a pension-fund manager believed a solar-panel manufacturer was going to generate superior returns given government subsidies and the demand for so-called "green energy." Under either the Trump or the Biden rule, investing in that company would be perfectly acceptable, because the intent would be to invest in a profitable company and to maximize returns for the pension fund's participants and beneficiaries. The fund manager would be buying the shares because he believed they were a sound investment—which is appropriate under either rule and ERISA's statutory language.

But what if the solar panel manufacturer's financial prospects were questionable? Under the Biden rule, consideration of the company's supposed environmental benefits would be permissible and could tip the scale in favor of investing in that company because of the "E" in ESG—even though the company had questionable returns potential. Rather than considering an ESG factor as part of determining the financial benefits of an investment, the fund manager would be investing to advance an agenda, irrespective of financial benefit or pain for the fund's beneficiaries.

Allowing the fund manager to advance a social and political agenda rather than the financial interests of the fund's beneficiaries in effect amends ERISA without the congressional action that our Constitution requires.

Under the Trump rule, such an investment would be impermissible, because investing in an underperforming company to advance the "E" in ESG violates ERISA's requirement that fiduciaries act "solely" on behalf of the plan's beneficiaries and "exclusively" for the purpose of maximizing their retirement benefits.

Of course, the Biden Administration's goal was to allow fund managers to place ESG's social and political goals above the financial

interests of pension-plan beneficiaries because those goals were synonymous with the Biden Administration's social and political goals.

That is exactly why I have referred to ESG as a "luxury belief." It
represents the willingness of financial elites to sacrifice the money
of other people—often financially vulnerable people—in the service of the social or political goals of the elites themselves, who,
needless to say, never have to worry about whether they can pay
their bills at the end of the month.

In fairness, some Democrats saw the danger and objected to
Biden's attempt to politicize pension-fund assets. Democratic senator Joe Manchin of West Virginia opposed the rule because, as his
website stated, "the Biden Administration's ESG rule ... prioritizes
politics over getting the best returns for millions of Americans' retirement investments."[44]

Speaking on the Senate floor, Manchin added that the Biden
administration's "ESG rule" was "just another example of how our
Administration prioritizes a liberal policy agenda over protecting
and growing the retirement accounts of 150 million Americans
that will be in jeopardy."[45]

So House Republicans passed a bill to nullify the Biden administration's attempt to rewrite ERISA. It passed the Senate on a bipartisan basis.

Biden, of course, vetoed it.[46] The Biden pro-ESG/anti-
shareholder rule took effect on January 30, 2023.[47] Score one for
those who would put politics over the financial interests of retirees.

As a result, the Trump-era rule never really saw the light of day.
But the public debate on the rule got the word out, and Scalia's
opinion piece in defense of it was both succinct and articulate.
People understood it, and that was a huge step forward in mobi-
lizing the ESG Resistance.

People were beginning to realize that something fishy was going
on—and it involved their retirement savings.

2. THE TEXAS SOLUTION

The next major counterattack on stakeholder capitalism came from Texas. On June 14, 2021, shortly after Exxon's May 26 proxy fight loss, Texas governor Greg Abbott signed Senate Bill 13, a law prohibiting the state from doing business with financial institutions that boycott energy companies. It became effective on September 1, 2021.[48]

The drafters modeled this law "after existing state laws prohibiting state contracts with companies that boycott, divest from, or sanction Israel," according to the Texas Public Policy Foundation, for which the bill was a legislative priority.[49]

The law bars any "state governmental entity," including Texas retirement and investment funds, from doing business with any "financial company" that the state comptroller determines "boycott[s] energy companies" including those that engage in "fossil fuel-based" energy production."[50]

The law defines boycotting broadly to include not only literal boycotting, but also "taking any action that is intended to penalize, inflict economic harm on, or limit commercial relations with a company because" it "does not commit or pledge to meet environmental standards beyond applicable federal and state law."[51]

The law does not prohibit ESG investing specifically, but it does strike at the heart of the ESG agenda—the attack on fossil fuels. In an October 2023 advisory memorandum on this law, Texas Attorney General Ken Paxton stated that "[w]hen considering whether a company is an energy company boycotter . . . particular notice should be taken of whether the company is a member of the Net Zero Alliance or a signatory of any other similar entity that espouses a commitment to the furtherance of so-called Environmental, Social and Governance policies."[52]

In August of 2022, Texas Comptroller Glenn Hegar announced[53] his list[54] of financial companies that boycott energy companies. According to Hegar's announcement, the ESG "movement has produced an opaque and perverse system in which some financial companies no longer make decisions in the best interest of their shareholders or their clients, but instead use their financial clout to push a social and political agenda shrouded in secrecy."[55]

Given the statute's language, however, his office's "review was limited to the boycott of energy companies, rather than a review of the entire ESG movement."[56]

The comptroller's list of energy company boycotters included BlackRock and individual funds from both BlackRock and State Street, among others. On November 1, 2023, Hegar updated[57] the list.[58] BlackRock and numerous individual BlackRock and State Street funds were still on it.

BlackRock objected to being included on the comptroller's list of boycotters. Relying on the colloquial use of the term "boycott," BlackRock argued that it has never actually boycotted oil or other fossil fuel companies. In fact, BlackRock must invest in such companies if they are part of an index on which BlackRock bases an investment product—such as the S&P 500, which includes every major US energy company.

As a May 13, 2022, letter from BlackRock to Comptroller Hegar stated, "We do not boycott energy companies."[59] Following the issuance of Hegar's August 2022 list, BlackRock told CNBC, "We disagree with the Comptroller's opinion. This is not a fact-based judgment. BlackRock does not boycott fossil fuels—investing over $100 billion in Texas energy companies on behalf of our clients proves that."[60] In fact, BlackRock is one of the largest investors in U.S. energy companies.

The problem is not that BlackRock or the Big Three literally boycott energy companies, in the colloquial sense. The problem is that they invest in them—and then can vote the shares they hold in those energy companies (including shares held for Texas government entities) against the best economic interests of those companies and in favor of a net-zero agenda (as occurred with Exxon). Or they can pressure energy companies to take such actions without a shareholder vote, in "stewardship" meetings.

In fact, the Big Three surely voted the Exxon shares they held for Texas government entities in 2021 to elect three Engine No. 1 director nominees and against Exxon's management team less than a month before the Texas boycott bill became law. The reasons BlackRock offered for that vote are revealing.

A 2021 document from BlackRock titled "Vote Bulletin: ExxonMobil Corporation," states that part of the justification for supporting Engine No. 1's nominees and voting against Exxon management was that BlackRock believed Exxon needed to do more "in relation to the energy transition in order to mitigate the impact of climate risk" and "that Exxon's energy transition strategy falls short of what is necessary to ensure the company's financial resilience in a low carbon economy."[61]

Voting against management-supported directors for failing to meet standards BlackRock sets to address "climate risk" certainly sounds like an "action intended to penalize" Exxon for failing to meet a standard that applicable law does not require. In fact, it sounds exactly like what the Texas law was drafted to prevent.

The law's intent is clear, and at least some government entities are acting accordingly. As the *Dallas Morning News* reported, the Teachers Retirement System of Texas (TRS) divested over $500 million from BlackRock and smaller positions from UBS Group, BNP Paribas, Nordea Bank, and several other boycotting financial institutions. "A spokesman for the TRS said the pension fund 'is abiding by the statute.'"[62]

On March 19, 2024, the Texas State Board of Education's Chairman Aaron Kinsey announced that the Texas Permanent School Fund leadership had delivered an official notice to BlackRock terminating its financial management of a massive $8.5 billion, ensuring "full compliance with Texas law." According to Kinsey, "BlackRock's destructive approach toward the energy companies that this state and our world depend on is incompatible with our fiduciary duty to Texans."[63]

In addition to these divestments, the Texas law has had a significant impact in raising public awareness, both inside and outside of Texas, of ESG's impact—particularly its impact on energy companies.

The Texas law has also restricted which banks can be involved in Texas municipal bond offerings. Banks the comptroller has identified as boycotters that handle municipal bond deals—such as Citigroup—lost business.[64]

Texas started a trend. Eleven states have enacted legislation targeting entities that oppose certain industries, primarily energy companies, according to Ropes and Gray's website Navigating State Regulation of ESG.[65]

3. THE STATE-FIDUCIARY-DUTY SOLUTION

With the Trump-era fiduciary-duty rule on President Biden's chopping block, in May of 2021 former congressman Diane Black and I published an opinion piece in the *Wall Street Journal* titled "Who Really Pays for ESG Investing?" We criticized BlackRock and other financial firms for using pensioners' assets to advance ESG, rebutted the notion that companies focused on politics could outperform those focused on profits, and noted that "ESG investing upends the fiduciary duties portfolio managers owe their clients."[66]

It was an unsuccessful effort to change the Biden administration's approach on this issue, but it did get me thinking about alternatives.

As I continued speaking (and I would work at least some ESG discussion into just about any speech I gave), what I would most commonly hear from those who understood the issue was—"This is terrible. What can we do?" At first, apart from "help get the word out," I did not have much of a response.

It was increasingly obvious that any effective resistance was going to need a means to stop the ESG train on its tracks—and given that train's momentum, we needed it soon.

It seemed to me that the fiduciary-duty approach was the strongest option. Fink knew this was a major impediment for his stakeholder capitalism/ESG effort. As we saw, his 2018 letter bent over backwards to find some justification for evading that duty, even claiming that "investors' increasing use of index funds [was] driving a transformation in BlackRock's fiduciary responsibility."[67]

Fink was claiming that the very people fiduciary duties were intended to protect were, by purchasing BlackRock's products, somehow forcing BlackRock to transform—read that evade—those duties. It made little sense but revealed a clear weakness in his stakeholder-capitalist house of cards.

At the federal level, it was obvious the Biden administration would never enforce the Trump-era fiduciary duty rule, would veto any federal legislation designed to address the threat, and would more likely attempt to legitimize both stakeholder capitalism and the ESG agenda—all of which eventually occurred. So a federal solution was off until a new president took office, or 2025 at the soonest.

We could not wait that long.

So it occurred to me that the best solution would be to combine the Texas approach of using state legislation with Scalia's fiduciary-duty approach.

Every state has laws governing fiduciary duties—either under common law or by statute. While the language may differ from state to state, the concept that fiduciaries have a legal—not to mention a moral—duty to act solely in the best financial interests of those whose funds they manage is a universal concept dating back centuries.

But there were two problems.

First, most of the monies invested with the Big Three came from pension funds, and ERISA preempted state regulation of private pension funds. So state legislation could neither set nor modify fiduciary obligations for private pension funds. But ERISA exempted state—or public—pension funds, which remained subject to state law.

In other words, while ERISA prevented states from legislating with respect to private pension funds, such as those for the Teamsters or the United Auto Workers, they were free to legislate with respect to their state-government pension funds, such as those for teachers or law-enforcement personnel.

So the first problem was solved. There was room to update state legislation and specifically prohibit fiduciaries from misusing (through investing, proxy voting, or "stewarding") state pension-fund assets for social or political purposes. In other words, the states could establish rules for their own entities similar to the Scalia rule at the federal level.

Addressing the issue at the public-pension-fund level was also important in a practical sense. Retirement benefits for millions of Americans who work for state and local governments are dependent upon returns that asset managers, primarily the Big Three, make on their behalf. The failure to prioritize returns puts those retirement benefits at risk.

"Unfunded state-pension liabilities total $6.96 trillion or just under $21,000 for every man, woman and child in the United States," according to a 2022 American Legislative Exchange Council (ALEC) analysis.[68] That is a massive shortfall, making a focus on investment returns critical. A state-fiduciary-duty bill could keep the focus on financial returns rather than politics or social activism by assuring that public-pension-fund assets were invested for, as Secretary Scalia stated, the "one 'social' goal" that "trumps all others—retirement security for American workers."[69]

The second problem was that every state already had laws governing fiduciary duties. Even blue states California[70] and New York[71] have laws requiring that fiduciaries exercise their duties "solely in the interest" of the beneficiaries of their funds and for the "exclusive purpose" of providing benefits.

So was it necessary to amend state laws to make it clear—or clearer—that investing, proxy voting, and "stewarding" for social or political purposes violated those laws? In other words, did state law already prohibit the Big Three from using their power to force ESG on companies in which they had invested state pension-fund assets?

The answer is that the existing state laws on fiduciary duties did not necessarily provide the needed protections, because the Big Three could argue that forcing their portfolio companies to adopt ESG policies would somehow benefit pension-fund beneficiaries.

In fact, they were already doing that.

The Big Three claim that their ESG investing, proxy voting, and stewarding are intended to produce long-term value for investors. Of course, their notion of long-term leaves open the question of how long is long-term, and how one distinguishes long-term value enhancements from politically biased prognostications about what may or may not happen in some distant future. The debate over what long-term means and whether a goal is too long-term or speculative to enhance value for investors raises issues that can obfuscate a fiduciary's actual intent.

Pursuing lawsuits on this issue against the extremely well-funded Big Three on a state-by-state basis would be very time-consuming, complex, and economically prohibitive, absent clear statutory language specifically precluding fiduciaries from prioritizing ESG's social or political goals over pension-fund beneficiaries' financial interests. State-fiduciary-duty legislation would simplify such cases and weaken the defense that ideologically based investing is somehow and in some future universe intended to create long-term value.

So in September of 2021, I began drafting a bill that combined ERISA's statutory language on fiduciary duties with text from Secretary Scalia's regulation and some language of my own. I intended this proposed State Fiduciary Duty Bill to make it clear that there had been no transformation of any investment firm's fiduciary duties, no matter what its executives, stakeholder capitalists, and ESG proponents claimed.

The first speaking engagement where I discussed this proposed legislation was, coincidentally, the first event where the sponsor had asked me to speak specifically about ESG. Derek Kreifels, the founding CEO of the State Financial Officers Foundation (SFOF) had asked me to speak at the group's November 2021 meeting. SFOF is a free-market organization for responsible financial management composed of state treasurers, auditors, comptrollers, and other financial officers. Under Derek's leadership, it would become a leading force in the ESG Resistance.[72]

I ran the fiduciary-duty/state-legislation idea by Derek, and he loved it. The reaction from the state financial officers in attendance at the meeting was overwhelmingly positive.

Following that meeting, I began sharing my draft legislation with individuals in state governments that I knew or who had expressed interest. Those efforts met with some success, but the momentum for this State Fiduciary Duty Bill accelerated in 2022, when the Heritage Foundation and the American Legislative Exchange Council (ALEC) got involved.

David Burton, Senior Fellow in Economic Policy at Heritage, and Will Hild from Consumer Research reviewed and improved my draft legislation's language. In April of 2022, both ALEC[73] and Heritage[74] adopted model state-fiduciary-duty legislation thanks to leadership from Jonathan Williams, Chief Economist and Executive Vice President of Policy at ALEC, Andy Olivastro, Chief Advancement Officer at Heritage, and Bridgett Wagner, Executive Director of the Edwin J. Feulner Institute at Heritage.

The ALEC and Heritage models differ in inconsequential ways. Both work to the same effect. Both the ALEC and Heritage models adopt ERISA's fiduciary-duty provisions and make it clear that "[a] fiduciary shall discharge his duties with respect to a plan solely in the pecuniary interest of the participants and beneficiaries for the exclusive purpose of . . . providing pecuniary benefits to participants and their beneficiaries."[75]

As was the case with Secretary Scalia's ERISA-based rule, the model statutes also make it clear that acting "solely" in the financial interests of a state pension fund's "participants and beneficiaries"—and for the "exclusive purpose" of benefiting them financially—prohibits managing those funds to further "non-pecuniary, environmental, social, political, ideological, or other goals or objectives" (ALEC's model language)[76] or with "any purpose whatsoever to further social, political, or ideological interests" (Heritage's model language).[77]

Contrary to what ESG proponents would argue when opposing such legislation, neither of these models would prohibit a fiduciary from considering ESG-related pecuniary or financial factors when evaluating an investment. That is a strawman argument that ignores the model legislation's language and intent.

Asset managers should consider *all* "pecuniary" or financial factors when evaluating investment returns—and many political and social considerations can affect pecuniary value and financial returns. What the model state-fiduciary legislation actually prohibits is *sacrificing* investment returns to *advance* political, social, or ideological goals—including ESG goals. A fiduciary's sole and exclusive focus must be on enhancing those returns for the fund's beneficiaries.

To clarify how this would work, let us look at three situations and see how the model legislation would apply to a fiduciary's actions—investing, proxy voting, and "engaging with portfolio companies"—a.k.a. "stewardship."

First, each model requires that fiduciaries *invest* pension fund assets solely and exclusively to advance the financial interests of the fund's beneficiaries and prohibits investing state pension-fund assets to advance ESG or other ideological, social, or political goals.

Yes, to the dismay of radical environmentalists, the models would prohibit asset managers from investing with the intent to advance a net-zero-carbon agenda. If an asset manager has a problem with that, it should not be investing assets for a pension fund.

This prohibition would primarily apply to active-portfolio managers, as passive funds generally invest based on pre-set criteria. However, investing pension fund assets in a passive index fund where the index itself was designed to advance non-financial political, social, or ideological goals would also violate the prohibitions of both models.

Second, the models each prohibit a fiduciary from *voting* the shares of a company it holds on behalf of pension-fund beneficiaries in a manner contrary to the financial interests of that company—and thus the financial interests of the fund's beneficiaries. A fiduciary obviously cannot be acting in the best financial interests of the beneficiaries whose funds it has invested if its actions are detrimental to the company in which it has invested those funds.

For example, as we saw above, there is no issue if a fund manager invested in a solar-panel manufacturer because the manager believed it would be profitable and generate positive returns for pension-fund beneficiaries. Nor does it violate any fiduciary duties to own such a company as part of a broader index for passive-investment purposes, where ESG factors were irrelevant to the company's inclusion in the index.

But let us say that a fund manager invested in a profitable solar-panel manufacturer—or held those shares in a passive index fund—but believed that the detrimental environmental impact of producing, placing, and disposing of solar panels outweighed the benefits of solar energy. So rather than encouraging management to increase its profitable solar-panel production, the fund manager used his proxy voting power to elect directors who supported imposing a "net-zero-solar-by-2050" policy on the company, potentially protecting the environment "long-term" but obviously reducing returns for the retirees whose funds had been used to buy this company's stock.

As absurd as it sounds, that is essentially what happened to Exxon in 2021 when—as we saw in chapter 4—BlackRock, State Street and Vanguard successfully helped elect directors that environmentalist hedge fund Engine No. 1 had nominated—following which Exxon adopted a "net-zero-carbon-by-2050" policy.

Obviously, when fiduciaries damage the business or prospects of companies in which they have invested pension fund assets in order to accomplish social or political goals, they are not acting either "solely in the interest of participants and beneficiaries" or "for the exclusive purpose of providing benefits." The model state-fiduciary legislation would—and should—prohibit such conduct.

Again, if an asset manager has a problem with that, the manager should not be investing assets for a pension fund.

Third, the models would prohibit investing pension fund assets in a company and then *stewarding* it to engage in conduct that advances political or social goals at the expense of that company's profits, lowering its stock price and the pension beneficiaries' returns.

Proxy voting is not the only arrow in the Big Three's quiver. It is just the most public. They do not need to actually vote the shares they hold. Just a visit to a CEO and the threat of an adverse vote is often enough to cow that CEO into advancing ESG goals. Even a pointed letter can do the trick.

Every CEO knows what happened to Exxon, and no CEO wants that to happen to him. If you are meeting with a company that is one of your major shareholders, wants to "steward" your business, and has bragged about voting against or withholding "votes from 4,800 directors at 2,700 different companies"[78] in a single year, you are certainly going to take that meeting seriously.

As I mentioned, "stewardship" is actually more effective and more insidious than proxy voting, as it occurs in C-suite conference rooms and on Zoom calls, beyond the purview of both investors and those who would protect their interests.

Forcing corporate behaviors that reduce returns in order to advance ESG's social or political goals is not acceptable just because it is done behind closed doors through so-called stewardship visits. It is still misdirecting pension-fund assets to advance a social or political ESG agenda, and the model state-fiduciary bills would prohibit those assets from being used in this manner.

Success to date: by the time this book went to print, thirteen states—including Arkansas, Florida, Georgia, Kansas, Kentucky, Indiana, Montana, North Carolina, North Dakota, South Carolina, Tennessee, Utah, and West Virginia—had passed some form of state-fiduciary-duty legislation rejecting the misuse of state pension-fund assets to advance ESG or other ideological goals.[79]

The legislative language and effectiveness have varied by state. Nine states have explicitly named ESG when outlining their new investing restrictions. Florida, Georgia, Indiana, and Kansas prohibit investing to advance "social, political, or ideological interests." South Carolina prohibits "environmental, social, or political goals, objectives, or outcomes." Montana and West Virginia added the phrase "or other similarly oriented considerations" to their ESG restrictions.

All are clear and consistent in their intent: those responsible for investing and shareholder voting must act solely in the financial interests of the pension funds' beneficiaries. Utilizing state pension funds' assets to advance ESG or other forms of socially or politically motivated investing is inconsistent with that duty.

In other words, the states enacting such legislation made it clear that passive investing has not transformed anyone's fiduciary duties in any respect, stakeholder capitalism notwithstanding.

The ESG Resistance was moving forward.

Chapter 8

THE PRESSURE INTENSIFIES, AND ESG FLOUNDERS

"Enlighten the people generally, and tyranny and oppressions of the body and mind will vanish like evil spirits at the dawn of day."

—*Thomas Jefferson*[1]

C ollectivist policies always build a house of cards. The only question is how long it will stand. As we saw with the Soviet Union, it can take decades of immeasurable human suffering before such a house topples. Failure rarely induces humility in collectivists, nor does it weaken their desire to impose on us what they believe is best for us—but is ultimately best for them.

To conceal their intentions, collectivists hide their goals behind innocuous or moralistic-sounding labels—stakeholder capitalism and ESG being prominent examples. So as elites gain power, the most effective weapon against them is public awareness.

"Gradually and Then Suddenly"

With respect to stakeholder capitalism and its ESG agenda, that awareness began to spread in 2021 and 2022 as the Resistance grew. It is difficult to say at what point it first took hold. To quote Hemingway, it seemed to happen "[g]radually and then suddenly."[2]

I first noticed a change in momentum at an ALEC meeting in July of 2022. I was on a panel with Vivek Ramaswamy and economist Stephen Moore, moderated by ALEC economist Jonathan Williams. Although Vivek and I had been writing, speaking, and appearing on panels about the stakeholder-capitalist/ESG threat for nearly two years, this panel was on the current state of the economy.

Vivek Ramaswamy and I first met in May of 2021, when we both testified on the dignity of work before the U.S. Senate Banking, Housing, and Urban Affairs Committee. We each wove the stakeholder-capitalism threat into our testimony, but the topic failed to generate much interest from the Democrat-majority panel. Nonetheless, we became fast friends, stayed in contact, and would appear on panels together over the next couple of years (until he became a presidential candidate). Vivek would play a significant role in spreading the word about this dangerous collectivist threat.

Ever the entrepreneur, in May of 2022, a few months before the ALEC event, Vivek had launched Strive Asset Management to compete with the Big Three. Its mission was to restore "the voices of everyday citizens in the American economy by leading companies to focus on excellence over politics."[3]

According to the press release announcing Strive's launch, the "'Big 3' firms bear a fiduciary duty to advance the best interests of their clients. Yet in the name of 'stakeholder capitalism,' they use their clients' funds to exercise decisive influence over nearly every U.S. public company to advance political ideologies that many of their clients disagree with."[4] Strive was to be an alternative index-fund manager focused solely on financial returns. Justin Danhof of the Free Enterprise Project was one of Vivek's early hires.

At the ALEC meeting about two thousand people, mostly state legislators, attended our panel on the economy. Afterwards, there was a panel on ESG. While neither Vivek nor I was on that panel, we both wanted to hear what was being said. I thought there would be plenty of open seats. But when we got to the room (which was relatively large), we could barely get in, and the seats were full. By the time the panel started, state legislators were lined up outside and down the hall, and there was no room for anyone else to attend.

We made our way close to the front, leaned against a wall, and listened as the panelists discussed state legislative options to defend capitalism—primarily the Heritage and ALEC fiduciary duty models and the Texas boycott legislation.

Two things struck me. First, hundreds of state legislators were lining up to hear about ESG. Second, there was not a glazed look in anyone's eyes as the panelists spoke. People actually seemed to be leaning forward in their chairs to hear what was being said, and the questions were generally well informed. I was surprised. Something had changed. Obviously, people were aware of the issue, anxious to act, and looking for solutions.

One issue the Resistance faced in its early days was convincing people that there was still time to stop the ESG juggernaut. While it was easy to despise what these elites were doing once you understood it, you had to respect how well they did it. Their efforts were insidious, rapid, and comprehensive. By 2022, they had already moved the ESG ball way downfield, significantly penetrating the financial community, while the Resistance had yet to put a full team on the field.

For example, recall the Net Zero Asset Managers initiative that BlackRock, State Street, and Vanguard joined in March and April of 2021, shortly before the Exxon/Engine No. 1 proxy-contest vote. As we have seen, NZAM is a powerful asset-manager coalition whose members commit to "supporting the goal of net zero green-house gas emissions by 2050 or sooner."[5] They also agree to "ensure that products and services available to investors are consistent with the aim of achieving net zero emissions," by engaging with financial institutions including "credit rating agencies, auditors, stock exchanges, proxy advisers, investment consultants, and data and service providers."[6]

It was no secret that the Big Three were key to the success of this effort. After they joined NZAM in 2021, the globalist World Economic Institute published an article titled "How BlackRock and Vanguard Can Advance the Net-Zero Emissions Movement." It acknowledged the significant role the Big Three could play in NZAM, noting that BlackRock and Vanguard alone managed an "amount equivalent to about three-fifths of U.S. GDP." So, "[g]iven their size" they had "tremendous market influence" and "the capacity to set the course for meaningful net-zero action within the asset management sector."[7]

By 2022, NZAM's effort to infect every aspect of the global financial system with stakeholder capitalism's ESG virus had met with considerable success. That May, it announced that 273 asset managers had joined the initiative "representing more than USD 61.3 trillion in assets under management."[8] The Big Three alone represented about a third of that total.[9]

Obviously, the forces behind the ESG agenda were enormous, organized, and moving forward. If the Resistance were going to succeed, it could not play whack-a-mole with every ESG advance. Rather, it needed to focus on the real power sources behind this movement—the entities with the assets under management, proxy-voting power, and influence to implement the ESG agenda—that is, the Big Three, with BlackRock in the lead position.

So the target was obvious. If the Resistance could increase public awareness of what the Big Three were up to, it could slow and perhaps prevent a terrifying "transformation of the entire economy."

The Word Spreads

In 2021 and 2022, the Resistance made considerable progress in this effort, thanks to numerous individuals who understood the serious threat that stakeholder capitalism and ESG posed and were willing to use whatever tools they had to oppose it. In addition to the efforts discussed in the previous chapter—and others too numerous to list—the following individuals and groups had a significant impact on that progress.

Florida Governor Ron DeSantis played an early and strong role in raising awareness of stakeholder capitalism, ESG, and all things "woke." In December of 2021, DeSantis acted against "woke corporations" through Florida's State Board of Administration and revoked "all proxy voting authority that has been given to outside fund managers, to clarify the state's expectation that all fund managers should act solely in the financial interest of the state's funds." DeSantis's concern was that such fund managers "may pursue social ideologies inconsistent with the state's values or the financial interests of the state's investments."[10]

In July of 2022, DeSantis "announced legislative proposals and administrative actions to protect Floridians from the environmental, social, and corporate governance (ESG) movement." According to the governor's announcement, "[f]rom Wall Street banks to massive asset managers and big tech companies, we have seen the corporate elite use their economic power to impose policies on the country that they could not achieve at the ballot box." His proposed actions were intended to protect "Floridians from woke capital" and to assert "the authority of our constitutional system over ideological corporate power."[11]

In December of 2022, Florida withdrew $2 billion of managed funds from BlackRock. Florida's chief financial officer, Jimmy Patronis, stated that "Florida's Treasury Division is divesting from BlackRock because they have openly stated they've got other goals than producing returns."[12] According to Reuters news service, Florida's actions were part of a broader "backlash against ESG investing" that was "gathering steam among Republican leaders in Florida, and elsewhere, who criticize corporations for focusing on matters like climate change or workforce diversity."[13]

Florida would enact a state-fiduciary-duty law in April of 2023.

In May of 2022, former vice president Mike Pence had published an influential opinion piece in the *Wall Street Journal* titled "Republicans Can Stop ESG Political Bias." He advised that "[s]tates with large employee pension funds invested in the stock market" should "rein in massive investment firms like BlackRock, State Street and Vanguard" that "are pushing a radical ESG agenda." He recommended that states "pass [ALEC's] model legislation" and, for a more permanent solution, that "the next Republican president and GOP Congress should work to end the use of ESG principles nationwide."[14]

On May 25, 2021 (the day before the Exxon/Engine No. 1 proxy vote), fifteen state financial officers, led by Treasurer Riley Moore of West Virginia and with support from Derek Kreifels and the SFOF, had sent a letter to Biden administration climate envoy John Kerry that struck at the ESG movement's radical environmentalist heart.[15] The letter said that Kerry and other members of the Biden administration were "privately pressuring U.S. banks and financial institutions to refuse to lend to or invest in coal, oil, and natural gas companies, as part of a misguided strategy to eliminate the fossil fuel industry in our country."[16] The financial officers urged banks and financial institutions "not to give in to pressure from the Biden Administration."[17]

That November, a group of sixteen state financial officers—again led by Riley Moore, with SFOF support—signed an open letter to the U.S. banking industry stating that the signatories would take "concrete steps" to "select financial institutions that support a free market and are not engaged in harmful fossil fuel industry boycotts for our states' financial services contracts."[18]

On January 17, 2022, Moore announced that West Virginia's Board of Treasury Investments would "no longer use a BlackRock Inc. investment fund as part of its banking transactions." According to Moore, "BlackRock has urged companies to embrace 'net

zero' investment strategies that would harm the coal, oil and natural gas industries, while increasing investments in Chinese companies that subvert national interests and damage West Virginia's
manufacturing base and job market."[19]

A group of red-state attorneys general were the next to react. On
August 4, 2022, nineteen AGs joined the Resistance by sending a
letter to Larry Fink asserting that BlackRock had violated its fiduciary duties under their states' laws when it invested to accomplish
ESG goals—net-zero in particular—rather than to generate financial returns.[20]

The AGs warned BlackRock that proxy voting to advance ESG,
or other ideological causes, violated their laws governing fiduciary
duties and that BlackRock's ESG investment policies appeared to
involve "rampant violations" of the well-established rule requiring
that fiduciaries act to maximize financial returns, rather than to
promote social or political objectives. The AGs stated that financial returns for investors must be a fiduciary's sole focus and that
BlackRock was sacrificing those returns to advance its net-zero
climate agenda.[21]

A month later, AGs Jeff Landry of Louisiana[22] and Todd Rokita
of Indiana[23] each went a step further and issued a letter warning
their state pension fund trustees that investing to advance ESG
goals was likely a violation of their respective state's laws governing fiduciary duties.

Advocacy groups also played a significant role. In addition to
having a strong voice in this fight, the Heritage Foundation led the
effort to coordinate Resistance efforts and assure that groups with
common goals were not working at cross purposes. As these advocacy groups became more effective, the media started to pay attention.

A February 2023 *Wall Street Journal* article titled "Conservatives Have a New Rallying Cry: Down With ESG" pointed out
that "[a] growing collection of conservatives. . . . argue that the
people whose retirement plans the big firms handle never con-
sented to having their money tied up in what they consider to be
liberal causes" and that their investments "should be based solely
on returns."[24]

The article identified Leonard Leo, a longtime leader at the Federalist Society, as overseeing a conservative nonprofit called Marble Freedom Trust that, along with its consulting firm, CRC Advisors, was "leading the anti-ESG push." Marble had "spent more than $10 million on the effort so far." The article quoted Leo as stating that "[t]he ESG movement is polluting our culture and assaulting the dignity and worth of people. Our enterprise stands with a growing group of Americans who are fighting to crush leftist dominance in this arena."[25]

The article identified "Consumers' Research, the Heritage Foundation, [and] the State Financial Officers Foundation" as "[s]ome of the major voices in the debate" that had received funding from Marble."[26]

In early 2022, Consumers' Research launched a website titled whoislarryfink.com,[27] deriding Fink as "woke." Later that year, it launched AboutBlackRock.com,[28] warning consumers to "be wary of investments managed by BlackRock.... Led by Chairman and CEO Larry Fink, the company uses its clout to push a radical agenda in coordination with other financiers through a network of international organizations." It concludes by warning that "BLACKROCK IS CRUSHING AMERICA FROM WITHIN."[29]

As a result of these and other actions—and in addition to eleven states passing boycott legislation and thirteen states passing fiduciary-duty legislation—during 2022 and 2023 nine states withdrew a total of about $8 billion from BlackRock over ESG concerns—Florida withdrew $2 billion,[30] Louisiana $794 million,[31] Arizona $543 million,[32] the Teachers Retirement System of Texas $521 million,[33] Missouri $500 million,[34] South Carolina $200 million,[35] Arkansas $125 million,[36] Utah $100 million,[37] and West Virginia $21.8 million.[38] Americans for Tax Reform has a BlackRock Divestment Tracker that lists withdrawals.[39] There may also be withdrawals that occur without an announcement, to avoid publicity. The SFOF estimates that number at an additional $3.2 billion.[40]

In 2024, the Texas Permanent School Fund withdrew an additional $8.5 billion.[41]

So a grand total of about $16.5 billion.

That $16.5 billion was but a dent in BlackRock's trillions, although it was a dent the BlackRock employees responsible for those accounts surely felt. In June of 2023, when the amount Black-Rock had lost was much lower, Larry Fink admitted that Black-Rock's "business was hurt. We lost $4 billion of mandates."[42]

But more important, divestment demonstrated that people in many red states were aware their funds were being used to advance progressive social and political goals rather than to generate returns for their states' pension beneficiaries. Apparently, and contrary to Fink's assertion in his 2018 CEO letter, not all of "[s]ociety" was insisting that each company "not only deliver financial performance, but also show how it makes a positive contribution to society."[43] In fact, a significant portion of "[s]ociety"—as represented by the people's democratically elected representatives in over a dozen states—believed that asset managers' investment decisions should be focused "solely" and "exclusively" on financial returns for retirees, as the law on fiduciary duties requires.

For the Big Three, the implications were daunting.

Would the divestments snowball in amount—and beyond BlackRock? Had the Big Three overreached? There were obvious litigation risks to the Big Three's actions on fiduciary duty grounds, particularly as states enacted legislation specifically prohibiting ideological investing. Perhaps the success of passive index investing had not transformed BlackRock's fiduciary obligations after all.

In that case, the Big Three had better be prepared to demonstrate that a focus on "stakeholders" and ESG goals actually enhanced returns for investors, as opposed to merely advancing goals these financial elites had determined were best for society.

After all, they had represented publicly that stakeholder capitalism and the ESG agenda would perform better than shareholder-focused free-market capitalism. Were those representations true and, if not, how many people had relied on them? There could be a significant class-action lawsuit waiting in the wings.

Recall the bold-type claims in Fink's 2020 CEO letter—that rapidly changing awareness of "climate change" was causing "**a**

fundamental reshaping of finance" and that "[c]ompanies, investors, and governments must prepare for a significant reallocation of capital."[44]

Fink was adamant that this "fundamental reshaping" was
going to occur, and with that justification he had announced that
BlackRock—the world's largest asset manager—was going to exit
"investments that present a high sustainability-related risk, such
as thermal coal producers" and launch new sustainable index
"products that screen fossil fuels." According to Fink, BlackRock's
"investment conviction [was] that sustainability- and climate-
integrated portfolios can provide better risk-adjusted returns to
investors" and BlackRock believed "sustainable investing is the
strongest foundation for client portfolios going forward."[45]

A year later, in his 2021 CEO letter, Fink claimed that this
climate-change-inspired reallocation of capital had "**accelerated
even faster than I anticipated.**" According to Fink, "the creation
of sustainable index investments ha[d] enabled a massive acceleration of capital towards companies better prepared to address
climate risk," and "companies with better ESG profiles [were] performing better than their peers, enjoying a '*sustainability premium*'" (emphasis mine).[46]

And then that house of cards collapsed. In 2022, merely a year
later, ESG funds were significantly underperforming the market.
And people noticed.

A March 2022 article in the *Harvard Business Review* by University of Colorado Provost Professor of Finance Sanjai Bhagat stated
that "ESG funds certainly perform poorly in financial terms."[47]

A June 2022 study by Aneesh Raghunandan of the London
School of Economics and Shiva Rajgopal of the Columbia Business School warned that "ESG funds appear to underperform financially relative to other funds within the same asset manager
and year, and to charge higher fees." Not surprisingly, asset managers find high fees very sustainable.[48]

A Bloomberg article in December 2022 entitled "Big ESG Funds
Are Doing Worse than the S&P 500," reported that in 2022 "[t]he
10 largest ESG funds by assets have all posted double-digit losses,

with eight of them falling even more than the S&P 500's 14.8% decline. The laggards include BlackRock Inc.'s $20.7 billion iShares ESG Aware MSCI USA exchange-traded fund (ESGU) and Vanguard Group's $5.9 billion ESG US Stock ETF (ESGV)."[49]

On December 27, RealClearEnergy published an article entitled "2022: The Year ESG Fell to Earth," in which economist and respected energy expert Rupert Darwall wrote that "[t]he year 2022 brings an end to an era of illusions" including "the first energy crisis of the enforced energy transition to net zero." It was "the year that brought environmental, social, and governance (ESG) investing down to earth with a thump." According to Darwall, "for the year to date, BlackRock's ESG Screened S&P 500 ETF lost 22.2% of its value, and the S&P 500 Energy Sector Index rose 54.0%."[50]

So with higher fees and inferior performance, it was no surprise when Reuters also reported in December of 2022 that investors had "pulled more money from funds marketed as 'sustainable' than they added for the first time in more than a decade" and that those funds "were also set to lag the performance of non-ESG funds for the first time in five years."[51]

So much for Larry Fink's "sustainability premium."

Stakeholder capitalism and ESG investing simply had not lived up to their promise. No one should be surprised. Those espousing the stakeholder-capitalism notion of businesses "doing well by doing good" had been missing the point—businesses must do well *before* they can do anyone any good, including their non-investor stakeholders. In reality, "doing well" requires making a profit.

To make that point, in a March 2023 *Wall Street Journal* opinion piece titled "Is ESG Profitable? The Numbers Don't Lie," my friend economist Mike Edleson and I published the results of our study on how companies focused on political or social activity performed financially versus those that were not so focused. Using third-party scoring on political and social activism, we evaluated each large- and mid-cap U.S. public company as either liberal, conservative, or neutral (only one-quarter of companies were rated "neutral").[52]

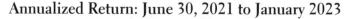

TABLE 6

Annualized Return: June 30, 2021 to January 2023

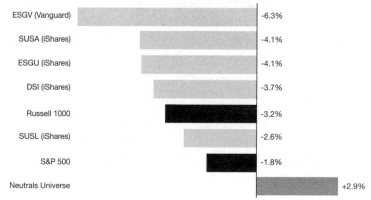

ESGV (Vanguard)	-6.3%
SUSA (iShares)	-4.1%
ESGU (iShares)	-4.1%
DSI (iShares)	-3.7%
Russell 1000	-3.2%
SUSL (iShares)	-2.6%
S&P 500	-1.8%
Neutrals Universe	+2.9%

The results were illuminating. During the period from June 30, 2021, through January 31, 2023, the market was down overall (−1.8 percent large-caps and −3.2 percent mid-caps). ESG funds performed even worse, with most losing between −2.5 percent to −6.3 percent. But the sample of neutral companies gained 2.9 percent. In other words, companies that were focused on profits performed better than those distracted by non-business political or social goals.

As it turns out, companies that focus on social and political causes are actually less profitable than companies that focus on profits. As a corollary, asset managers will not maximize share-holder returns if that is not their focus. It is hard enough to maximize those returns when that is your focus, let alone when you are trying to change the world. It really is not rocket science.

Investors noticed, and investors cared. ESG performance in 2023 would make that point in spades.

The Big Three React

By the end of 2022, the executives at the Big Three were certainly aware that the wheels were coming off the ESG train, and there were strong signs that ESG's momentum was slowing. At that point, all that was needed to get the ball rolling for the Resistance was a good push, and Consumers' Research was about to provide it.

VANGUARD

On December 1, 2022, Consumers' Research and thirteen red-state AGs filed a complaint with the Federal Energy Regulatory Commission (FERC) urging it to deny Vanguard's request for authorization to acquire voting shares of publicly traded utilities. The complaint alleged that Vanguard was "meddling with the energy industry to achieve progressive political goals at the expense of market efficiency."[53]

In an opinion piece for the *Wall Street Journal*, Consumers' Research executive director Will Hild pointed out that, as a member of NZAM, Vanguard had had to "commit to implementing a 'stewardship and engagement policy' consistent with 'achieving global net zero emissions by 2050.'" Given the fact that Vanguard had "publicly committed to pressuring utilities to lower their emissions," Hild said that "FERC should investigate Vanguard's activities to determine exactly what the asset manager has been telling utilities," as it appeared "to be not only putting America's critical infrastructure at risk but violating its agreement only to control utility company shares passively."[54]

The complaint hit a nerve.

Days later, on December 7, 2022, Vanguard announced that it was withdrawing from NZAM membership.[55]

Vanguard's press release announcing that withdrawal was a concise and well-written explanation of passive index investing and its associated fiduciary duties. It first noted that 80 percent of Vanguard's "clients' assets are invested through index funds, which provide broadly diversified access to stock and bond markets at minimal cost."[56]

The press release then acknowledged the simple proposition underlying passive index investing—"[i]ndex fund managers don't choose the securities in a fund or dictate a portfolio company's strategy or operations. Instead, they buy and hold all securities included in the benchmark index and capture the return that the market provides." The release quoted Vanguard's founder, Jack Bogle, who was instrumental in popularizing passive index investing and who advised, "rather than searching for the needle in the haystack, buy the whole haystack."[57] Implied, I suppose, is that you should not burn the haystack down.

Vanguard explained that while it believed climate change was "a material and multifaceted financial risk," its membership in NZAM had resulted in "confusion" about its views, "particularly regarding the applicability of net zero approaches to the broadly diversified index funds favored by many Vanguard investors."[58]

To avoid that confusion, Vanguard had "decided to withdraw from NZAM" in order to "provide the clarity our investors desire about the role of index funds and about how we think about material risks, including climate-related risks—and to make clear that Vanguard speaks independently on matters of importance to our investors."[59]

There were no complaints—à la Larry Fink's 2018 letter to CEOs—about being unable to remove companies from an index or claims that this had somehow magically transformed Vanguard's fiduciary duties.

It was about time.

Finally, one of the Big Three was conceding that a collectivist net-zero-policy approach to the multifaceted issue of climate change might not be in the best interests of all the companies in which it invested on behalf of its clients. In other words, passive index-fund managers who invest in a "whole haystack" of companies should not collectively compel all the companies in that haystack to advance social or political issues that damage their profitability. That certainly made sense—if your goal was to prioritize your clients' financial interests as opposed to advancing social or political policy.

In a *Financial Times* interview the following February, Vanguard CEO Tim Buckley clarified his views. The article, titled "Vanguard Chief Defends Decision to Pull Asset Manager Out of Climate Alliance," quoted Buckley as saying, "We don't believe that we should dictate company strategy. . . . It would be hubris to presume that we know the right strategy for the thousands of companies that Vanguard invests with. We just want to make sure that risks are being appropriately disclosed and that every company is playing by the rules."[60]

So much for passive index-fund managers "forcing behaviors"—to quote Larry Fink.[61] On the contrary, Buckley's approach was that companies in Vanguard's passive index products should make a profit, provide a financial return, and play by the rules, which sounded very Milton Friedman–ish.

Of course it was "hubris" for passive index managers to assume they know "the right strategy for the thousands of companies" in which they invest. They simply do not know and cannot know. So it is better for their investors if they remain passive and let the profit-focused CEOs who run those companies deal with strategy. That is, after all, what passive investing has always been about. Collectivist policies fly in the face of that notion.

As for whether Buckley had anyone in mind when he mentioned passive-index-manager "hubris," we may never know.

But what about Fink's "sustainability premium"? ESG-compliant companies were supposed to outperform non-ESG-compliant companies, right? Was he really smarter than the collective wisdom of the market?

By early 2023, it was obvious that there was no such premium. Buckley confirmed the obvious—"We cannot state that ESG investing is better performance wise than broad index-based investing. Our research indicates that ESG investing does not have any advantage over broad-based investing."[62]

Yes, he said "does not have any advantage." He might also have mentioned that, although there was no advantage performance-wise for investors, asset managers had an advantage with respect to the higher fees they could charge for such "sustainability" products.

Following this interview, the *Wall Street Journal* published an opinion piece by former BlackRock executive Terrence Keeley titled "Vanguard CEO Bucks the ESG Orthodoxy: Tim Buckley Pulls Out of the Net Zero Managers Initiative and Affirms His Fiduciary Duty to Clients."[63] The title said it all.

To be clear, Vanguard does have ESG-based products. According to Buckley, those ESG index funds exist to "allow investors to express their values and preferences" but this "has to be an individual investor's choice."[64] In other words, while Vanguard offers passive index products that set ESG qualifications as the criteria for being included in or excluded from the index, it will not compel corporations in its broader index-fund products (such as S&P 500 products) to advance ESG goals because Vanguard—wisely—is not in the business of micromanaging America's private sector or ramming ESG strategies down the throats of its investors.

There is certainly nothing wrong with offering ESG-based products if they are what clients want—and assuming the asset manager is not a fiduciary investing on behalf of people who have expressed no preference and simply expect the manager to get the highest possible passive return. Nor is there anything wrong with Vanguard catering to a niche market by offering products that keep socially focused progressives happy. Offering clients options is how businesses survive and succeed. If a product a client requested underperforms, that is on the client who requested or knowingly chose the product.

Offering such products is quite different from threatening to vote against director nominees or management teams to compel all corporations in a broad index—such as the S&P 500—to collectively advance non-financial social or political goals, particularly goals that will impede financial performance for those companies and, by extension, the whole index—or haystack.

That is true whether the client supports or opposes those goals. Obviously, there are progressives who support the political goals of ESG yet still want their money invested for the greatest return. But the situation is obviously more egregious when an asset manager is using its clients' monies to advance social or political goals they oppose.

The situation is also different when a fiduciary knowingly provides or purchases on behalf of others an ESG-based product rather than a product designed to generate returns. Absent the legally sanctioned consent of its beneficiaries or authorization in the documents establishing the trust, it is difficult to see how doing so would not be a breach of that fiduciary's duties.

Bottom line: it is not the role of passive index-fund managers to advance social or political policy, liberal or conservative. To function as they should, the financial markets must be a transparent, honest, level playing field focused on investor returns. Stakeholder capitalism and ESG are the antithesis of the level-playing-field concept. Vanguard obviously knows this—as does every other passive index fund manager.

In February of 2024, Vanguard announced that Tim Buckley was retiring as CEO.[65] In May, Vanguard announced "that its Board of Directors ha[d] appointed Salim Ramji" as the company's new CEO. Ramji's resume includes "a decade as a senior leader at BlackRock Inc., leaving in January 2024."[66] According to Buckley, Ramji has "has a strong fiduciary ethos."[67] But whether Ramji will follow Tim Buckley's or Larry Fink's approach to fiduciary obligations and ESG investing is yet to be seen.

SSGA

So let us look at how another member of the Big Three reacted to changing circumstances—State Street Global Advisers.

In July of 2021, SSGA's CEO, Ron O'Hanley, took a very Larry Fink–like approach to stakeholder capitalism and ESG. Asked about ESG's implications in a podcast with McKinsey & Company, he stated that "[t]he big index funds were early on this, which is a bit counterintuitive because they are supposed to be passive investors."[68]

Good point. As he well knew, the Big Three are, in fact, passive investors who are supposed to set up index-based products and then let the CEOs of the companies in that index perform. But for O'Hanley, like Fink, that was too constraining. (He had obviously been reading Fink's CEO letters.)

O'Hanley complained that he couldn't just "get upset with a company and say, 'From now on, it's the S&P 499. We're not going to own that stock.'" Of course, O'Hanley surely knew that passive index managers were supposed to be, well, passive, but he preferred to take a page from Fink's 2018 CEO letter. According to O'Hanley,

"Index managers had said, 'We don't have the tool of divestment, so we have to be engaged with these portfolio companies.'"[69]

In other words, O'Hanley had adopted Fink's circular logic, concluding that the inability of *passive* index fund managers to sell an individual company's stock meant they had to *actively* engage with companies to compel them to adopt the policies the *passive* managers wanted them to adopt. "Active" was apparently the new "passive."

As Tim Buckley had observed, that was the "hubris" of passive index managers who assume they know "the right strategy for the thousands of companies" in which they invest. And "the right strategy" was as clear to O'Hanley as it was to Fink—"engagement meant starting to push on these ESG factors."[70]

According to O'Hanley, the reason it was important to push "these ESG factors" was stakeholder capitalism. "The idea of stakeholder capitalism has become a lightning rod," he said, "but my view is simple: we are not going to maximize shareholder value if we disregard the rest of the stakeholders."[71]

It certainly was a simple view. It was also simply wrong. No one was or is claiming corporations should "disregard" stakeholders. They are essential to any successful company. The issue is whether businesses should prioritize the interests of non-investor stakeholders over the interests of actual investors—or shareholders—in order to advance social and political goals, thereby diminishing their focus on profit, and thus the returns for SSGA's clients.

At the end of the interview, O'Hanley discussed his opinion of whether companies and CEOs should even take positions on social or political issues. Rhetorically, he asked, "Is it even the role of corporate CEOs to do that? I go back to the idea that you will not satisfy the shareholders if you don't satisfy the rest of the stakeholders."[72]

He then let the collectivist cat out of the bag—it was all about power. According to O'Hanley, "It becomes difficult for firms to ignore these issues when people know that they have power and influence." But having the power is not enough, you must use it— "if you are going to use your power, you need to make sure that you can make a difference and are willing to follow through. The real danger is that most firms underestimate the difference they can make."[73]

Does anyone seriously believe that the "real danger" is the Big Three underestimating their power? On the contrary, the "real danger" is that they know they have the power and have found it too intoxicating to ignore. In fact, according to Larry Fink, they have been pursuing policies that demanded "a transformation of the entire economy." That does not sound like they are underestimating anything.

A year and a half later, SSGA's tone had changed.

In December of 2022, the Texas Senate Committee on State Affairs held a hearing on ESG in which Senator Bryan Hughes (a Resistance stalwart) questioned Lori Heinel, SSGA's Global Chief Investment Officer, about a letter from SSGA with a section headed "The March from Shareholder to Stakeholder Capitalism." Consistent with O'Hanley's views, the letter stated, "The traditional paradigm of shareholder primacy is shifting towards one in which companies must be seen to act in the best interests of all stakeholders."[74]

The senator asked if he had read it correctly. In response, Heinel took a position far different from that of either Fink or her own CEO. She answered, "We hold deeply that the primary reason for a corporation to exist is to generate profits and to generate returns for its shareholders. So, we are absolutely steadfast in that. We are actually quite concerned about the rise of stakeholder capitalism as a class of investing."[75]

Well, that was a switch.

But what about the ESG agenda? Eighteen months earlier, SSGA's CEO had said that "engagement meant starting to push on these ESG factors." Did SSGA believe that ESG really enhances profits—which Heinel had just said were "the primary reason for a corporation to exist"?

Nope.

According to Heinel, "Over the years, we've debated whether ESG is a perfomance enhancement, and as CIO I've been steadfast in saying, by definition, imposing a constraint on a portfolio—if you just do basic investment principles, that's a constraint—and so I've steadfastly encouraged our teams to not think of ESG as a performance enhancer. . . ."[76]

In other words, ESG is a constraint on performance, and under basic investment principles a constraint on performance lowers profitability. So collectivist ESG policies do not enhance value. Again, not rocket science.

I have never spoken with Lori Heinel, but a reasonable conclusion from her testimony is that it would be in the best interests of investors if the CEOs running companies in passive index products were able to make decisions concerning which strategies will enhance profits for their individual companies rather than having the Big Three impose them collectively.

The winds were shifting.

WHAT ABOUT BLACKROCK?

So where was BlackRock in all this repositioning? Well, in June of 2023 Larry Fink was interviewed at the Aspen Ideas Festival. Asked about ESG investing, he said, "I don't use the word ESG anymore because it's been entirely weaponized . . . weaponized by the far left and weaponized the by far right. . . . But it's been totally weaponized." Fink then pointed out that in his "last CEO letter the phrase ESG was not uttered once." Why? Well, according to Fink he was "ashamed of being part of this conversation."[77]

Let that sink in. Over the previous five and a half years, Fink had been the number-one proponent of ESG. The progressive media and progressive financial community praised him for his groundbreaking rebuttal to Milton Friedman. He was the darling of the World Economic Forum crowd. Thanks to the Big Three, Exxon had environmentalist hedge fund director nominees on its board. Fink was using the "E" in ESG to transform the entire economy. He had aggressively used his power and influence to weaponize ESG against hundreds of companies and their leaders.

Just two years earlier, following the Exxon/Engine No. 1 proxy vote battle, Charles Gasparino, a journalist with an inside track on Wall Street, had written that "sources inside BlackRock say that over the past year, Fink has transformed the place into an ESG cultural center. Fink talks ESG nonstop at company town halls. Seminars on ESG investing seem to take place every week."[78]

Then, suddenly, he is ashamed to be a part of the discussion?

It was his discussion! Did he read his CEO letters?

What was going on?

Fink's outspokenness on stakeholder capitalism and ESG had made BlackRock a target. As he acknowledged—"Our business was hurt. We lost $4 billion of mandates." But he also noted that it was not a huge loss, taken in perspective. According to Fink, "Net last year BlackRock raised a third of all asset flows in asset management," and in the United States alone it was "awarded over $200 billion in net flows, so . . . one of the best years ever."[79]

What was there to be ashamed about?

Perhaps simply making BlackRock a target was part of the problem, even apart from the financial implications. According to the *Wall Street Journal*, Fink faced not only "backlash from conservative pundits," but also criticism "in the finance industry, from people who said he was moralizing, playing God and stepping beyond BlackRock's fiduciary duty to maximize financial returns for clients."[80] That had to hurt.

Another explanation is that Fink knew that, contrary to his guidance, ESG investing had turned out to be a disaster. Fink's Aspen interview was in June of 2023, at which time he was certainly aware that sustainable investing products were underperforming—big time—including BlackRock's flagship model ESG products.

And according to a January 2024 report from Morningstar, "Investors continued their flight from sustainable funds" in 2023's third quarter "making 2023 [the] worst calendar year on record" for ESG investments. In total, investors pulled $13 billion from ESG or "sustainable" funds in 2023 "amid lagging performance, continued political scrutiny in the United States, and a bad year for an iShares fund."[81]

Morningstar reported that in 2023 BlackRock's iShares ESG Aware ETF lost $9.3 billion. "Roughly two thirds of the outflows occurred in 2023's first quarter (matching a change in BlackRock's flagship target-allocation ETF model portfolios, which mostly replaced iShares ESG Aware MSCI USA ETF with iShares MSCI USA Quality Factor ETF QUAL)."[82]

In other words, early in 2023, a few months before Larry Fink's "I don't use the word ESG anymore" Aspen interview, BlackRock and its investors intentionally moved funds from an ESG product that Fink had been promoting as the wave of the future into a "quality" non-ESG product focused on profits and returns.

For 2023 overall, BlackRock was both the firm with the most assets under management in sustainable funds—$59.2 billion—and the asset manager with the most outflows. In total, BlackRock's sustainable-funds portfolio lost $8.7 billion in 2023. It was not a good year for "sustainable investing"—one of the terms being tested to replace ESG investing. To borrow a 1950s movie title, you could say it was "a bad day at Black Rock."[83]

The *New York Times* ran an article titled "Investors Pull Billions from Sustainable Funds amid Political Heat: A New Report Showed That $13 Billion Was Withdrawn Last Year from Funds that Invest in Companies with Environmental, Social and Governance Principles." According to the *Times*, "The money flowing out of funds that invest in companies with environmental, social and governance principles has gone from a trickle to a torrent as investors sour on a sector hit by green-washing concerns, red-state boycotts and boardroom debates."[84] The article failed to mention withdrawals from investors who preferred returns over social policy goals.

Bloomberg published an article titled "US Investor Exodus Deals Historic Blow to Global ESG Fund Market," stating that "for the first time ever, ESG funds suffered net global outflows" primarily attributable to "a major exodus by US investors from environmental, social and governance strategies."[85]

One reason that Bloomberg noted for the exodus was investor skepticism of "the strategy's staying power, after an extended period of poor financial returns on a relative basis." According to Bloomberg, for 2023, "ESG fund withdrawals in the US coincided with a huge slump in traditional green stocks, with the S&P Global Clean Energy Index down more than 20% . . . compared with a 24% increase in the S&P 500."[86]

By the end of 2023, being ashamed to discuss ESG was understandable, particularly if you had been leading the discussion.

Maybe Milton Friedman was right after all.

2024

At the beginning of 2024, in addition to still being NZAM members, BlackRock and SSGA belonged to a United Nations–backed climate group known as Climate Action 100+ (CA100). According to its website, CA100+ is the "largest ever global investor engagement initiative on climate change"[87] and has "over 700 investors responsible for $68 trillion in assets under management."[88] The group was launched in December 2017 as "an investor-led initiative to ensure the world's largest corporate greenhouse gas emitters take necessary action on climate change."[89]

BlackRock and SSGA joined CA100+ in 2020. Vanguard never joined.[90]

According to the *Wall Street Journal*, "Members are supposed to 'engage' 170 'focus companies' such as Boeing, Home Depot and American Airlines—that is, threaten to vote against noncompliant corporate directors and back shareholder resolutions that pressure management," which is exactly what the Big Three had been doing. The campaign had "great success with 75% of targeted companies committing to 'net zero.'"[91]

In March of 2022, Republican Arizona attorney general Mark Brnovich published an opinion piece in the *Wall Street Journal* explaining why CA100+ leading the ESG movement was an antitrust violation. According to Brnovich, CA100+ would use "its coordinated influence to compel companies" to advance "a political agenda, such as compliance with the Paris Climate Accord," which could "include pushing climate goals at shareholder meetings and voting against directors and proposals that don't comport with the agenda, even if other decisions may benefit investors."[92]

Brnovich then explained that because money managers' influence over these companies comes from their investing on behalf of others, "your retirement funds are likely helping facilitate these political campaigns to advance far-left policy goals, with consumers bearing the costs of increased energy prices."[93]

On March 30, 2023, twenty-one concerned red-state attorneys general sent an open letter to fifty-three major asset-management firms informing them that the AGs were investigating asset managers for colluding on climate issues. The letter specifically mentioned CA100+, stating that "[p]otential unlawful coordination appears throughout Climate Action 100+'s documents."[94]

According to the AGs' letter, CA100+ "members clearly speak for the group as they commit to communicate 'a central message' to companies: 'inaction by companies following engagement may result in investors taking further action.'" The AGs found this coordination "a transparent attempt to push policies through the financial system that cannot be achieved at the ballot box."[95]

Despite this opposition, in June of 2023, CA100+ announced a "second phase" in which it was upping the ante on climate goals and would shift from pressuring companies to disclose net-zero progress to getting them to actually reduce emissions. The group would now demand "its members to publish information on their 'engagements' and to explain how and why they voted on shareholder resolutions flagged by the outfit." According to the *Journal*, "The point was to embarrass asset managers that climate scolds accuse of being insufficiently committed to the cause."[96]

For SSGA, that was a step too far. In a statement, SSGA said that it "has concluded the enhanced Climate Action 100+ phase 2 requirements for signatories are not consistent with our independent approach to proxy voting and portfolio company engagement."[97] Note the use of the word "independent," in light of the Arizona AG's anti-trust collusion allegations.

According to the *Financial Times*, "BlackRock said in a note that it was dropping its corporate membership because it believes the phase 2 strategy, which takes effect in June, conflicted with U.S. laws requiring money managers to act solely in clients' long-term economic interest."[98] Yes, BlackRock used the word "solely." However, BlackRock would remain involved through an international subsidiary or division.

For CA100+, it was a major setback, but not a defeat. Globalists rarely surrender in their war on free peoples and markets.

The Fat Lady Is Not Singing

The Resistance has without doubt had substantial success to date in slowing the stakeholder capitalist/ESG train. ESG investing is back on its heels, and few people are even using the term much anymore. In February of 2024, Bloomberg published an article titled "Climate Investors Warn the Right Is Winning the War on ESG."[99] It was good to see.

Only a sustained effort, however, will topple the stakeholder capitalists' house of cards. The collectivists really believe that their agenda is necessary for our good—whether we want it or not—and, being true believers, they will not stop just because they encounter obstacles or suffer setbacks.

C. S. Lewis had them pegged: "Of all tyrannies, a tyranny sincerely exercised for the good of its victims may be the most oppressive. It would be better to live under robber barons than under omnipotent moral busybodies. The robber baron's cruelty may sometimes sleep, his cupidity may at some point be satiated; but those who torment us for our own good will torment us without end, for they do so with the approval of their own conscience."[100]

If you believe the collectivists will discontinue their efforts to use their massive financial leverage in order to achieve their authoritarian vision of utopia, you are wrong. They have discovered a significant source of power; they will continue to use it; and they will not capitulate—unless and until free-market capitalism is their only alternative.

They will change the names they use and the messaging they rely on—in fact, they have already done that—but it will be the same old wine in different bottles. To quote an old song by The Who—"Meet the new boss, same as the old boss." The question is whether we will "get fooled again."[101]

The opposition to these stakeholder-capitalism/ESG efforts must be continuous and comprehensive. This is a long-term effort. If the Resistance loses focus, it will fail. The Left counts on that, and they are far from surrendering.

Chapter 9

THEIR WORDS MAY CHANGE, THEIR POLICIES DO NOT

"We need to keep switching up the language around climate change."

—*Cate Blanchett, actress*[1]

The Resistance has made tremendous progress in a brief period of time. The Big Three have had to change both their language and what they are willing to do publicly. Most prominently, stakeholder capitalists are attempting to distance themselves from the term ESG like it is the plague, after so recently employing it with reverence.

ESG was always just an innocuous-sounding label used to conceal a destructive agenda. The collectivist Left is now discarding it because—thanks to the Resistance—people are beginning to understand what it really means. But these collectivists are definitely not discarding their commitment to stakeholder capitalism and ESG's underlying social and political goals. Their aim is still an economic transformation and the alluring control that would come with it.

There is no better evidence of collectivists dumping the ESG label than Larry Fink's statement in his June 2023 Aspen interview that he did not "use the word ESG anymore because it's been entirely weaponized" and that he was "ashamed of being part of this conversation."[2] Unfortunately, his statement did not mean he was embracing free-market capitalism.

In that same interview he said, "I never said I was ashamed. I'm not ashamed." That statement was half true and half false. Clearly, he had said he was ashamed, and clearly, he was not in fact ashamed when he said he was. He ended that comment with, "I do believe in conscientious capitalism."[3]

So, what is conscientious capitalism?

As defined by the Leavey School of Business at Santa Clara University, "Conscientious Capitalism is the application of personal virtue, purpose, and accountability to individual leadership of business organizations and to the critical decisions that inspire employees and companies to drive innovation, market leadership, and profits by serving employees, customers, stakeholders, and the community."[4]

In other words, conscientious capitalism *is* stakeholder capitalism. Fink switched his terminology in yet another attempt to make collectivist goals sound both moral and free-market-oriented when they are neither.

An equally misleading descriptor is "conscious capitalism," a phrase that *Forbes* explained in an August 4, 2022, article titled "How and Why to Apply 'Conscious Capitalism' to Your Business." According to *Forbes*, conscious capitalism "emphasizes the idea that businesses should serve the interests of all stakeholders, including employees, customers, suppliers, communities and the environment, rather than solely focusing on maximizing the shareholders' value. . . ."[5]

ESG, stakeholder capitalism, conscious or conscientious capitalism: they are all just different labels for the Big Three's attempt to transform the economy along collectivist lines.

Don't believe me?

In his June 2023 Aspen interview Fink also said that while his last CEO letter had "not uttered" the phrase ESG once, BlackRock did still "talk a lot about decarbonization, we talk a lot about governance, when we have governance issues, or social issues, if that's something we need to address."[6] That means BlackRock is promoting ESG in its stewarding meetings, whether they use the term or not.

In March of 2024, Larry Fink released his "2024 Annual Chairman's Letter to Investors."[7] He is no longer issuing annual letters to CEOs. Perhaps someone informed Fink that it is not a good look for the CEO of a passive-investment firm to be actively instructing CEOs how to run their businesses.

His 2024 letter to investors is a good PR effort, focuses on returns for retirees—which seems like a wise move—and even has heartwarming references to Fink's parents. It also uses variants of "decarbon" (as in decarbonization) thirteen times.[8] On climate, he just cannot help himself.

To get a better idea of what CEOs are hearing from the Big Three these days, let us take a look at their proxy-voting guidelines. The Big Three issue these guidelines annually. They inform the management teams of the companies in which the Big Three invest how they intend to vote the shares they hold.

When looking for insights on how they address ESG-related issues, keep in mind that by 2024, the Big Three had already made significant inroads into the U.S. corporate culture. As a result, there was far less heavy lifting to be done on ESG issues than had been the case in 2018, when Larry Fink sent his infamous stakeholder-capitalist letter informing CEOs that they needed to serve a social purpose. The Big Three have already voted in favor of thousands of ESG-based shareholder resolutions and against thousands of directors who stood in the way of their ESG agenda—and they have not been alone.

Climate Action 100+ boasts that it "is made up of 700 global investors across 33 markets"[9] and that, as a result of its actions, "[n]early 80% of the world's 150 top CO_2 emitting companies have stated net zero ambition for Scope 1 and 2 emissions by 2050 or sooner."[10] As we have seen, though Vanguard was never a member, BlackRock and SSGA were members until early 2024.

And even after Vanguard withdrew from the Net Zero Asset Managers coalition in December of 2022, NZAM still touts its 315 asset manager signatories that have committed to achieving net-zero by 2050 or sooner—with $57 trillion under management. BlackRock and SSGA remain members.[11]

Not surprisingly, by 2023, nearly two-thirds of the stocks in the S&P 500 were also in the S&P ESG index.[12] So the need for the Big Three to aggressively advocate for ESG goals in their 2024 proxy-voting guidelines was far less pressing than had been the case in 2018. Prisoners had already been taken.

It is also important to keep in mind that the Big Three drafted their 2024 proxy voting guidelines while facing counterattacks and intense criticism for their political and social activism. So they were incentivized to skillfully craft protective language to fend off accusations that they were breaching their fiduciary duties. I will not discuss all their protective language because the question is whether they were still conveying activist ESG messages to the CEOs of the companies in which they invest despite that language. CEOs—and most other people—can generally see through that kind of thing pretty easily.

So, when looking at the language from the Big Three's proxy-voting guidelines below, think about what you are reading as if you were the CEO of a company and the Big Three were your largest and most powerful shareholders. Beyond any protective and legalistic language on investment risk and disclosure, ask yourself what suggestive messages the Big Three's guidelines send on the issues formerly known as ESG?

Governance

On governance and board composition, BlackRock's 2024 proxy-voting guidelines make it clear that its Investment Stewardship team is "interested in diversity in the boardroom." They ask "boards to disclose how diversity is considered in board composition, including," among other things "demographic characteristics such as gender, race/ethnicity, and age."[13]

BlackRock then sets the rules for staying under its diversity radar—"In the U.S., we believe that boards should aspire to at least 30% diversity of membership" and that "an informative indicator of diversity for such companies is having at least two women and a director who identifies as a member of an underrepresented group."[14]

Of course, BlackRock warns, "To the extent that, based on our assessment of corporate disclosures, a company has not adequately explained their approach to diversity in their board composition, we may vote against members of the nominating/governance committee."[15]

Any CEO who has been paying attention knows what that means. How about SSGA and Vanguard?

SSGA's proxy-voting guidelines state that "effective board oversight of a company's long-term business strategy necessitates a diversity of perspectives, especially in terms of gender, race and ethnicity."[16] Clear enough. So are there consequences if you fail to meet SSGA's standards?

SSGA expects "boards of all listed companies to have at least one female board member," and if a company fails to meet that expectation for three years running, SSGA "may vote against all incumbent members of the nominating committee or those persons deemed responsible for the nomination process."[17]

SSGA also expects "the boards of companies in the following indices to be composed of at least 30-percent female directors. • Russell 3000 • TSX • FTSE 350 • STOXX 600 • ASX 300." (That is a whole lot of companies).

If a company fails to meet that expectation, SSGA "may vote against the chair of the board's nominating committee or the board leader in the absence of a nominating committee."[18]

Finally, SSGA "may withhold support from the chair of the nominating committee when a company in the S&P 500 or FTSE 100 does not have at least one director from an underrepresented racial/ethnic community on its board."[19]

No ambiguity there.

Vanguard's guidelines also make clear the importance of race and sex in selecting directors, although with one encouraging addition. Along the same lines as BlackRock and SSGA, Vanguard's proxy-voting guidelines state that its funds "seek to ensure. . . . [d]iversity of thought, background, and experience, as well as personal characteristics (such as gender, race, ethnicity, and age)."[20] But they also state that boards should be "fit for purpose," which means "reflecting sufficient diversity of skills, experience, perspective, and personal characteristics (such as gender, age, race, and ethnicity) resulting in cognitive diversity" among the directors.[21]

That Vanguard acknowledges the importance of cognitive diversity is encouraging. Unfortunately, there is no reference to factors such as political, religious, or educational diversity that might produce some actual cognitive diversity (of the kind that could have helped Silicon Valley Bank's investors). Rather, Vanguard states that in addition to a "diversity of attributes," boards "should also, at a minimum, represent diversity of personal characteristics, inclusive of at least diversity in gender, race, and ethnicity on the board."[22]

For any CEO reading these guidelines the message is clear: to stay under the Big Three's radar in 2024, you need to put people on your board based on their gender, race, and ethnicity. Whether that requirement is even legal is questionable, as we shall see.

Social

How about the "S" or social element of ESG—which is really the "E" or equity element in DEI?

One section of BlackRock's proxy-voting guidelines is headed "Human Capital Management," which is essentially how a business manages its workforce. Under that heading, the guidelines state that "[s]ome components of HCM are consistent across most companies such as the approach to diversity, equity, and inclusion ('DEI')."[23]

That is a veiled collectivist demand for DEI. Absent any guidance as to which business strategies or needs would exempt a company from DEI, BlackRock is telling CEOs that every company must abide by DEI's ideological mandates. BlackRock's guidelines then instruct all "companies to disclose their approach to DEI as well as workforce demographics."[24]

And CEOs had better be ready to discuss how they are implementing DEI policies in their upcoming stewardship meetings, lest they become painful struggle sessions. A related three-page BlackRock Investment Stewardship Team document entitled "Our Approach to Engagement on Human Capital Management" states that in such engagements, discussions may "include how a company's business practices foster a diverse and inclusive workforce culture" and that BlackRock "may signal continuing concerns through our voting."[25]

Given BlackRock's aggressive activist voting history, CEOs would certainly know what that warning means.

SSGA's guidelines have a section titled "Workforce Diversity," stating that it "may vote against the chair of the compensation committee at companies in the S&P 500 that do not disclose their EEO-1 reports."[26] The Equal Employment Opportunity Commission's (EEOC) EEO-1 report is "a mandatory annual data collection that requires all private sector employers with 100 or more employees . . . to submit workforce demographic data, including data by job category and sex and race or ethnicity, to the EEOC."[27]

Ironically, the EEO-1 was meant to ensure that companies were not misbehaving by illegally considering race, sex, or ethnicity in their hiring practices.

Of course, if the report discloses a violation of the law, the EEOC can bring an enforcement action, whether the company publicly discloses the report or not. Passive fund managers play no role in that process. However, few CEOs would wonder why SSGA was requesting the information—an SSGA enforcement action requires no hearing.

SSGA's guidelines also state that "quality public disclosure" includes articulating "[e]fforts to advance diversity, equity, and inclusion" as well as "the role that diversity (of race, ethnicity, and gender, at minimum) plays in the company's broader human capital management practices and long-term strategy" and "what diversity, equity, and inclusion-related goals exist, how these goals contribute to the company's overall strategy, and how they are managed and progressing."[28]

ESG may be dying, but DEI is alive and well.

Vanguard's guidelines contain an encouraging caveat with respect to supporting "[e]nvironmental/social proposals." Vanguard's funds may support shareholder proposals that address "a shortcoming in the company's current disclosure" or reflect "an industry-specific, materiality-driven approach," but with the caveat that such proposals are "not overly prescriptive in dictating company strategy or day-to-day operations, or about time frame, cost or other matters."[29] This sounds encouragingly like a proper focus on profits.

Unfortunately, Vanguard goes on to state that, with respect to "a social risk proposal" and assuming compliance with its caveat, its funds are likely to support a shareholder proposal that "[r]equests disclosure of workforce demographics inclusive of gender, racial, and ethnic categories" which could include "publishing EEO-1 reports."[30]

Lifting the veil, Vanguard then states that it is likely to support a shareholder proposal that "[r]equests disclosure of the board's role in overseeing material diversity, equity, and inclusion (DEI) risks or other material social risks."[31] So maybe not a proper focus on profits, after all.

A word search of each of the Big Three's proxy-voting guidelines discloses that while all three contain the word "equity," none contains the word "equality."

The Big Three's 2024 message to CEOs is clear—you had better address DEI.

Are Forced Board and Workforce DEI Even Legal?

It is disconcerting that in 2024 the Big Three would continue their emphasis on forced board diversity and workforce DEI following the Supreme Court's July 2023 decision in *Students for Fair Admissions v. Harvard*[32] holding that race-based affirmative-action programs in college admissions violate the Fourteenth Amendment's Equal Protection Clause.

That is particularly so, considering Justice Gorsuch's concurring opinion pointing out that Title VII of the Civil Rights Act—which applies to private businesses—also bars discrimination in hiring "because of such individual's race, color, religion, sex, or national origin."[33] It is difficult to conclude that the Court will define discrimination differently than it did in *Students for Fair Admissions* when a case reaches it under Title VII involving a private-sector business.

In a *Wall Street Journal* opinion piece following that decision titled "Is Your Company's DEI Program Lawful?," labor attorney Michael Toth wrote that U.S. corporations should be cautious following *Students for Fair Admissions*, as many of them "have pushed racial preferences and quotas under the guise of 'diversity, equity and inclusion' policies that run contrary to the justices' warning against choosing 'winners and losers based on the color of their skin.'" In addition, Toth warned that businesses "should also ensure that diversity training doesn't create a hostile workplace environment, a well-recognized form of employment discrimination under Title VII."[34]

These are warnings businesses would be wise to heed.

As a young trial attorney, I took part in cases involving claims of racial and sexual discrimination. One problem for the plaintiffs in those cases was that the businesses involved never made any overt admissions acknowledging that their hiring practices discriminated against women or certain races. No business ever admitted, *We hire based on race and sex* or *We make sure a certain number of whites and men are on our board and part of our workforce.* Quite the contrary. Their personnel manuals always stated that race, sex, and age played no role in hiring or promotions.

Such obvious racism was not only illegal; it was also widely accepted as immoral. So victims of discrimination had to rely on data related to recruitment, selection, and employment processes to demonstrate patterns of racial or sexual bias in hiring outcomes.

Today, with the encouragement of—if not direction from—their major institutional shareholders, most major U.S. companies have issued statements confirming that they are hiring or promoting people based on race or sex, to advance DEI or some other social or political goal, in direct contravention of the Civil Rights Act.

The hiring data demonstrate that they have done what they were encouraged to do. For example, a 2023 article at Bloomberg titled "Corporate America Promised to Hire a Lot More People of Color. It Actually Did" states that "[t]he year after Black Lives Matter protests, the S&P 100 added more than 300,000 jobs—94% went to people of color."[35]

This is not something the trial bar will long ignore.

Yet the Big Three seem to believe that exposing the businesses in their funds to this litigation risk is in the best financial interests of the businesses' actual owners—their clients.

In 2024, that is highly likely not the case.

Climate

How about ESG's core element—climate change, which justifies the transition to net-zero? This is the factor that "demands a transformation of the entire economy," to quote Larry Fink.

BlackRock's 2024 proxy-voting guidelines have a section headed "Material Sustainability–Related Risks and Opportunities" as well as one headed "Climate Risk"—apparently in case the "Material Sustainability–Related Risks" section missed something. Let us look at both sections.

On "Sustainability Risks," BlackRock's guidelines are clear. When it is "assessing how to vote—including on the election of directors and relevant shareholder proposals"—it wants "robust disclosures" in order to understand "how companies are integrating material sustainability risks and opportunities across their business and strategic, long-term planning." When "a company has failed to appropriately provide the necessary disclosures and evidence of effective business practices," then BlackRock's Investment Stewardship team "may express concerns through our engagement and voting."[36]

In summary, BlackRock wants "robust disclosures" on "sustainability" so it can do an "assessment" of how "effective" the "business practices" are for each of the thousands of companies in which it invests. Should a company come up short in that assessment, BlackRock will let management know in its "stewardship" meetings and vote against management-supported directors or in favor of ESG shareholder proposals to which management objects.[37]

Recall that Vanguard's CEO defended withdrawing from the Net Zero Asset Managers Coalition—with its commitment to net-zero by 2050—by calling it "hubris" for an asset manager to presume it knows "the right strategy for the thousands of companies" in which it invests.[38] Larry Fink and BlackRock's Stewardship Team either missed that comment or disagreed with it, but it certainly applies here.

Just look at the "robust" level of disclosure BlackRock wants from the thousands of companies in which it invests. According to its guidelines, "The International Sustainability Standards Board (ISSB) standards, IFRS S1 and S2, provide companies with a useful guide to preparing this disclosure."[39] Perhaps not surprisingly, ISSB says that it "builds on the work of"—among other climate reporting initiatives—"the World Economic Forum's Stakeholder Capitalism Metrics."[40] They actually mention that, assuming it is a positive.

IFRS S1[41] and S2[42] are, shall we say, a comprehensive set of sustainability-related financial and climate disclosures with a clear goal—achieving net-zero.

But these disclosures are voluntary and will only become binding legal requirements in jurisdictions that adopt them. So why would a passive index-fund manager impose them independent of government action? Surely management teams can individually determine whether it is best for their companies to disclose sustainability risks in compliance with voluntary standards and the extent to which they should disclose them.

Perhaps it is because BlackRock needs to know which companies are falling in line with its "sustainability" requirements. It is hard to transform an entire economy if you do not know what the companies in your portfolio are doing.

How about the additional "Climate Risk" section of BlackRock's guidelines? Well, this section has some interesting prophylactic language, demonstrating that the Resistance has had an impact and BlackRock knows it has a problem. According to its guidelines, BlackRock is "typically a minority" shareholder and so "does not tell companies what to do." Rather, "It is the role of the board and management to set and implement a company's long-term strategy to deliver long-term financial returns."[43]

While that is stating the obvious, it is good to hear. It is also significant that BlackRock thought something so obvious needed to be said. A friend of mine familiar with BlackRock calls this "strategic ambiguity," meaning BlackRock wants to appear on both sides of every issue, to make all of its clients and regulators happy.

So despite this protective language, BlackRock stresses the elevated level of importance it places on so-called "climate risk" and the need for a collectivist approach. According to its guidelines, BlackRock's "research shows that the low-carbon transition is a structural shift in the global economy . . . which may be material for many companies."[44]

"Many companies?" Is that really what BlackRock meant?

It is difficult to imagine any company for which a "structural shift in the global economy" would be immaterial. In fact, it would be kind of a big deal for literally every company. While BlackRock's statement did not say "every company," it certainly did not exclude any companies. Most important, it is unlikely that any CEOs questioned whether BlackRock intended to include their companies.

BlackRock then encourages "companies to publicly disclose, consistent with their business model and sector, how they intend to deliver long-term financial performance through the transition to a low-carbon economy."[45] "[L]ong-term" is undefined, although the net-zero goal is by 2050, so twenty-six years out—which is extremely long-term (nearly an eternity) in the investment world.

And, by the way, BlackRock would "appreciate companies publishing their transition plan" in a manner "[c]onsistent with the ISSB standards" so that BlackRock is "better able to assess preparedness for the low-carbon transition."[46]

Again, BlackRock wants "robust disclosure" enabling it to do an "assessment" of how "effective" the "business practices" are for each of the thousands of companies in which it invests in case any is failing to adequately prepare "for the low-carbon transition"— read that, to toe the line on net-zero.

Hubris.

In case the sections on "Sustainability" and "Climate Risk" were insufficient to make BlackRock's point, it also published an additional five-page document titled "Climate-Related Risks and the Low-Carbon Transition," which sets forth a detailed discussion of "[c]limate-related risks and opportunities as an investment issue"[47] and explains how BlackRock will be "[a]ssessing companies' long-term resilience through disclosures on climate-related risks and opportunities,"[48] how it engages "with companies on the low-carbon transition," and how companies should approach "material climate-related risks and opportunities."[49]

It is an enforcement plan and an environmental extremist's dream come true. For "a minority" shareholder that "does not tell companies what to do," BlackRock sure provides a lot of detail about what it expects from those companies—and the consequences of failing to meet its expectations.

This document does contain prophylactic language stating that "it is not [BlackRock's] role to engineer a specific decarbonization outcome in the real economy."[50] That clearly needed to be said, because the extensive information BlackRock requests and the description of how it will engage with companies on this issue could easily lead a reader to believe that engineering "a specific decarbonization outcome in the real economy" is exactly how Black-Rock views its role.

In fact, CEOs might be forgiven for reading BlackRock's guidelines as directing them to come up with a plan, which BlackRock will approve or disapprove, to get to net-zero, and to create a story for investors on how this will actually benefit them—or else.

Of course, this document also warns that BlackRock "may signal continuing concerns through our voting," with the caveats that it will do so "where clients have authorized us to vote on their behalf" and that "[i]n all cases, our voting is intended to advance the long-term financial interests of our clients as shareholders."[51]

I guess that needed to be said, as well. The Resistance was at least having some impact.

SSGA's guidelines state that while it "is not prescriptive on target setting,"[52] it does "expect companies that have adopted net zero ambitions to disclose interim climate targets."[53] For those companies that choose "not to disclose any climate targets," SSGA expects "the company to provide an explanation on how the company measures and monitors progress on managing climate-related risks and opportunities in line with the recommendations of" the Taskforce for Climate-Related Financial Disclosures (TCFD).[54]

Another distinction without much of a difference.

SSGA "may take voting action against directors" of companies in the "• S&P 500 • S&P/TSX Composite • FTSE 350 • STOXX 600 • ASX 200 • TOPIX 100 • Hang Seng • Straits Times Index" (so just about every major company) if they "fail to provide sufficient disclosure regarding: (i) board oversight of climate-related risks and opportunities; (ii) total direct and indirect [Green House Gas] emissions ("Scope 1" and "Scope 2" emissions); and, (iii) climate-related targets, in accordance with the TCFD."[55]

For an asset manager that claims not to be "prescriptive" on carbon emissions "target setting," SSGA sure wants a lot of information on those targets—and threatens to enforce its non-prescriptive prescriptions with extreme prejudice.

As I noted above, Vanguard's guidelines have a caveat that applies to both environmental and social proposals. Assuming compliance with that caveat, Vanguard's guidelines focus on disclosure. Its funds are likely to support shareholder proposals that request "disclosure related to the company's Scope 1 and Scope 2 emissions data,'" as is also the case with BlackRock.[56] But Vanguard goes beyond Scope 1 and 2 data and adds "Scope 3 emissions data," which includes not only your business's emissions but those of your suppliers, "in categories where climate-related risks are deemed material by the board."[57]

That is not encouraging, and it is difficult to envision a circumstance where those requirements would satisfy Vanguard's caveat that shareholder proposals not be "overly prescriptive in dictating company strategy or day-to-day operations."[58] Roping in suppliers is very heavy-handed and disruptive.

Vanguard also states that its funds may support a shareholder proposal that "[r]equests an assessment of a changing climate's impact on the company, disclosing appropriate scenario analysis and related impacts on strategic planning."[59]

While to differing degrees and with differing caveats, the Big Three send a clear message to any CEO reading their 2024 guidelines—they want to assure that the thousands of companies in which they invest are toeing the line on climate change and net-zero—financial returns be damned.

Why Are the Big Three Pushing "Decarbonization," the Low-Carbon "Transition," and the "Net-Zero" Climate Agenda?

For most businesses, "decarbonization," the low carbon "transition," or the "net-zero" agenda will diminish success—that is, profits and investors' returns—by driving up energy costs and diverting resources to a degree that crushes future economic growth. You may or may not believe that we need to reduce carbon emissions, but the reality is that inexpensive and dependable fossil fuels are going to be a major source for meeting the world's energy needs for many decades to come. Countries and companies that produce, refine, and utilize them will have a competitive advantage over those that do not. Ignoring their continuing importance is ignoring reality.

In March of 2024, about eight thousand people attended the annual "CERAWeek by S&P Global" energy conference "to hear about the latest in next-wave emissions-reduction technologies" and "to hear speeches from titans of oil and gas." As Yahoo!Finance reported, "one message came through: Fossil fuels aren't going anywhere anytime soon."[60]

In fact, demand is increasing. Yahoo! reported that Pierce Norton, CEO of pipeline operator ONEOK, "highlighted that demand is increasing even more rapidly because of the computing power needed for artificial intelligence and painted a picture of 'energy addition' rather than 'energy transition.'"[61]

The *New York Times* pointed out that in 2023 "electric utilities have nearly doubled their forecasts of how much additional power they'll need by 2028" because of "an unexpected explosion in the number of data centers, an abrupt resurgence in manufacturing driven by new federal laws, and millions of electric vehicles being plugged in."[62]

The result is an increase in states building new natural gas–powered plants and slowing the shutdown of existing plants that rely on other fossil fuels. As the *Times* stated, "A boom in data centers and factories is straining electric grids and propping up fossil fuels."[63]

At that same energy conference, Saudi Aramco CEO Amin Nasser said what energy-industry people have long understood but have been reluctant to state—"We should abandon the fantasy of phasing out oil and gas and instead invest in them adequately reflecting realistic demand assumptions." The audience reaction was applause.[64] According to the *New York Times*, "To some, it felt like the oil executive blurted the quiet part out loud."[65] Indeed he had.

In addition to booming demand for fossil fuels in developed countries, Nasser noted that developing nations in the global South "will drive oil and gas demand as prosperity rises in those nations, which represent more than 85% of the world's population."[66]

In October of 2023, the International Energy Agency published its "World Energy Outlook Report 2023," which projected that global demand for coal, oil, and natural gas will hit an all-time high by 2030.[67] While that would mean increasing reliance on fossil fuels for the next seven years (which is long term in the investment world), Nasser believes demand will not peak for a much longer time and stated that "[p]eak oil and gas are unlikely for some time to come, let alone 2030."[68]

Exxon CEO Darren Woods said, "We're not on the path" to reaching net-zero emissions by 2050. "One of the challenges here is that while society wants to see emissions reduced, nobody wants to pay for it."[69]

The problem for passive index-fund investors is that the Big Three seem determined to make their clients "pay for it"—and there's the rub.

Nasser, Woods, and Norton are energy-sector executives who have a personal stake in promoting long-term fossil-fuel profitability, which arguably diminishes their credibility. So let us look at what energy-company executives are doing rather than just what they are saying. Are they putting their money where their mouths are on the continuing and long-term future of fossil fuels?

How people invest their money is an indicator of what they believe that is far more reliable than what they espouse.

In October of 2023, Chevron announced plans to acquire oil and gas company Hess for $53 billion,[70] and Exxon announced it was acquiring oil company Pioneer Natural Resources for $59 billion.[71] Investing in the future of fossil fuels was so obviously the right decision that even the directors that the environmentalist hedge fund Engine No. 1 had nominated to Exxon's board—and who were elected with the votes of the Big Three—supported the acquisition.[72] It really is difficult to overstate how wrong both Engine No. 1 and BlackRock were about the future of fossil fuels. Even their hand-picked directors have backtracked.

That same month, speaking in a CNBC interview, Larry J. Goldstein, a trustee with the not-for-profit Energy Policy Research Foundation and former president of the Petroleum Industry Research Foundation, stated that Chevron's and Exxon's acquisitions demonstrated that the large oil companies "do not see an end to oil demand any time in the near future." In fact, "they see oil demand in fairly large volumes existing for at least the next 20, 25 years."[73]

Shon Hiatt of the USC Marshall School of Business told CNBC that Chevron and Exxon's "strategy suggests that in emerging economies marked by population and economic expansion, the adoption of low-carbon energy sources may be prohibitively expensive, while hydrocarbon demand in European and North American markets, although potentially reduced, will remain a significant factor."[74]

Of course it will. The world cannot function without fossil fuels. In the real economy, the energy sector's investing paints a clear picture of the future for fossil fuels, although it is not the one the Big Three and their environmental extremist allies are painting—and attempting to compel. Wishful thinking is neither a plan nor a strategy.

Compelling American businesses to embrace a net-zero transition—at a time when fossil-fuel production and demand are soaring—is a politically motivated move to bring about a result the progressive elites have determined is in our "long-term" best interest, whether we want it or not.

Their claim that it is really about "long-term" value creation for investors distorts the meaning of "long-term" beyond human recognition. Even the most talented financial analysts and economists can only predict the future a few years out, and even then, there is no guarantee that they are correct.

The financial world's quintessential "long-term" investors are private equity firms. According to Investopedia, "The returns in private equity are typically seen after a few years. It's considered a longer-term investment."[75] Holding periods for companies in a private equity firm's funds are typically three to seven years. In any rational investment context, quarterly results are short-term, three to five years is long-term, seven years is a stretch, and twenty to thirty years is an eternity.

While passive index funds are also long-term investments—as investors do not trade individual companies in the index—the actual investment horizon is shorter than people may imagine. For example, the S&P 500 is a stable index because "S&P Indices believes turnover in index membership should be avoided when possible."[76] Nonetheless, even that stable index's historical turnover rate is 4.4 percent annually, which is about twenty-two additions/subtractions per year.[77] At that rate, nearly a third (30 percent) of the companies in that index today were not in it seven years ago.

Looking out seven years, the International Energy Agency has concluded that oil prices and demand will not even peak until 2030, and no one knows if that hopeful date is correct. As we have seen, Amin Nasser believes the IEA is likely understating when that peak may occur. In either event, inexpensive and reliable fossil fuels are here for the long term, and companies that fail to take advantage of them will suffer financially—as will their investors.

Of course, these energy-sector executives may be wrong, just as the elite financial managers at the Big Three and their radical environmentalist allies may be wrong. In reality, no one can accurately predict what will happen this year, let alone during the next twenty.

But whichever side is proven correct, passive index investors should suffer the least, as they diversify risk by investing in a group of companies, each of which addresses risk as its management team deems in the best interests of its individual company. That is, of course, unless the financial elites at the Big Three impose collectivist policies across their funds, stifling the competitive behavior of the companies in those funds, eliminating the benefits of diversified indexes, and increasing financial risks for their clients.

Hubris.

Here is the truth. The net-zero "transition" is a classic example of a luxury champagne-socialist belief. Larry Fink and his friends have the luxury to push for policies that drive energy prices through the roof because they can and will afford to ride in limousines, yachts, and private jets no matter how high prices get. Their wealth walls them off from the concerns of their inferiors—concerns like paying the rent, staying warm, buying food, or filling up the tank. So they make themselves feel morally superior by forcing policies on their portfolio companies that will hurt everybody else, including their clients—policies that must eventually be abandoned because they bear no relationship to the real world that the rest of us have to inhabit.

The Big Three's net-zero climate-change transition demands are neither investment-based nor an effort to protect their clients' realistic "long-term" financial interests. They are an attempt to achieve control and collectively advance an environmental-extremist net-zero agenda which, as Larry Fink stated, "demands a transformation of the entire economy."

That transformation will not occur in any rational "long-term" investment horizon—if ever—and the unelected financial elites at passive asset-management firms should neither be collectively compelling American businesses to advance such a transition nor foisting the costs of it on their investors. That is putting progressive social and political policy over the financial interests of their clients.

But unfortunately, while ESG may be a term stakeholder capitalists are deserting in 2024, the "E" policy goals—now known as decarbonization goals—are alive and well.

Chapter 10

THIS IS NOT OVER, BUT THERE IS HOPE

"Now this is not the end. It is not even the beginning of the end. But it is, perhaps, the end of the beginning."

—*Winston Churchill, 1941*[1]

I wish I could have subtitled this book "The Story of How Financial Elites Tried to Transform America—and How America Defeated Them." That is very close to being true, but it is not as yet true. If the Resistance becomes complacent, I fear that it may never be true.

The real battle is not over how the Big Three invest. It is about unseemly power and control. It is about how they vote the shares they hold for others and how they use those shares in meetings where they "steward" the managements of the companies in which they invest. The keys to their power in stewarding meetings are their share ownership and the threat that they will use their votes at shareholder meetings on the election of directors or shareholder resolutions.

Like the language they use in their proxy-voting guidelines, the Big Three's actual proxy voting has changed. In this respect, the Resistance has had a measurable impact and some success in slowing the ESG juggernaut. Let us take a look at both the Big Three's recent voting patterns and the future of proxy voting as a lever of collectivist control.

Proxy Voting

Including protective language in their proxy-voting guidelines is not the only action the Big Three have taken to safeguard themselves from criticism and potential litigation. According to an article published by the influential financial-services company Morningstar, "Increasing hostility from the political arena toward the consideration of environmental, social, and governance issues in investing appears to be translating into sharply declining support for ESG shareholder resolutions from the biggest U.S. fund companies."[2]

From 2021 through 2023, each of the Big Three clearly shifted its proxy voting away from support for environmental and social proposals—although, as I noted above, it is important to keep in mind that by 2022–2023, much of the ESG work had been done. Recall that the Business Roundtable issued its stakeholder-capitalism surrender in 2019 and Exxon's proxy contest loss to Engine No.1 occurred in 2021. Add to that the fact that proxy contests are messy and very public, so most of the real negotiating takes place behind closed doors in stewardship meetings. But the Big Three's proxy-voting adjustments over the past two years nonetheless show an important shift in momentum.

A report by Diligent Marketing Intelligence titled "Investment Stewardship 2024" showed the extent of this shift. According to Diligent, in the U.S., the drop in Vanguard's support for environmental and social proposals was the most precipitous—going from 29.6 percent in the 2020–2021 voting season, to 12 percent in 2021–2022, to a mere 3 percent in 2022–2023. BlackRock's support also dropped significantly, going from 41.3 percent, to 23.7 percent, to a much reduced 8.7 percent. SSGA dropped less but still meaningfully, going from 43.7 percent to 28.6 percent to 21.2 percent.[3]

Based on these voting results, *Fortune* magazine published an October 2023 article titled "BlackRock, Vanguard, and State Street Turned against Environmental and Social Proposals This Year, a Clear Sign of Backlash." It stated that the "most surprising finding is how thoroughly the 'Big 3' . . . turned against environmental and social shareholder proposals in the past year," calling their votes "[c]lear signs of a backlash." I guess "turned back to supporting their investors" would not have sold as many magazines.[4]

Going forward, the Resistance will need to keep a close eye on the Big Three so it can publicize any socially or politically motivated proxy voting, particularly in states that have passed legislation making it clear that such voting is a breach of fiduciary duty. In this respect, the Resistance will have the benefit of two reports that take a deep dive into how asset managers vote on ESG issues.

The first comes from the Committee to Unleash Prosperity (CTUP), whose mission is "to educate policy makers and the public about government policies that have been proven, in practice, to maximize economic growth and equitable prosperity in America and around the world."[5] The CTUP will be publishing an annual report on proxy voting titled "Politics over Pensions."

The first CTUP report, issued in May of 2023, examined "4,814 non-ESG branded funds"[6] to see how asset managers cast proxy votes on "50 of the most extreme ESG-oriented shareholder proposals from 2022."[7] It graded each asset manager from A to F. Vanguard received an A, BlackRock a C, and SSGA a D.[8]

The CTUP's second report, which came out in May of 2024, found that in 2023 major money managers were around 25 to 30 percent less likely to vote for hostile ESG resolutions than was the case in 2022.[9] Nonetheless, according to the 2024 report, "The bad news is that the large investment firms are STILL violating their fiduciary duty by supporting ESG resolutions more than half the time."[10] Vanguard maintained its A status, while BlackRock improved to a B, and SSGA moved up to a C.[11]

The other report is from the 1792 Exchange, whose "[m]ission is to preserve freedom by partnering with allies to steer public companies back to neutral on ideological issues."[12] In September of 2023, 1792 launched a database to analyze and monitor the proxy-voting records of "over 100 of the nation's largest asset managers including BlackRock, SSGA, and Vanguard across hundreds of ESG-related resolutions."[13]

The first 1792 Exchange report found that each of the Big Three lowered its support for ESG in 2023, with SSGA's ESG support going from 50 percent in 2022 to 18 percent in 2023, BlackRock's from 30 percent down to 7 percent, and Vanguard's from 21 percent to 6 percent.[14] The proxy-vote monitoring from 1792 will also be ongoing.

In contrast to 2021, when the Exxon vote got meaningful public attention only after it had occurred, today the Resistance has its eye on the Big Three's proxy voting.

Sunlight is the best disinfectant.

But make no mistake, there are still plenty of leftists working at the Big Three who are determined to circumvent our democratic processes and our free markets to impose their arbitrary ESG standards on American corporations and the American people—even if they are now somewhat cleverer in promoting their agenda.

Proxy Voting "Choice"

With their proxy-voting practices coming under increased scrutiny and state legislation making it clear that fiduciaries are obligated to vote a company's shares in the actual investors' best financial interest, BlackRock,[15] SSGA,[16] and Vanguard[17] have also initiated what they call "voting choice" programs. They are letting their clients in some select funds exercise some choice on how to vote proxies for the underlying companies, in an effort to at least appear to distance themselves from those decisions.

Voting-choice programs work by offering investors broad options on how to vote their proportional shares in certain pooled investment vehicles (that is, certain passive index funds). The options differ among the Big Three, as these programs are still developing.

BlackRock was the first to adopt what it calls "voting choice" for institutional investors, in 2022.[18] In 2023 it expanded that program to retail investors in its S&P 500 ETF, which is, according to Black-Rock, its "largest ETF and one of the most widely held."[19] Both SSGA and Vanguard announced similar voting choice programs, at the end of 2022 and in 2023, respectively.[20]

The key to how meaningful these programs will be is the range of available voting options. If you do not support net-zero goals over profits or equity over equality, is there a voting-choice vehicle for you? Unfortunately, there currently is not.

The reality is that these so-called "voting choice" programs offer little, if any, actual choice—if you believe in free-market cap-italism. On ESG issues, the options the Big Three currently offer would result in proxy voting either consistent with or worse than if the Big Three's simply continued voting the shares. In that sense, "voting choice" is a ruse that will have virtually no voting impact on proxy voting results.

The first option is to allow the Big Three to continue voting the shares. This is also the fallback if the investor makes no choice. When BlackRock's proxy-voting guidelines state that it will vote shares a particular way "where clients have authorized us to vote on their behalf,"[21] it includes both investors who have specifically authorized that and those who have not chosen any option.

The remaining options come from the two major proxy-advisory firms, Institutional Shareholder Services (ISS)[22] and Glass Lewis.[23] For those who are unfamiliar with proxy-advisory firms, they have infrastructure and personnel dedicated to ana-lyzing board nominees and shareholder proposals across a broad swath of companies.

They serve a legitimate purpose. Because of the thousands of companies in which institutional investors own shares—particu-larly in large passive index funds—there are a tremendous number of director elections and shareholder proposals they must consider annually. Few investors have the ability to knowledgeably vote this number of proxies. So investors often outsource share voting to proxy-advisory firms.

The investors instruct these firms how they want their shares voted, pursuant to voting options that each firm offers or specific instructions from the investor. Like the Big Three, ISS and Glass Lewis each offers a benchmark option where it votes shares pursuant to its in-house proxy-voting guidelines.[24]

While an in-depth discussion is beyond the scope of this book, ISS and Glass Lewis collectively dominate 97 percent of the U.S. proxy-advisory business.[25] Although foreign-owned, they have extensive influence over the election of directors and passage of shareholder proposals in the United States. ISS and Glass-Lewis are ESG supporters, as their proxy-voting guidelines make clear.[26] Any alert investor would and should be concerned. Red-state officials have openly questioned their voting bias.

In January of 2023, twenty-one red-state attorneys general wrote to ISS and Glass Lewis stating that evidence regarding their "climate change advocacy and goals suggest[ed] potential violations of [their] contractual obligations and legal duties." According to the AGs' letter, ISS and Glass Lewis had each "pledged to recommend votes on company directors and proposals based on whether a company is implementing 'net zero emissions' goals and related climate commitments."[27] The AGs questioned whether "such recommendations, and the policies that led to them, are based on the financial interests of the investment beneficiaries rather than other social goals"[28] and pointed out that they "appear unsupported by your duty to consider only the economic value of investments."[29]

In October of 2023, eighteen state financial officers wrote to ISS and Glass Lewis in a similar vein, expressing concerns about their objectivity on ESG and their treatment of shareholder proposals by conservatives.[30]

According to the CTUP, both ISS and Glass Lewis "give awful advice" to the money-management firms they advise, and that advice "is often contrary to these firms' fiduciary duty of earning a high return for their clients."[31] In CTUP's 2023 "Politics over

Pensions" report, Glass Lewis and ISS received grades of D and F—lower than BlackRock's C.[32]

In CTUP's 2024 report, Glass Lewis received a D and ISS received an F as they continued "to advise their client firms to vote in favor of ESG resolutions." According to the CTUP report, "ISS endorsed nearly every ESG resolution. Money management firms would be doing a great service to the clients whose money they manage to stop taking advice from these ultra-liberal firms on proxy voting."[33]

In his April 2024 annual "Letter to the Shareholders, Jamie Dimon, the Chairman and CEO of JPMorgan Chase, questioned the reliance of stewardship committees at most major asset-management firms on the advice of ISS and Glass Lewis. He noted "that ISS is owned by Deutsche Boerse, a German company, and Glass Lewis is owned by Peloton Capital, a Canadian private equity firm" and questioned "whether American corporate governance should be determined by for-profit international institutions that may have their own strong feelings about what constitutes good corporate governance."[34]

For his part, Dimon stated, "By the end of 2024, J.P. Morgan Asset Management generally will have eliminated third-party proxy advisor voting recommendations from its internally developed voting systems." In addition, it "will work with third-party proxy voting advisors to remove their voting recommendations from research reports they provide to J.P. Morgan Asset Management by the 2025 proxy season."[35]

The ISS and Glass Lewis proxy-voting options that the Big Three offer, particularly their benchmark options, should be read in light of their bias towards progressive issues and the ESG agenda.

Beyond the benchmark options (which are both strongly pro-ESG), the Big Three offer ISS and Glass Lewis options that essentially fall into two categories—sustainability options and board/management-aligned option—both of which are also pro-ESG and neither of which is pro-shareholder, other than coincidentally.

According to a Morningstar article on the Big Three's "New Proxy-Voting Options," the sustainability options include "the

ISS Sustainability and Socially Responsible Investment policies offered by BlackRock and SSGA, and the Glass Lewis ESG policy offered by SSGA and Vanguard. BlackRock also allows investors to choose Glass Lewis' Climate Policy." These options are even "more likely to recommend votes in support of ESG shareholder proposals, or against board director elections, compared with the house policy at any of the [Big Three] firms."[36]

BlackRock describes the ISS sustainability option as generally supporting "shareholder proposals advocating environmental, social & governance disclosure or universal norms/codes of conduct."[37]

BlackRock and SSGA also offer the option to select ISS's and Glass-Lewis's in-house benchmark policies, which, according to Morningstar, "are more likely to support ESG shareholder resolutions" than even the Big Three's policies.[38]

If you are looking for less ESG- and more shareholder-returns-oriented policies, the sustainability options and ISS/Glass Lewis's benchmark options have nothing to offer. To the extent these options would produce different results on ESG issues from the Big Three's in-house options, the results for investors would be worse.

As a possible alternative, all three firms also offer board-aligned options that, according to Morningstar, "simply reflect the board's voting recommendation at each company, which means they will almost never support a shareholder proposal or oppose director elections or other management proposals." There is also a related option that is "[c]orporate governance-focused" and generally sides "with management on most issues that come to a vote."[39]

BlackRock describes the board-aligned option as generally following "the board's recommendation around environmental and social matters." It describes the corporate-governance options as generally voting "in alignment with management on shareholder proposals."[40]

According to the proxy consulting firm Bowyer Research, however, neither the ISS nor the Glass Lewis board-aligned options are ESG-neutral. They both "impose penalties in the form of adverse votes in cases in which the advisor deems the board insufficiently diverse according to race and gender (and, in the case of one of the advisors, 'gender identity')."[41]

In addition, on environmental and social factors, the board-aligned policies do "default towards siding with management" but "may possibly vote against the board on environment and social disclosure proposals based on industry standard practices" even though "ESG-skeptical fiduciary entities may feel that industry standards have been overly influenced by ESG activists."[42]

Apart from the options themselves, recall that the Business Roundtable has come out in support of stakeholder capitalism, and the companies in that group can no longer be universally trusted to act in their shareholders' best interests. Many companies have already boarded the stakeholder-capitalism train. In fact, as we have seen, nearly two-thirds of the stocks in the S&P 500 are already in the S&P ESG index.[43]

In addition, to make sure board members and management stay on that train, the Big Three still have their behind-the-scenes "investment stewardship" or "engagement" programs, both terms being euphemisms for compulsion on ESG issues. This substantially diminishes the value of the board/management-aligned options.

On March 14, 2024, sixteen state financial officers sent a letter to SSGA's CEO Ron O'Hanley encouraging SSGA "to promote traditional fiduciary duty (advancing all clients' objective economic interests), instead of serving the demands of global bodies and a subset of clients whose interests align with anti-fiduciary actions." It alleged that SSGA is misleading its clients by claiming to offer eight different "voting choice" policies, when all of them prioritize ESG goals over financial goals.[44]

The letter explains that even SSGA's management-aligned policy supports ESG because SSGA will continue to punish board members who are insufficiently pro-ESG, so it is not actually a neutral policy for clients who are interested in maximizing financial value. The letter asks SSGA to offer, in time for the 2024 proxy-voting season, "at least one voting choice option that endorses 'pro-fiduciary' proposals while opposing ESG-supporting proposals, and that does not punish boards or directors for being insufficiently ESG-motivated, but rather for failing to address the issues and concerns of pro-fiduciary proponents."[45]

The board-aligned options certainly sound better than the patently ESG alternatives, but generally would not produce results significantly different from simply allowing the Big Three to continue voting the shares.

BlackRock and SSGA also offer a specialty option aligned with Catholic-faith-based voting.[46] BlackRock describes this option as supporting both "social justice" and "environmental stewardship"[47]—so, ESG.

They also both offer "Taft-Hartley Act" options based on AFL-CIO proxy-voting guidelines and voting-choice options for "public fund" investors.[48] BlackRock describes both options as generally supporting "shareholder proposals on social" and "environmental" issues.[49] So, again, ESG.

Vanguard offers an option where the shares are not voted.[50] Of the current options, it is perhaps the best. The medical profession's "First, do no harm" commitment comes to mind.

So investors can pick the least of these elitist evils. Bottom line, the Big Three's voting-choice options currently offer no truly pro-investor-returns or pro-shareholder options.

So perhaps it is no surprise that, as Morningstar has noted, while the Big Three "are currently rolling out 'pass-through voting,' which will enable more investors to have greater choice over how their funds are voted . . . many—perhaps most—investors are expected to continue to rely on their asset manager to make these decisions."[51]

As investors, we have long trusted asset managers to do what we pay them for—to act in our best interests. For many investors, the idea that these asset managers are working against our best financial interests is news.

In any event, for those who want to see their shares voted differently, these voting-choice plans offer no options that would produce results meaningfully different—in a positive sense—from simply letting the Big Three vote the shares pursuant to their ESG-supportive proxy-voting guidelines. So they are not particularly popular.

For example, BlackRock's voting-choice program has been around the longest, and it is not making much of a dent in

BlackRock's proxy-voting power. At the end of 2023, BlackRock had total index equity of $5.2 trillion. Of that amount, only $2.6 trillion (or half) was available for voting choice. And of that amount, only $598 billion (or 11.5 percent of BlackRock's total equity) was "exercising Voting Choice."[52]

Under BlackRock's expanded 2024 program, an additional $249 billion was "newly committed," increasing the total committed to voting choice to $847 billion or 16 percent of BlackRock's total equity index holdings.[53] Even if every vote in the 16 percent was pro–shareholder returns and anti-ESG (which is absolutely the opposite of reality), BlackRock would still be voting the shares purchased with 84 percent of the monies it invests. That is a lot of power to transform our economy.

Faced with limited acceptance of its so-called voting choice efforts and amidst growing criticism of both Glass-Lewis and ISS, BlackRock announced that it would add "Egan-Jones as the third proxy advisor on its Voting Choice platform beginning in July 2024."[54] While it is much smaller than either ISS or Glass-Lewis, BlackRock noted that "[f]or more than 20 years, Egan-Jones has provided retail, institutional and governmental investors with proxy voting coverage."[55]

BlackRock offers two Egan-Jones "proxy voting guidelines. "The first is Egan-Jones's Wealth-Focused Policy, which seeks to 'protect and enhance the wealth of investors' and 'does not prioritize environmental or social goals.' The second is Egan-Jones' most popular voting guidelines, the Standard Policy."[56]

So what does this mean for investors in the ESG resistance?

Well, on ESG the Egan-Jones "Standard Policy" does not differ meaningfully from the ISS or Glass-Lewis standard policies. For example, under certain circumstances, it would allow votes in favor of shareholder proposals "on establishing a climate change committee" or asking for a company "report describing if, and how, it plans to integrate ESG metrics into the performance measures of named executive officers under the Company's compensation incentive plans."[57] So no real ESG or DEI relief here.

The "Wealth Focused" guidelines do recommend voting against most ESG and DEI initiatives, which is certainly an improvement. However, they do not appear to support any initiatives designed to get back to shareholder-focused/politically neutral investing, such as shareholder proposals to consider the risk of decarbonization, whether net-zero commitments are truly fiduciary, or the risks of DEI policies. For example, the guidelines recommend voting against "shareholder proposals requesting that the Company . . . conduct a review of any and all of its policies to ensure that there are none that have the effect of encouraging divestment from the [oil and gas] sector."[58]

Offering shareholders the option to support ESG/DEI–reversing proposals is extremely important. As we have seen, the Big Three have already voted to replace hundreds—if not thousands—of corporate directors, nearly two-thirds of the companies in the S&P 500 are now in the S&P ESG Index, the Business Roundtable has aligned itself with both BlackRock and the World Economic Forum on so-called stakeholder capitalism, and over twenty-five hundred CEOs—including those at virtually every major American corporation—have pledged to promote DEI initiatives in their companies.

The bottom line is that a vast array of ESG and DEI policies already in place across corporate America must be dislodged if we are to get back to politically neutral/shareholder-focused investing. It does not appear that the Egan-Jones Wealth Focused guidelines will meaningfully advance that goal.

While perhaps an effective PR tool, voting choice is little more than a ruse that marginally empowers investors without meaningfully diminishing the Big Three's power to impose the agenda formerly known as ESG on American businesses or to preserve their progress to date. The voting-choice programs are an attempt to create a defense against breach-of-fiduciary-duty claims. They are an effort to avoid blame and liability for pro-ESG proxy voting by making it appear that the Big Three have seen the error of their ways and are returning proxy-voting power to investors. That simply is not the case.

THIS IS NOT OVER, BUT THERE IS HOPE

A Real Choice

The good news is that there is now a viable option for shareholder-focused free-market capitalists, should the Big Three opt to offer it in support of investor returns.

In March of 2024, the proxy-consulting firm Bowyer Research announced "the release of its new proxy voting guidelines designed for investors who wish to counter the promotion of ESG ideology by political activists through the use of the proxy voting system and to reassert the traditional understanding of shareholder primacy as their fiduciary duty."[59]

ISS is offering the Bowyer guidelines as a custom option only "for government-based funds (e.g. public pensions, etc.)" for the current proxy-voting season (ending mid-2024).[60] It could be available as an option for the Big Three's voting-choice programs after that point, should they choose to adopt it. Although none has yet agreed to do so, the potential is encouraging. It would turn their voting-choice programs into programs with an actual choice.

Reuters News Service used the term "ESG Skeptic" to describe the new guidelines in an article titled "Proxy Adviser ISS Expands Offerings for 'ESG Skeptic' Clients."[61] That name understates their relevance, perhaps intentionally. They are far more than merely skeptical.[62]

As the Bowyer Research press release states, the intent is to take "a crucial step in restoring the primacy of shareholders in modern business" and offer "a back-to-neutral framework that prioritizes an approach to business's fiduciary responsibility intended to put shareholders, not stakeholders, first."[63]

I will refer to these guidelines as the "shareholders-first" option, which I believe more accurately reflects their potential impact.

With respect to net-zero, the shareholders-first option "actively oppose[s] corporate commitments to divest from fossil fuels or adopt climate change/decarbonization pledges, as well as other non-business-relevant pro-ESG proposals, whether they come from shareholders or management."[64] According to

Bowyer Research's website, the guidelines would also "support anti-ESG shareholder proposals that seek to rescind past decarbonization proposals."[65]

On social-justice issues, the guidelines urge "corporations not to opine on divisive social/political issues" and "require corporations to resist activist demands to pressure them into making public statements on hot-button topics, ranging from abortion and LGBTQ+ issues to climate change and Second Amendment issues." The intent is to remind "companies that shareholders do not benefit when companies take sides on issues that are not part of their core-business focus."[66]

According to the Bowyer Research website, the guidelines also "[s]upport proposals which examine the risk that DEI programs create legal risk in light of the Harvard SCOTUS ruling regarding race and gender quotas." They would not "impose penalties by voting against board members based on lack of racial and gender diversity." Instead, "[v]otes against board members [would be] based entirely on the financial underperformance of the company compared to peers." The guidelines "support anti-ESG shareholder proposals that seek to rescind . . . past racial equity audit proposals.[67]

With respect to corporate governance and accountability, the guidelines take an "aggressive approach" by recommending "voting against the boards and pay packages of severely underperforming companies" and actively opposing "moves to diminish shareholder voting rights or insulate corporate management from corrective investor action."[68]

Significantly, shareholders-first is a back-to-neutral approach to social and political issues. According to Bowyer Research's website, the shareholder-first guidelines "do not offer universal support for proposals from anti-ESG groups" and actually oppose "proposals which seek to impose conservative politics on the company in the same way that we oppose proposals which seek to impose liberal ideology on companies." In fact, the guidelines will support "pro-ESG proponents" when they "identify genuine risk factors, for example sexual predation in online forums or risks arising from sexual harassment in companies with a problematic history."[69]

According to Bowyer Research president Jerry Bowyer, "Our goal in this product launch was to employ win-win business thinking instead of win-lose political thinking. Clients wanted something that previously had not been available. ISS is giving those clients what they want. Both sides win. Capitalism wins."[70] I would add that, finally, investors can also win.

ISS's global head of investment stewardship, Lorraine Kelly, stated that the Bowyer Research option is "in keeping with our longstanding mission to provide a wide array of voting policy choices." Well, as I said, it is an actual choice—so, more than that.[71]

The longer the Big Three wait to allow pro-shareholder-capitalism clients to choose a viable investor-friendly proxy-voting option, the longer they risk claims that they are abdicating their fiduciary duties and are responsible for underperforming investment portfolios. Bowyer's shareholders-first option presents them with an opportunity to end the wait. If they decline to offer it, the no-choice nature of their voting "choice" programs will be all the more obvious.

No general voting option will ever be perfect, but shareholders-first is an actual option for those who want an abundant and promising future—and do not want their monies used to threaten our democracy, economic freedom, or individual liberty.

CONCLUSION

"Power always thinks it has a great soul and vast views beyond the comprehension of the weak."

— *John Adams*[1]

T he next round in the fight between the Big Three and the Resistance has now begun, and on a higher plane. It is expanding into a more explicitly ideological struggle. The Resistance has recognized what has always been true about the fight over stakeholder capitalism and ESG—that there is far more at stake than attacks on disfavored business sectors or the integrity of pension and retirement benefits. The question is whether America's economy will continue along capitalist lines or be hijacked by financial elites determined to destroy the foundation of our profit-based, opportunity-driven free-market system.

At this point, the Big Three are responding with subterfuge, mischaracterizing what the Resistance is doing, and misleading the public about what the elites have always intended to accomplish with their ESG agenda. They are now careful not to say the quiet parts out loud.

The tactic of the Resistance in this new phase is to force the Big Three out from their hiding place so they must either abandon stakeholder capitalism and ESG or explicitly proclaim and defend them on honest terms. We will now see whether Larry Fink and his allies have the gumption for an open fight—whether they are prepared to defend stakeholder capitalism and ESG and what they always intended for them to foster—a tyranny for the good of its victims.

In his infamous 2018 CEO letter, Fink stated that society was demanding that American businesses "respond to broader societal challenges," and "serve a social purpose."[2] Perhaps he actually thought everyone in America wanted him, Larry Fink, to remake our free-market economy in the image of an ESG totem. At any rate, he is now fully aware that this was simply untrue.

In reality, most investors want nothing to do with stakeholder capitalism, the ESG agenda, or collectivism in general. Rather, they want BlackRock and its Big Three allies to be what they advertise themselves to be—passive-product firms that invest money and vote shares solely and exclusively to advance their clients' best financial interests, as traditional fiduciary duty requires. They get paid a lot for fulfilling that important role. Enough already with social and political activism designed to transform the economy.

BlackRock's 10-K— We've got a Problem

BlackRock does seem to understand that it has a problem. In its 2024 annual Form 10-K filing with the Securities and Exchange Commission, BlackRock acknowledged the risks its ESG activism poses for its business. This filing states that, if BlackRock is unable "to successfully manage ESG-related expectations across varied stakeholder interests, it may adversely affect BlackRock's reputation, ability to attract and retain clients, employees, shareholders and business partners or result in litigation, legal or governmental action, which may cause its AUM, revenue and earnings to decline."[3]

That is a mouthful of consequences.

BlackRock's 10-K attributes the increased negative focus on its ESG activism to the success of the Resistance in passing state legislation "restricting or prohibiting state government entities from doing certain business with entities identified by the state as 'boycotting' or 'discriminating' against particular industries or considering ESG factors in their investment processes and proxy voting."[4]

Honestly, it was good to see an acknowledgement that the Resistance legislation was having an effect on the Big Three. But even in that admission, BlackRock conveniently misrepresented both the Texas contracting legislation and the state-fiduciary-duty legislation. Either BlackRock is unable to fathom that there is opposition to its activism, so they have difficulty responding to it; or, more likely, they understand it full well and are intentionally mischaracterizing it.

For example, as BlackRock surely knows, while the Texas model contracting legislation does use the term "boycott," it defines that term very broadly. As used in that statute, boycotting includes actions that "penalize, inflict economic harm on, or limit commercial relations with a company because" that company "does not commit or pledge to meet environmental standards beyond applicable federal and state law."[5]

That covers far more than the colloquial definition of "boycotting" and goes well beyond "'discriminating' against particular industries" as BlackRock's 10-K claims. The Texas model prohibits punishing—which is an intentional and affirmatively harmful act—fossil-fuel companies for failing to adopt social and political positions that are neither in the best interests of their business nor required by law.

The problem with BlackRock and its Big Three allies is not and has never been that they "boycott"—as commonly defined—fossil-fuel companies, or refuse to invest in them. In fact, everyone knows that they must own certain fossil-fuel companies as part of various indexes, such as the S&P 500.

The problem is that the Big Three invest in fossil-fuel companies and then punish them for their pro–fossil fuels business models by voting the shares they hold—or pressuring these companies in so-called stewardship meetings—to force those companies to adopt net-zero or other damaging decarbonization policies. Such policies are obviously not in the best interests of either fossil-fuel companies or those who have invested in them, as they promote reducing reliance on—if not eliminating—the very products that justify the companies' existence.

If that is not the kind of conduct in which BlackRock and its allies are engaging, they should have nothing to fear from the Texas model contracting legislation. But of course, that is precisely what the Big Three are doing. The whole point of the "E" in ESG is to punish companies for failing to adopt net-zero goals, regardless of whether doing so is required by law or is in the companies' best financial interests. Just ask Exxon. As defined by Texas law, that is boycotting oil companies, even if you have invested in them.

The real issue is that Texas has called BlackRock out for doing what its laws prohibit, and BlackRock does not like it.

Nor does state-fiduciary-duty legislation prohibit consideration of "ESG factors" in a state's "investment processes and proxy voting," as BlackRock's 10-K filing claims.[6] Such legislation requires that, as fiduciaries, the Big Three act "solely" in the financial interests of a state pension fund's "participants and beneficiaries"—and for the "exclusive purpose" of benefiting them financially.[7] This is really not something any fiduciary should find either objectionable or difficult to understand.

To further that requirement, state-fiduciary-duty legislation prohibits fiduciaries from investing to advance "non-pecuniary" or "ideological" goals including—but certainly not limited to—the goals formerly known as ESG. Managing funds primarily to advance ESG goals, however, differs significantly from "considering" ESG factors that may affect the beneficiaries' financial interests. Despite BlackRock's claim, the fiduciary-duty legislation does not compel asset managers to ignore such factors.[8]

As fiduciaries, asset managers violate the law when they demand that companies in which they have invested prioritize serving "a social purpose"—to quote Fink's 2018 CEO letter—over the financial interests of their investors.[9] Fiduciaries simply cannot sacrifice returns, or accept additional risk, by stewarding companies or voting their shares to prioritize a social or political end over their clients' financial interests.

This is really a simple concept that BlackRock may not like, but surely understands.

To paraphrase Secretary Scalia, a fiduciary's duty is to the beneficiaries of the funds it manages alone, and one "social" goal trumps all others—their financial and retirement security.[10] To advance that goal, and that goal alone, a fiduciary may *consider* anything relevant to the investment's "pecuniary" or financial performance, even ESG factors. But it cannot ignore its clients' financial interests to advance ESG or any other social or political goals these financial elites support—the interests of any so-called "stakeholders" to the contrary notwithstanding.

BlackRock Seems Confused—but Is Not

In addition to mischaracterizing the Texas contracting and state fiduciary-duty legislation in its 10-K, BlackRock coyly feigns an inability to understand how anyone could possibly decline to do business with BlackRock based on its social and political advocacy.

For example, as we have seen, on March 19, 2024, which was shortly after BlackRock filed its 10-K, the Texas Permanent School Fund (TPSF) struck a major blow for the Resistance by withdrawing $8.5 billion from BlackRock. In a letter to BlackRock, TPFS Chairman Aaron Kinsey explained the reason for this withdrawal.[11] I should first note that the TPSF had no legal obligation to inform BlackRock why it was divesting funds. Absent any conflict of interest or other legal impediment, investors are free to move their funds from one asset manager to another for any reason or no reason. BlackRock is not entitled to the TPSF's business. Chairman Kinsey's letter was a courtesy.

Substantively, Chairman Kinsey's letter did not discuss BlackRock's performance. Rather, Chairman Kinsey stated that "BlackRock's dominant and persistent leadership in the ESG movement immeasurably damages our state's oil & gas economy" and that "BlackRock's destructive approach toward the energy companies that this state and our world depend on is incompatible with our fiduciary duty to Texans."[12]

That is pretty clear. BlackRock's response, on the other hand, was tone-deaf.

First, it accused the TPSF of putting "short term politics" over "long-term fiduciary duties" because BlackRock claimed it had delivered "consistently strong performance."[13] Of course, past underperformance was not the stated reason the TPSF divested its funds. Nor is there any reason to believe that other asset managers are or would be incapable of matching or exceeding BlackRock's fees or performance, particularly given the over-promotion and underperformance of its highly touted ESG products.

BlackRock's claim that the TSPF was acting for political purposes was blatantly and self-servingly hypocritical. Let's face it, Blackrock wants carte blanche to use the funds it invests for others to advance ESG political goals while simultaneously accusing states of acting politically if they object to BlackRock's political activism. It has long been a leftist tactic to accuse opponents of doing what the leftists themselves are actually doing—to create confusion and obscure evidence of their culpability.

Apparently aware that its you're-acting-politically argument lacks both consistency and merit, BlackRock then reiterates its fallback argument that because it invests in oil and gas companies it cannot be discriminating against oil and gas companies.[14] Again, no one denies that BlackRock invests in oil and gas in the literal sense. That really is not and never was the issue. For BlackRock to suggest otherwise is a deliberate mischaracterization of Texas law rather than a misunderstanding of what the Texas law clearly provides.

The issue is that BlackRock is trying to transform the economy, and in pursuit of that goal is punishing energy companies for producing energy. Texas is boycotting BlackRock because Texas does not want to degrade or transform the economy, and especially does not want oil companies to be punished for producing oil. As defined by Texas law, that is boycotting.

The real issue, as Chairman Kinsey's letter clearly states, is BlackRock's ESG leadership.[15]

If BlackRock finds that in any way confusing, it would do well to recall its net-zero advocacy, Fink's statement that such advocacy "demands a transformation of the entire economy," and Black-Rock's vote against Exxon, a Texas energy company, in its proxy battle with Engine No.1. These were attacks not only on Texas pensioners, but also against all Texan investors, workers, consumers, and citizens generally.

Or perhaps BlackRock should reread Fink's 2018 statement that "a company's ability to manage environmental, social, and governance matters demonstrates the leadership and good governance that is so essential to sustainable growth, which is why we are increasingly integrating these issues into our investment process."[16] Fink may have abandoned the term ESG now that people are coming to understand what it entails, but he is still committed to discussing "decarbonization" with company management and, as we have seen, used that term (or a derivative of it) thirteen times in his 2024 Investors letter.[17] Does BlackRock really expect us to believe that it does not understand that "decarbonization" is an issue for Texas's "oil and gas economy"?

As I said, BlackRock's response was tone-deaf.

BlackRock did make one nice concession in its response, stating, "We are fiduciaries with a mandate to maximize performance for the people that entrust us to manage their money."[18] In context, I guess that needed to be said. They might have mentioned that their duty was to maximize performance as a passive—not an activist—investor and that they would indeed follow that mandate. It is good that they got the general concept, in any event. Baby steps.

It is also worth noting that BlackRock is also facing at least two state lawsuits for fraud in connection with its ESG advocacy.

In December of 2023, Tennessee brought an action against BlackRock under Tennessee's consumer-protection laws for misleading investors with respect to ESG investing. According to the seventy-three-page complaint, "BlackRock marketed many of its funds as devoid of ESG considerations and has admitted that ESG aims—in particular, radically reducing portfolio companies' carbon output 'do not provide an indication of current or future performance nor do they represent the potential risk and reward profile of a fund.'" Nonetheless, the state alleges, "BlackRock committed to global organizations that it would pursue these aims across all assets under management. And it did." As a result, for years, "BlackRock has misled consumers about the scope and effects of its widespread ESG activity."[19]

In March of 2024, Mississippi sued BlackRock for fraud, alleging that it engaged in ESG activism even with client money invested in non-ESG funds. Basically, the state alleges that BlackRock defrauded investors by claiming its traditional non-ESG passive funds did not employ ESG-investing strategies, while as a member of groups such as Net Zero Asset Managers it had pledged to advance net-zero goals. Mississippi also alleges that BlackRock defrauded investors by claiming ESG investing improved financial performance, when the evidence was that it did not.[20]

In both cases, BlackRock denies liability.

Finally, the common sense of our cause has reached as far as Bloomberg's editorial board, which published an opinion piece in May of 2024 titled "Index Funds Need to Be Passive, Not Political,"[21] which called for federal legislation that would "strictly limit the role of any asset manager that's claiming to act as a 'passive' shareholder" and that "[proxy-v]oting decisions should be devolved to end investors as much as possible" or "default to either supporting management or else be cast at the last minute as 'mirror votes' that simply replicate the voting patterns of all other stockholders."[22] As for so-called "stewardship," the editorial board stated that "[e]ngagement with company leaders should be restricted to ensuring effective corporate governance and rigorously documented and disclosed."[23]

For the Resistance, it was a clear win. Any arguments that the Resistance was a politically motivated movement outside of financial norms died with that editorial.

It's a Team Effort

While BlackRock and Fink have put themselves willingly at the center of this fight, they have not acted alone. The rise of passive investing inadvertently concentrated economic power in the hands of a few asset managers—primarily the Big Three—and they all pursued stakeholder capitalism and the ESG agenda. Their most recent proxy-voting guidelines, while couched in protective language, continue to emphasize their underlying ESG goals and show no real departure from their efforts to impose those goals on American businesses and—by proxy—on all of us.

In fairness, Vanguard has at least claimed it will take a more passive role. Explaining Vanguard's withdrawal from the Net Zero Asset Managers coalition, CEO Tim Buckley said, as we have seen, that Vanguard does not believe it "should dictate company strategy" and that "[i]t would be hubris to presume that we know the right strategy for the thousands of companies that Vanguard invests with." Rather, Vanguard "just want[s] to make sure that risks are being appropriately disclosed and that every company is playing by the rules." And, by the way, Vanguard's "research indicates that ESG investing does not have any advantage over broad-based investing."[24]

That was all very positive, and the Committee to Unleash Prosperity's "Politics over Pensions" report did grade Vanguard an A on proxy voting.[25] Hopefully, Vanguard's new CEO (a former BlackRock executive) will maintain Vanguard's A status.

And in fairness to SSGA, its chief investment officer, as we have also seen, has stated that SSGA holds "deeply that the primary reason for a corporation to exist is to generate profits and to generate returns for its shareholders." She also said that SSGA was "actually quite concerned about the rise of stakeholder capitalism as a class of investing."[26] And, by the way, ESG is a "constraint" on performance, so she has "steadfastly encouraged our teams to not think of ESG as a performance enhancer."[27]

Nevertheless, the Committee to Unleash Prosperity's 2023 "Politics over Pensions" report gave SSGA a D on proxy voting, below even BlackRock's C.[28] Notably, SSGA did move up to a C in 2024.[29]

Unfortunately, the most recent proxy-voting guidelines from BlackRock, SSGA, and Vanguard call into question whether there has been any real change in the ESG messages they are sending to America's CEOs. If they were endeavoring to get back to neutral on social and political issues, as is their proper role as passive asset managers, the simple solution would be to stop requiring disclosures and setting performance metrics on ESG's radical net-zero environmental policies and DEI's discriminatory equity-based board composition and workforce-hiring practices—and any other ideological goal, whether progressive or conservative.

They could—and should—get back to passive investing focused solely on their clients' financial interests, allowing CEOs to independently run their companies while voters and consumers guide our government and our economy. Our Republic and our free-market economy have produced unparalleled prosperity for over two hundred years. If we can resist the collectivists of this generation, they may well do so for the next two hundred.

The Resistance came together to defend our representative democracy from stakeholder capitalism's autocratic dictates, to defend our free-market economy from stakeholder capitalism's prosperity-destroying collectivism, and to defend our individual liberty from the stakeholder-capitalist elites who would use our money to impose their collectivist ideology on us—whether we want it or not.

We are not going away.

Nonetheless, it is important to keep in mind that the collectivists are not going away either. We are not the first generation to face a collectivist threat, nor will we be the last. Preserving freedom and prosperity, keeping our economy and our Republic strong will require high levels of both diligence and commitment. But if there were ever a nation capable of defending economic freedom and individual liberty, it is America. They are both essential parts of our national DNA.

While stakeholder capitalism has global advocates, they have no chance of success without the support of America's business sector.

If we internally desert free-market capitalism for a collectivist economic system, it will be tantamount to economic suicide for all but the elites who advocate that transformation. President Abraham Lincoln once stated, "If destruction be our lot, we must ourselves be its author and finisher. As a nation of freemen, we must live through all time, or die by suicide."[30]

I wrote this book in the hope that we will remain free through all time.

ACKNOWLEDGEMENTS

"There is no limit to what a man can do or where he
can go if he doesn't mind who gets the credit."

—from a small plaque on the desk of
President Ronald Reagan[1]

irst and foremost, I want to thank my wife of thirty-seven years for her support during the months I spent researching, writing and—I'm sure—incessantly talking about stakeholder capitalism, ESG, and the evils of collectivism. I have included her comments (at least the printable ones). There would be no book without her.

Three other individuals took the time to review, comment on, or edit what I wrote as I went along, keeping me on track and helping improve both what I said and how well I said it. It was a privilege to have their assistance.

First, my long-time friend, former Missouri Senator James Talent's thoughtful and astute review, revisions, and comments were essential to this book's message and completion. Jim's involvement meaningfully improved this book. We have been discussing stakeholder capitalism, ESG, and collectivism, among other topics, since at least 2020. His friendship, insights, and communicative skills have been invaluable.

Second, my friend Dr. Michael Edleson, the retired chief risk officer of the University of Chicago's endowment, former managing director of risk management for Morgan Stanley Smith Barney and several other Morgan Stanley divisions, and former chief economist of Nasdaq and the National Association of Security

Dealers (NASD), among his many other impressive qualifications. I truly appreciate Mike's taking the time to help me with this project. He has many other responsibilities that occupy his valuable time (including a new Corvette). His friendship, diligence, knowledge, and wisdom made this book much better than it would otherwise have been.

Third, my friend Al Neubert, known to his friends as the Godfather of Indexing, is the former director of business development for the S&P Index Products and Services unit at Standard & Poor's. He also was on the S&P Index Committee and oversaw the management of the S&P 500 for twenty years. Al is currently a consultant in the index-business industry and is considered a leading world authority on index development, management, and maintenance protocols. It was a privilege to have him reviewing and commenting on this book. His comments and edits were invaluable. I sincerely appreciate his taking the time and making the effort.

I would be remiss if I did not thank my editor Elizabeth Kantor, whose professional and thorough work on this book made it more accurate, well stated, and easier to read. I also enjoyed our conversations about the book and politics in general.

Many other friends and fellow Resistance members were also very helpful when I had questions and needed suggestions, or served as inspiration. If we survive this attack on our values, these individuals will be prominent on the list of those who defended our personal liberty and economic freedom.

They include, in alphabetical order, Brent Bennett (Texas Public Policy Foundation), Jerry Bowyer (Bowyer Research), David Burton (Heritage Foundation), Jeff Chasney (former CIO, CKR Restaurants), Justin Danhof (Strive Asset Management), Paul Fitzpatrick (1792 Exchange), Catherine Gunsalus (Heritage Action), Will Hild (Consumers' Research), Jason Isaac (American Energy Institute and the Texas Public Policy Foundation), Terrence Keeley (CEO of Impact Evaluation Lab), Derek Kreifels (State Financial Officers Foundation), Stephen Moore (Committee to Unleash Prosperity), Andy Olivastro (Heritage Foundation), Pat Pizzella (former Deputy Secretary and Acting Secretary of Labor;

Mayor, Pinehurst, North Carolina), Vivek Ramaswamy (entrepreneur and politician), Kevin Roberts (Heritage Foundation), Eugene Scalia (former Secretary of Labor), Nick Schulz (Exxon), Scott Shepard (National Center for Public Policy Research), Jeff Sherman (Strive Asset Management), Stephen Soukup (author and publisher of The Political Forum), Mike Thompson, Bridgett Wagner (Heritage Foundation), Noah Wall (State Financial Officers Foundation), Paul Watkins, Jonathan Williams (American Legislative Exchange Council)—and all the governors, state financial officers, attorneys general, and legislators who are taking and have taken action to protect the assets of their taxpayers and public institutions.

Also I would like to thank, in particular, Glenn Beck, Cameron Sholty, and Justin Haskins of the Heartland Institute for being on the stakeholder-capitalism/ESG issue early and aggressively.

Finally, I would like to thank Roger Kimball, a true lover of freedom, a defender of liberty, and an inspiration to all Americans. Thank you for convincing me to write this book.

NOTES

Dedication

[1]   Milton Friedman, *Capitalism and Freedom* (Chicago: University of Chicago Press, 1962), 15.

Introduction

[1]   "Thomas Jefferson Quotes," AZ Quotes, accessed May 6, 2024, https://www.azquotes.com/quote/559886#google_vignette; "Thomas Jefferson," Wikiquotes, accessed May 6, 2024, https://simple.wikiquote.org/wiki/Thomas_Jefferson.

[2]   Saijel Kishan, "How to Fix 'ESG' by Changing Its Name," Bloomberg, January 29, 2024, https://www.bloomberg.com/news/articles/2024-01-29/a-finance-professor-s-guide-to-fixing-esg-starts-with-its-name.

[3]   Larry Fink, "Larry Fink's 2018 Letter to CEOs: A Sense of Purpose," BlackRock, 2018, https://www.blackrock.com/corporate/investor-relations/2018-larry-fink-ceo-letter.

[4]   Larry Fink, "Larry Fink's 2019 Letter to CEOs: Purpose & Profit," BlackRock, 2019, https://www.blackrock.com/corporate/investor-relations/2019-larry-fink-ceo-letter.

[5]   "Declaration of Independence: A Transcription," National Archives, July 4, 1776, https://www.archives.gov/founding-docs/declaration-transcript.

6   "September 17, 1787: A Republic, If You Can Keep It," National Park Service, accessed May 6, 2024, https://www.nps.gov/articles/000/constitutionalconvention-september17.htm.

7   F. Eugene Heath, "Invisible Hand," Britannica Money, updated March 22, 2024, https://www.britannica.com/money/invisible-hand.

8   Larry Fink, "Larry Fink's 2017 Letter to CEOs," BlackRock, 2017, https://www.blackrock.com/corporate/investor-relations/2017-larry-fink-ceo-letter.

9   "Larry Fink's 2018 Letter to CEOs."

Chapter 1: Power Too Intoxicating to Resist

1   Edmund Burke, "Speech on the Middlesex Election" (February 7, 1771), Oxford Reference, https://www.oxfordreference.com/display/10.1093/acref/9780191826719.001.0001/q-oro-ed4-00002268.

2   "Index Industry Association Survey Reveals 3.7 Million Indexes Globally," Business Wire, November 14, 2018, https://www.businesswire.com/news/home/20181114005124/en/Index-Industry-Association-Survey-Reveals-3.7-Million-Indexes-Globally.

3   "S&P U.S. Indices Methodology," S&P Dow Jones Indices: A Division of S&P Global, accessed May 6, 2024, 4, https://www.spglobal.com/spdji/en/documents/methodologies/methodology-sp-us-indices.pdf.

4   Ryan Jackson, "Actively Managed Funds Surprise in Market Rebound," Morningstar, September 11, 2023, https://www.morningstar.com/etfs/actively-managed-funds-measured-up-well-market-rebound.

5   Tim Edwards et al., "SPIVA U.S. Scorecard: Year-End 2022," S&P Dow Jones Indices: A Division of S&P Global, accessed May 6, 2024, https://www.spglobal.com/spdji/en/documents/spiva/spiva-us-year-end-2022.pdf.

6   "Distribution of Active and Passive Investment Funds in the United States in 2012 and 2022, by Type," Statista, June 12, 2023, https://www.statista.com/statistics/1262209/active-passive-investment-funds-usa.

7   Ibid.

8   Adam Saban, "It's Official: Passive Funds Overtake Active Funds," Morningstar, January 17, 2024, https://www.morningstar.com/funds/recovery-us-fund-flows-was-weak-2023.

9   Dan Morenoff, "Break Up the ESG Investing Giants," *Wall Street Journal*, August 31, 2022, https://www.wsj.com/articles/break-up-the-esg-investing-giants-state-street-blackrock-vanguard-voting-ownership-big-three-competitor-antitrust-11661961693.

10   Jan Fichtner, Eelke M. Heemskerk, and Javier Garcia-Bernardo, "Hidden Power of the Big Three? Passive Index Funds, Re-Concentration of Corporate Ownership, and New Financial Risk," Cambridge Core: Cambridge University Press, April 25, 2017, https://www.cambridge.org/core/journals/business-and-politics/article/hidden-power-of-the-big-three-passive-index-funds-reconcentration-of-corporate-ownership-and-new-financial-risk/30AD689509AAD62F5B677E916C28C4B6.

11   "Acquiring More than 5% of a Publicly Traded Company," *Pillsbury Investment Fund Law Blog*, accessed May 6, 2024, https://www.investmentfundlawblog.com/resources/investments-by-funds/acquiring-5-publicly-traded-company.

12   Graham Steele, "The New Money Trust: How Large Money Managers Control Our Economy and What We Can Do about It," American Economic Liberties Project, November 23, 2020, https://www.economicliberties.us/our-work/new-money-trust/#.

13   "Proxy-Voting Insights: BlackRock, Vanguard, State Street," Morningstar, June 13, 2023, https://corpgov.law.harvard.edu/wp-content/uploads/2023/06/blackrock-vanguard-state-street-esg-proxy-voting-FINAL061223.pdf.

14   Fichtner, Heemskerk, and Garcia-Bernardo, "Hidden Power of the Big Three?"

15   Kirsten Grind, "Vanguard and BlackRock Plan to Get More Assertive with Their Investments," *Wall Street Journal*, March 4, 2015, https://www.wsj.com/articles/vanguard-and-blackrock-plan-to-get-more-assertive-with-their-investments-1425445200.

16   Andrew Ross Sorkin, "BlackRock's Message: Contribute to Society, or Risk Losing Our Support," *New York Times*, January 15,

2018, https://www.nytimes.com/2018/01/15/business/dealbook/
blackrock-laurence-fink-letter.html.

17 Ibid.

18 Burke, "Speech on the Middlesex Election."

19 Larry Fink, "Larry Fink's 2018 Letter to CEOs: A Sense of
Purpose," 2018, https://www.blackrock.com/corporate/investor-
relations/2018-larry-fink-ceo-letter.

20 John Frank, "Larry Fink 'Ashamed' to Be Part of ESG Political Debate," Axios, June 25, 2023, https://www.axios.
com/2023/06/26/larry-fink-ashamed-esg-weaponized-desantis.

21 "Larry Fink's 2018 Letter to CEOs."

22 Adam Hayes, "Fiduciary Definition: Examples and Why They
Are Important," Investopedia, updated March 19, 2024, https://
www.investopedia.com/terms/f/fiduciary.asp.

23 "Blackrock Investment Stewardship (BIS) Annual Report: January 1–December 31, 2022" ("abbreviated version"), Blackrock,
April 28, 2023, https://www.blackrock.com/co/literature/publica-
tion/annual-stewardship-report-2022-summary.pdf.

24 "Energy Investing: Setting the Record Straight," BlackRock,
accessed May 6, 2024, https://www.blackrock.com/corporate/
newsroom/setting-the-record-straight/energy-investing.

25 "Larry Fink's 2018 Letter to CEOs."

26 Ibid.

27 Ibid.

28 Ibid.

29 Josh Jones, "George Orwell Explains How 'Newspeak' Works,
the Official Language of His Totalitarian Dystopia in 1984," Open
Culture, January 24, 2017, https://www.openculture.com/2017/01/
george-orwell-explains-how-newspeak-works.html.

30 End Wokeness (@EndWokeness), "Why has everything gone
woke these days? ESG scores. Here is BlackRock CEO Larry
Fink along with the CEO of AmEx explaining his desire to 'force
behaviors' (2017)," X, June 4, 2023, 1:46 p.m., https://twitter.com/
EndWokeness/status/1665414711188287489.

31 "Larry Fink's 2018 Letter to CEOs."

32 Ibid.

33   "BlackRock Investment Stewardship: Protecting Our Clients' Assets for the Long Term," BlackRock, 2020, 4, https://www.blackrock.com/corporate/literature/publication/blk-profile-of-blackrock-investment-stewardship-team-work.pdf.

34   Ibid.

35   "Larry Fink's 2018 Letter to CEOs."

36   Sorkin, "BlackRock's Message."

37   Eric Roston, "Fink's Letter to CEOs Upends a Half-Century of Business Thought," Bloomberg, January 17, 2018, https://www.bloomberg.com/news/articles/2018-01-17/fink-s-letter-to-ceos-upends-a-half-century-of-business-thought.

38   Milton Friedman, "A Friedman Doctrine—the Social Responsibility of Business Is to Increase Its Profits," *New York Times*, September 13, 1970, https://www.nytimes.com/1970/09/13/archives/a-friedman-doctrine-the-social-responsibility-of-business-is-to.html.

39   Ibid.

40   Ibid.

41   Ibid.

Chapter 2: Corporate Governance

1   Andy Lin, "2023 Berkshire Shareholders Meeting Transcript and Video," *Andy Lin's Blog*, May 9, 2023, https://www.granitefirm.com/blog/us/2023/05/09/shareholders-meeting.

2   Michael Keenan, "The 15 Biggest Bank Failures in US History," GOBankingRates, April 14, 2023, https://www.gobankingrates.com/banking/banks/biggest-bank-failures-history.

3   Lawrence H. Summers, "Opinion: The Biden Stimulus Is Admirably Ambitious. But It Brings Some Big Risks, Too.," *Washington Post*, February 4, 2021, https://www.washingtonpost.com/opinions/2021/02/04/larry-summers-biden-covid-stimulus.

4   See, for example, Stephen Rattner, "Too Many Smart People Are Being Too Dismissive of Inflation," *New York Times*, March 5, 2021, https://www.nytimes.com/2021/03/05/opinion/fed-inflation-markets.html; Michael Strain, "Biden's Stimulus Risks

Shortening the Recovery," *National Review*, February 19, 2021, https://www.nationalreview.com/corner/bidens-stimulus-risks-shortening-the-recovery.

[5] Board of Governors of the Federal Reserve System, "Federal Reserve Issues FOMC Statement," press release, March 16, 2022, https://www.federalreserve.gov/newsevents/pressreleases/monetary20220316a.htm.

[6] Max Zahn, "Silicon Valley Bank: How a Digital Bank Run Accelerated the Collapse," ABC News, March 14, 2023, https://abcnews.go.com/Business/silicon-valley-bank-digital-bank-run-accelerated-collapse/story?id=97846569#:~:text=The%20collapse%20of%20Silicon%20Valley%20Bank%2C%20the%20second-biggest,deposits%20--%20within%20a%20single%20day%20last%20week.

[7] Noah Barsky, "Silicon Valley Bank Proxy Shows Board's Secret Yearlong Risk Panic," *Forbes*, March 12, 2023, https://www.forbes.com/sites/noahbarsky/2023/03/12/silicon-valley-bank-proxy-shows-boards-secret-yearlong-risk-panic/?sh=7a1a4db11e7b.

[8] "SVB Hires Kim Olson as Chief Risk Officer," SVB (Silicon Valley Bank), January 4, 2023, https://ir.svb.com/news-and-research/news/news-details/2023/SVB-Hires-Kim-Olson-as-Chief-Risk-Officer/default.aspx.

[9] *Bank Oversight: Testimony before the U.S. Senate Committee on Banking, Housing, and Urban Affairs*, 118th Cong. (2023) (statement of Michael S. Barr, Vice Chairman for Supervision), https://www.federalreserve.gov/newsevents/testimony/barr20230328a.htm; Andrew Ackerman, David Harrison, and Andrew Duehren, "Lawmakers Scold Fed over Silicon Valley Bank Collapse," *Wall Street Journal*, March 28, 2023, https://www.wsj.com/articles/top-bank-regulators-to-face-senate-questions-over-svb-signature-collapses-d50a50e0.

[10] Ibid.

[11] *Bank Oversight*.

[12] Ackerman, Harrison, and Duehren, "Lawmakers Scold Fed."

[13] Janet Paskin, "SVB Failure Becomes Fodder for Anti-ESG Crowd in US Culture Wars (2)," Bloomberg Law, March 14, 2023, https://

news.bloomberglaw.com/esg/svb-failure-becomes-fodder-for-anti-esg-crowd-in-us-culture-wars.

14   Brianna Herlihy, "Former Dems including Clinton Donor, Obama Official Dominated SVB's Board of Directors," Fox News, March 14, 2023, https://www.foxnews.com/politics/former-dems-including-clinton-donor-obama-official-dominated-svbs-board-directors.

15   SVB Financial Group, "United States Securities and Exchange Commission Schedule 14A: Proxy Statement Pursuant to Section 14(a) of the Securities Exchange Act of 1934," 2022, https://s201.q4cdn.com/589201576/files/doc_downloads/2022/SVB-2021-Form-DEF14A-(1).pdf.

16   Joshua Rhett Miller, "Obama Aide, Hillary Donors, Improv Act: Meet SVB's Board of Directors," *New York Post*, March 14, 2023, https://nypost.com/2023/03/14/obama-aide-hillary-donors-improv-actor-meet-svbs-board.

17   Ibid.

18   SVB Financial Group, "United States Securities and Exchange Commission Form 10Q: Quarterly Report Pursuant to Section 13 or 15(d) of the Securities Exchange Act of 1934," November 7, 2022, 50, https://d18rnop25nwr6d.cloudfront.net/CIK-0000719739/dffa5746-7f80-4d88-9d3a-65b793df5d52.pdf; Jonathan Weil, "Rising Interest Rates Hit Banks' Bond Holdings," *Wall Street Journal*, November 11, 2022, https://www.wsj.com/articles/rising-interest-rates-hit-banks-bond-holdings-11668123473.

19   Christiaan Hetzner, "SVB Collapse Highlights $620 Billion Hole Lurking in Banks' Balance Sheets," Yahoo!Finance, March 10, 2023, https://finance.yahoo.com/news/svb-collapse-highlights-620-billion-172512701.html.

20   Barsky, "Silicon Valley Bank Proxy."

21   Miller, "Obama Aide, Hillary Donors, Improv Act."

22   Samuel O'Brient, "5 Investors That Are Betting Big on Silicon Valley Bank (SIVB) Stock," InvestorPlace, March 10, 2023, https://investorplace.com/2023/03/5-investors-that-are-betting-big-on-silicon-valley-bank-sivb-stock.

23   Simply Wall St, "What You Need to Know about SVB Financial

Group's (NASDAQ:SIVB) Investor Competition," Nasdaq, August 20, 2021, https://www.nasdaq.com/articles/what-you-need-to-know-about-svb-financial-groups-nasdaq%3Asivb-investor-composition-2021-08.

24 End Wokeness (@EndWokeness), "Why has everything gone woke these days? ESG scores. Here is BlackRock CEO Larry Fink along with the CEO of AmEx explaining his desire to 'force behaviors' (2017)," X, June 4, 2023, 1:46 p.m., https://twitter.com/EndWokeness/status/1665414711188287489.

25 Larry Fink, "Larry Fink's 2018 Letter to CEOs: A Sense of Purpose," BlackRock, 2018, https://www.blackrock.com/corporate/investor-relations/2018-larry-fink-ceo-letter.

26 Larry Fink, "Larry Fink's 2019 Letter to CEOs: Purpose & Profit," BlackRock, 2019, https://www.blackrock.com/corporate/investor-relations/2019-larry-fink-ceo-letter.

27 Larry Fink, "Larry Fink's 2020 Letter to CEOs: A Fundamental Reshaping of Finance," BlackRock, 2020, https://www.blackrock.com/corporate/investor-relations/2020-larry-fink-ceo-letter.

28 Saijel Kishan, "BlackRock Voted against 255 Directors for Climate Issues," Bloomberg, July 20, 2021, https://www.bloomberg.com/news/articles/2021-07-20/blackrock-voted-against-255-directors-for-climate-related-issues.

29 "Investment Stewardship: 2022 Policies Update Summary," BlackRock, 2022, https://www.blackrock.com/corporate/literature/fact-sheet/blk-responsible-investment-guidelines-us.pdf, omitting internal citations.

30 Ross Kerber, "Vanguard Seeks More Boardroom Diversity and Wants Details," Reuters, August 30, 2019, https://www.reuters.com/article/us-vanguard-boards-idUSKCN1VK1FU/#:~:text=%E2%80%9CWe%20are%20expanding%20our%20focus%20to%20more%20explicitly,race%2C%20ethnicity%2C%20national%2intoorigin%2C%20and%20age%2C%E2%80%9D%20Vanguard%20wrote.

31 "Vanguard Investment Stewardship Insights: Voting Insights: Diversity-Related Proposals, January–June 2021," https://www.ie.vanguard/content/dam/intl/europe/

documents/investment-stewardship/voting-insights-diversity-proposals-2021.pdf.

32   Ibid.

33   "Asset Stewardship: Guidance on Diversity Disclosures and Practices," State Street Global Advisors, January 2022, 1, https://www.ssga.com/library-content/pdfs/asset-stewardship/racial-diversity-guidance-article.pdf.

34   Ibid., 2

35   Ibid, 3.

36   "2021 Proxy Statement: Notice of 2021 Annual Meeting of the Shareholders," Silicon Valley Bank, March 4, 2021, 2, https://www.svb.com/globalassets/library/uploadedfiles/content/corporate/2021-proxy-statement.pdf.

37   IShares Trust, "United States Securities and Exchange Commission Form N-PX: Annual Report of Proxy Voting Record of Registered Management Investment Company," December 22, 2022, https://www.sec.gov/Archives/edgar/data/1100663/000119312521258978/d176642dnpx.txt.

38   Vanguard Index Funds, "United States Securities and Exchange Commission Form N-PX: Annual Report of Proxy Voting Record of Registered Management Investment Company," December 22, 2021, https://www.sec.gov/Archives/edgar/data/36405/000110465921110322/tm2121856d11_npx.txt.

39   SPDR Series Trust, "United States Securities and Exchange Commission Form N-PX: Annual Report of Proxy Voting Record of Registered Management Investment Company," December 22, 2021, https://www.sec.gov/Archives/edgar/data/1064642/000119312521259029/d199722dnpx.htm.

40   Antoine Gara and Brooke Masters, "Silicon Valley Bank Was Warned by BlackRock That Risk Controls Were Weak," *Financial Times*, March 18, 2023, https://www.ft.com/content/fbd9e3d4-2df5-4a65-adbd-01e5de2c5053.

41   Max Zahn, "A Timeline of the Silicon Valley Bank Collapse," ABC News, March 14, 2023, https://abcnews.go.com/Business/timeline-silicon-valley-bank-collapse/story?id=97846565.

42   Alastair Marsh and Saijel Kishan, "SVB Collapse Exposes

'Lazy' ESG Funds as Hundreds Bought into Doomed Bank,"
Bloomberg, March 14, 2023, https://www.bloomberg.com/news/
articles/2023-03-14/svb-exposes-lazy-esg-funds-as-hundreds-
bought-into-doomed-bank?sref=yv2coi81.

43   Bentley Kaplan, "ESG Now Podcast: 'Was SVB All
about That ESG?,'" transcript, MSCI, March 31, 2022,
https://www.msci.com/documents/1296102/25589897/
Was+SVB+all+about+that+ESG+-+Transcript.pdf/dc55f292-
ca28-96d5-9856-4c9e0753443f?t=1680265569920#:~:text=At%20
the%20time%20of%20its%20collapse%2C%20MSCI%20
ESG,and%20an%20%E2%80%9CA%E2%80%9D%20put%20
SVB%20just%20above%20average.

44   Katherine Klein, "Does Gender Diversity on Boards Really Boost Company Performance?," Knowledge at Wharton, May 18, 2017, https://knowledge.wharton.upenn.edu/
article/will-gender-diversity-boards-really-boost-company-
performance/#:~:text=Despite%20the%20intuitive%20
appeal%20of%20the%20argument%20that,improve%20-
%E2%80%94%20or%20worsen%20%E2%80%94%20a%20
firm%E2%80%99s%20performance.

45   Renée B. Adams and Daniel Ferreira, "Women in the Boardroom
and Their Impact on Governance and Performance," *Journal
of Finance Economics* 94, no. 2 (November 2009), https://
www.sciencedirect.com/science/article/abs/pii/S0304405X-
09001421?via%3Dihub.

46   Jesse M. Fried, "Will Nasdaq's Diversity Rules Harm Investors?
European Corporate Governance Institute—Law Working Paper
No. 579/2021,", March 26, 2021, 2, https://deliverypdf.ssrn.com/
delivery.php?D=&EXT=pdf&INDEX=TRUE.E.

47   Alex Edmans, Caroline Flammer, and Simon Glossner, "Diversity, Equity, and Inclusion: Finance Working Paper No. 913/2023,"
European Corporate Governance Institute, September 2023, 2, 9,
https://papers.ssrn.com/sol3/papers.cfm?abstract_id=4426488.

48   Ibid, 29.

49   Ibid., 1.

50   Sarah Todd, "Is McKinsey Wrong about the Financial Benefits of

Diversity?," Quartz, July 29, 2021, https://qz.com/work/2038103/
is-mckinsey-wrong-about-the-financial-benefits-of-diversity.

51 Jeremiah Green and John R. M. Hand, "McKinsey's Diversity
Matters/Delivers/Wins Results Revisited," *Econ Journal Watch* 21,
no. 1 (March 2021): 28, 26, https://econjwatch.org/File+down-
load/1296/GreenHandMar2024.pdf?mimetype=pdf.

52 Jeremiah Green and John R. M. Hand, "McKinsey's Diversity
Matters/Delivers/Wins Results Revisited: Abstract," *Econ Journal
Watch* 21, no. 1 (March 2021), https://econjwatch.org/articles/
mckinsey-s-diversity-matters-delivers-wins-results-revisited.

53 "Lifting Financial Performance by Investing in Women: Long-
Term Capitalism at BlackRock," BlackRock, November 2023, 5,
https://www.blackrock.com/corporate/literature/whitepaper/
lifting-financial-performance-by-investing-in-women.pdf.

54 Alex Edmans, "Does Gender Diversity Really Boost Financial Performance?," May Contain Lies, November 2, 2023,
https://maycontainlies.com/does-gender-diversity-really-
boost-financial-performance/?utm_campaign=Fiduciary%20
Focus&utm_source=hs_email&utm_medium=email&utm_
content=281581768&_hsenc=p2ANqtz---JMqToxBP1BjYCxrFgB-
9T7Yg6zNdsfhUyX52PxltPcnzbjDvwt1YUXiILfwypMrjasPeMyf-
nz4BM7QWa4mCuovfWr8NzZdI6McIiGHA_bkCE2Ubg.

55 "Larry Fink on ESG, the Economy and the State of Democracy,"
transcript, WSJ Podcasts, October 18, 2023, https://www.wsj.
com/podcasts/opinion-free-expression/larry-fink-on-esg-the-
economy-and-the-state-of-democracy/f2e25649-e49b-4792-b025-
ff4496d346f5.

56 Hamilton v. Dallas County, 21-10133, 2023 WL 5316716 (5th Cir.
2023), at 24, https://www.ca5.uscourts.gov/opinions/pub/21/21-
10133-CV2.pdf.

57 Students for Fair Admissions, Inc. v. President and Fellows of
Harvard College, 600 U.S. 81 (2023), https://www.supremecourt.
gov/opinions/22pdf/20-1199_hgdj.pdf.

58 Ibid., at 15, omitting internal citations.

59 Ibid. (Gorsuch J. concurring opinion), at 4, citing Title VII of the
Civil Rights Act of 1964, U.S. Equal Employment Opportunity

Commission, accessed May 6, 2024, https://www.eeoc.gov/statutes/title-vii-civil-rights-act-1964.

Chapter 3: Social Injustice

[1] "Aleksandr_Solzhenitsyn: Quotes: Quotable Quote," Goodreads, accessed May 6, 2024, https://www.goodreads.com/quotes/7563989-human-beings-are-born-with-different-capacities-if-they-are; "Talk: Aleksandr_Solzhenitsyn," Wikiquotes, accessed May 6, 2024, https://en.wikiquote.org/wiki/Talk:Aleksandr_Solzhenitsyn.

[2] Elon Musk (@elonmusk), "DEI must DIE," X, December 15, 2023, 2:54 a.m., https://twitter.com/elonmusk/status/1735568882499211557?s=20.

[3] "What Is the 'S' in ESG?," S&P Global, February 24, 2020, https://www.spglobal.com/en/research-insights/market-insights/what-is-the-s-in-esg.

[4] Larry Fink, "Larry Fink's 2021 Letter to CEOs," BlackRock, 2021, https://www.blackrock.com/corporate/investor-relations/2021-larry-fink-ceo-letter.

[5] "Larry Fink on ESG, the Economy and the State of Democracy," transcript, WSJ Podcasts, October 18, 2023, https://www.wsj.com/podcasts/opinion-free-expression/larry-fink-on-esg-the-economy-and-the-state-of-democracy/f2e25649-e49b-4792-b025-ff4496d346f5.

[6] Martin Luther King Jr., "I Have a Dream" (speech, Washington, DC, August 28, 1963), American Rhetoric, https://www.americanrhetoric.com/speeches/mlkihaveadream.htm.

[7] Juliana Menasce, "Americans See Advantages and Challenges in Country's Growing Racial and Ethnic Diversity," Pew Research Center, May 8, 2019, https://www.pewresearch.org/social-trends/2019/05/08/americans-see-advantages-and-challenges-in-countrys-growing-racial-and-ethnic-diversity/?utm_source=link_newsv9&utm_campaign=item_317006&utm_medium=copy.

[8] "Online Survey among 1,600 Registered Voters," CRC Advisors,

NOTES

February 16–20, The Daily Caller, accessed June 5, 2024, 1, https://cdn01.dailycaller.com/wp-content/uploads/2023/03/Feb-16.pdf.

9   Students for Fair Admissions, Inc. v. President and Fellows of Harvard College, 600 U.S. 81 (2023), at 29, https://www.supreme-court.gov/opinions/22pdf/20-1199_hgdj.pdf.

10   Justin McCarthy, "Post–Affirmative Action, Views on Admissions Differ by Race," Gallup, January 16, 2024, https://news.gallup.com/poll/548528/post-affirmative-action-views-admissions-differ-race.aspx.

11   Andrew Prokop, "The Equity Wars: Equity Is Everywhere. But What Exactly Is It—and Why Is It So Controversial?," *Vox*, May 4, 2023, https://www.vox.com/policy/2023/5/4/23644810/equity-social-justice-equality-sanders-biden.

12   Kamala Harris (@KamalaHarris), "There's a big difference between equity and equality," X, November 1, 2020, 1:06 p.m., https://twitter.com/kamalaharris/status/1322963321994289154?lang=en.

13   Kate Sullivan, "Joe Biden Says He Will Pick Woman to Be His Vice President," CNN, updated March 15, 2020, https://www.cnn.com/2020/03/15/politics/joe-biden-woman-vice-president/index.html; Sarah Mucha, "Biden Says He Would Prefer a Person of Color or a Woman as His Vice President," CNN, updated August 30, 2019, https://www.cnn.com/2019/08/28/politics/joe-biden-potential-vp-pick/index.html.

14   End Wokeness (@EndWokeness), "Senator Bernie Sanders didn't know the difference between equity & equality. When he was told the difference (equal opportunity vs outcomes), he instantly rejected equity (outcomes)," X, January 16, 2024, 8:16 a.m., https://twitter.com/EndWokeness/status/1747246381683683833.

15   Ron Haskins and Isabel V. Sawhill, "Creating an Opportunity Society," Brookings, September 3, 2009, https://www.brookings.edu/books/creating-an-opportunity-society.

16   Price v. Valvoline, 23-20131 (5th Cir. 2023), at 9, 10, https://law.justia.com/cases/federal/appellate-courts/ca5/23-20131/23-20131-2023-12-18.html.

17   Elon Musk (@elonmusk), "'Diversity, Equity and Inclusion' are propaganda words for racism, sexism and other -isms [sic]. This is just as morally wrong as any other racism and sexism," X, December 15, 2023, 7:38 p.m., https://twitter.com/elonmusk/status/1735821713688940843?lang=en.

18   "Solzhenitsyn: Quotes"; "Talk: Aleksandr Solzhenitsyn."

19   End Wokeness (@EndWokeness), "Why has everything gone woke these days? ESG scores. Here is BlackRock CEO Larry Fink along with the CEO of AmEx explaining his desire to 'force behaviors' (2017)," X, June 4, 2023, 1:46 p.m., https://twitter.com/EndWokeness/status/1665414711188287489.

20   Voices for Freedom, "BlackRock's CEO and billionaire businessman Larry Fink on ESG. . . .," LinkedIn, June 2023, https://www.linkedin.com/posts/voices-for-freedom_blackrocks-ceo-and-billionaire-businessman-activity-7072013063649955840-wlEl.

21   Larry Fink, "Larry Fink's 2018 Letter to CEOs: A Sense of Purpose," BlackRock, 2018, https://www.blackrock.com/corporate/investor-relations/2018-larry-fink-ceo-letter.

22   Larry Fink, "Larry Fink's 2019 Letter to CEOs: Purpose & Profit," BlackRock, 2019, https://www.blackrock.com/corporate/investor-relations/2019-larry-fink-ceo-letter.

23   Larry Fink, "Larry Fink's 2021 Letter to CEOs," BlackRock, 2021, https://www.blackrock.com/corporate/investor-relations/2021-larry-fink-ceo-letter.

24   "BlackRock Investment Stewardship: Protecting Our Clients' Assets for the Long Term," BlackRock, 2020, 4, https://www.blackrock.com/corporate/literature/publication/blk-profile-of-blackrock-investment-stewardship-team-work.pdf.

25   Ibid., 3.

26   "Vanguard Investment Stewardship Insights," Vanguard, May 2021, no longer available at https://corporate.vanguard.com/content/dam/corp/advocate/investment-stewardship/pdf/perspectives-and-commentary/INVDEIS_052021.pdf, but screenshots can be viewed at https://onedrive.live.com/?authkey=%21AB2Ym74RdwNn26s&id=9E7E9E5515BD1287%2120542&cid=9E7E9E5515BD1287&parId=root&parQt=sharedby&o=OneUp.

27   Ibid.

28   Ibid.

29   "Insight: Asset Stewardship: Guidance on Diversity Disclosures
      and Practices," State Street Global Advisors, January 2022, 2,
      https://www.ssga.com/library-content/pdfs/asset-stewardship/
      racial-diversity-guidance-article.pdf.

30   Ibid, 2–4.

31   Ibid, 2.

32   "Asset Stewardship Report," State Street Global Advisors, May
      2023, https://www.ssga.com/us/en/intermediary/etfs/insights/
      asset-stewardship-report.

33   Alex Edmans, Caroline Flammer, and Simon Glossner, "Diversi-
      ty, Equity, and Inclusion: Finance Working Paper No. 913/2023,"
      European Corporate Governance Institute, September 2023, 29,
      https://papers.ssrn.com/sol3/papers.cfm?abstract_id=4426488..

34   Ibid., 1.

35   "Diversity, Equity& Inclusion," SVB (Silicon Valley Bank),
      November 2021, 5, https://www.svb.com/globalassets/library/
      uploadedfiles/dei-at-svb-november-2021.pdf

36   "Webinar: The Diversity, Equity & Inclusion Forum 2021," SVB
      (Silicon Valley Bank), December 15, 2021, https://www.svb.com/
      trends-insights/webinars/diversity-equity-inclusion-forum-2021.

37   "Environmental, Social, and Governance Report 2022, SVB (Sil-
      icon Valley Bank), 2022, 12, https://www.svb.com/globalassets/
      library/uploadedfiles/svb_environmental_social_governance_re-
      port_2022.pdf.

38   Tabby Kinder and Antoine Gara, "'It Is Not Cut-Throat like
      Goldman Sachs': SVB's Culture in Focus," *Financial Times*,
      March 16, 2023, https://www.ft.com/content/6e23a2fb-484e-
      418d-b309-bf558b3a6a17.

39   Ibid.

40   "We Pledge to ACT on Supporting More Inclusive Workplaces,"
      CEO Action for Diversity and Inclusion, accessed May 7, 2024,
      https://www.ceoaction.com/pledge.

41   "We're Leading to ACT ON Diversity and Inclusion," CEO
      Action for Diversity and Inclusion, accessed June 5, 2024, 34,

https://www.ceoaction.com/ceos/?page=34.

42   "General Information," Boeing, accessed May 7, 2024, https://www.boeing.com/company#general-information.

43   Clement Charpentreau, "Japan Airlines Boeing 777 Turns Back after Engine Failure," AeroTime Hub, December 4, 2020, https://www.aerotime.aero/articles/26620-japan-airlines-boeing-777-turns-back-after-engine-failure.

44   "Infrequent Inspection of Fan Blades Led to a United Jet Engine Breaking Up in 2021, Report Says," CBS News Colorado, September 9, 2023, https://www.cbsnews.com/colorado/news/infrequent-inspection-fan-blades-led-united-jet-engine-breaking-up-2021.

45   "The Boeing Company (BA): Major Holders," Yahoo!Finance, https://finance.yahoo.com/quote/BA/holders?fr=sycsrp_catchall.

46   Loren Thompson, "Boeing Releases First-Ever Diversity Report, Moves to Bolster Inclusion Efforts," *Forbes*, April 30, 2021, https://www.forbes.com/sites/lorenthompson/2021/04/30/boeing-releases-first-ever-diversity-report-moves-to-bolster-inclusion-efforts.

47   Ibid.

48   Ibid.

49   Ibid.

50   "2022 Annual Meeting of Shareholders: Proxy Summary," Boeing, March 11, 2022, 51, https://s2.q4cdn.com/661678649/files/doc_financials/2021/ar/Boeing-2022-Proxy-Statement.pdf.

51   Ibid.

52   Ibid.

53   "Global Equity, Diversity & Inclusion 2023 Report," Boeing, 2023, https://www.boeing.com/content/dam/boeing/boeingdotcom/principles/diversity-and-inclusion/assets/pdf/Boeing_GEDI_Report_FINAL.pdf.

54   Shannon Thaler, "Boeing Prioritizing Diversity and Inclusion over Flier Safety, Elon Musk Says after Near-Catastrophic Alaska Airlines Mishap," *New York Post*, January 11, 2024, https://nypost.com/2024/01/11/business/

elon-musk-rips-boeing-they-prioritized-dei-over-safety/amp;
Joe Cadotte, "All Boeing 737s Grounded after Alaska Airlines
Incident," January 6, 2024, Alaska's New Source, https://www.
alaskasnewssource.com/2024/01/06/65-boeing-737s-grounded-af-
ter-alaska-airlines-incident.

55   Elon Musk (@elonmusk), "Do you want to fly in an airplane where they prioritized DEI hiring over your safety?,"
X, January 10, 2024, 2:01 p.m., https://twitter.com/elon-
musk/status/1745158868676546609?ref_src=twsrc%5Etf-
w%7Ctwcamp%5Etweetembed%7Ctwterm%5E17451597851445
94547%7Ctwgr%5Edbca31d52d8e904a49c0531627a29c5d2a76f-
6f4%7Ctwcon%5Es2_&ref_url=https%3A%2F%2Fthepostmillen-
nial.com%2Felon-musk-says-people-will-die-due-to-dei-as-air-
lines-revealed-to-prioritize-diversity-hiring-over-safety.

56   Ibid.

57   Elon Musk (@elonmusk), "People will die due to DEI,"
X, January 10, 2024, 2:04 p.m., https://twitter.com/
elonmusk/status/1745159785144594547?ref_src=tws-
rc%5Etfw%7Ctwcamp%5Etweetembed%7Ctwter-
m%5E1745159785144594547%7Ctwgr%5E84000c950761d-
ca93e68c492c091caf60081c517%7Ctwcon%5Es1_&ref_
url=https%3A%2F%2Fwww.blackenterprise.
com%2Felon-musk-attacks-airlines-dei-efforts-prompting-cri-
ticism-from-civil-rights-leaders%2F.

58   Nicki Zink, "Trust in Boeing Continues to Dip, but It's Not
Impacting Airlines," Morning Consult, March 5, 2024, https://
pro.morningconsult.com/analysis/boeing-airlines-trust-
february-2024.

59   Andrew Afifian, "Is Boeing Prioritizing DEI Over Safety?," *Dallas
Express*, March 8, 2024, https://dallasexpress.com/business-
markets/is-boeing-prioritizing-dei-over-safety.

60   Sharon Terlep, "Boeing to Tie More of Employees' Incentive Pay
to Safety," *Wall Street Journal*, March 7, 2024, https://www.wsj.
com/business/boeing-to-tie-more-of-employees-pay-to-safety-
15c27813.

61   "Global Equity, Diversity & Inclusion Strategic Pillars & Goals,"

Boeing, accessed May 26, 2024, https://www.boeing.com/
content/dam/boeing/boeingdotcom/principles/diversity-and-
inclusion/assets/pdf/2023_GEDI_Strategy.pdf.

62 Eric Edholm, "Colin Kaepernick Explains Why He Won't Stand
during National Anthem," Y!Sports, August 27, 2016, https://
sports.yahoo.com/news/colin-kaepernick-explains-why-he-
wont-stand-during-national-anthem-145653015.html.

63 "Nike Sales Defy Kaepernick Ad Campaign Backlash," BBC, September 10, 2018, https://www.bbc.com/news/business-45472399.

64 "Nike 'Proud' of Kaepernick Campaign," BBC, September 25,
2018, https://www.bbc.com/news/business-45643845.

65 Khadeeja Safdar, "Meet the New Nike Boss: Trading Tech for
Air Jordans," *Wall Street Journal*, February 8, 2020, https://www.
wsj.com/articles/meet-the-new-nike-boss-trading-tech-for-air-
jordans-11581166802.

66 Jared Pope, "What DEI in the Workplace Means to LGBTQ
Employees, *Work Shield* (blog), June 8, 2021, https://workshield.
com/what-dei-in-the-workplace-means-to-lgbtq-employees.

67 "Insight: Asset Stewardship," 2.

68 "Corporate Equality Index 2023–2024," Human Rights Campaign, November 2023, https://www.hrc.org/resources/
corporate-equality-index?linkId=253550164.

69 Ibid.

70 Ibid.

71 "Diversity, Equity, and Inclusion," State Street Global Advisors,
2024, https://www.ssga.com/us/en/intermediary/ic/about-us/
careers/diversity-equity-and-inclusion.

72 Christopher F. Rufo (@realchrisrufo), "SCOOP: I've obtained
video from inside Disney's all-hands meeting about the Florida
parental rights bill. . . .," X, March 29, 2022, 5:03 p.m., https://
twitter.com/realchrisrufo/status/1508912865293619202?s=20&t=
wyv445jyzeM81sbM3S8uqg.

73 Janon Fisher, "Disney Executive Who Is the Mother of a Trans-
gender and a Pansexual Child Says She Wants at Least Half of
ALL Future Characters to Be LGBTQIA or Racial Minorities:
Theme Parks Are Now Banned from Saying 'Hello Boys and

Girls,'" *Daily Mail*, March 30, 2022, https://www.dailymail.co.uk/news/article-10666065/Disney-prez-says-mom-transgender-pansexual-children-wants-diverse-characters.html?ns_mchannel=rss&ns_campaign=1490&ito=1490.

74 Christopher F. Rufo (@realchrisrufo), "SCOOP: Disney diversity and inclusion manager Vivian Ware says the company has eliminated all mentions of 'ladies,' 'gentlemen,' 'boys,' and 'girls' in its theme parks. . . .," X, March 29, 2022, 6:41 p.m., https://twitter.com/realchrisrufo/status/1508937431520890888?ref_src=twsrc%5Etfw%7Ctwcamp%5Etweetembed%7Ctwterm%5E1508937431520890888%7Ctwgr%5E5b92a5735b41317d-ba2da049aa0f92fe7c87435f%7Ctwcon%5Es1_&ref_url=https%3A%2F%2Fd-19263040372762164426.ampproject.net%2F2308112021001%2Fframe.html.

75 "Disney Earns Top Score in HRC Foundation Corporate Equality Index," Human Rights Campaign, January 28, 2022, https://thewaltdisneycompany.com/disney-earns-top-score-in-hrc-foundation-corporate-equality-index/#:~:text=The%20Walt%20Disney%20Company%20proudly%20announces%20that%20for,policies%20and%20practices%20related%20to%20LGBTQ%2B%20workplace%20equality.

76 "ESG Reporting Center: 2023 Sustainability and Social Impact Report," The Walt Disney Company, 2023, https://impact.disney.com/esg-reporting.

77 "World of Belonging: Our Commitment to Diversity, Equity & Inclusion," The Walt Disney Company, accessed May 7, 2024, https://impact.disney.com/diversity-inclusion.

78 "Disney Employees' Open Letter in Favor of a Politically Neutral Disney," May 7, 2024, https://docs.google.com/forms/d/e/1FAIpQLSdueiXmPfww_2iQttbvfxTIcC7i-JOq5awsHNI2Q6X-W46UT7Q/viewform?pli=1.

79 Alexandra Canal, "'Spider-Man,' 'Super Mario Bros' Signal 'New Era' of Competition for Disney," Yahoo!Finance, June 30, 2023, https://finance.yahoo.com/news/spider-man-super-mario-bros-signal-new-era-of-competition-for-disney-194220682.html.

80 Caroline Reed, "The 4 Flops Of 2023 That Cost Disney $1

Billion," *Forbes*, August 4, 2023, https://www.forbes.com/sites/
carolinereid/2023/08/04/the-four-flops-of-2023-that-cost-
disney-1-billion/?sh=3720f24f3bed; Jasmine Kocon, "Bob Iger
Comments on Disney's 'Woke Agenda,' Says Creators Have 'Lost
Sight' of Goals," *Disney Food Blog*, accessed June 5, 2024, https://
www.disneyfoodblog.com/2023/11/29/bob-iger-comments-on-
disneys-woke-agenda-says-creators-have-lost-sight-of-goals/;
Lauren Williams, "Disney Director Issues Damning Warning
to Company over Politically Correct Priorities: Course Cor-
rection,'" GB News, May 2024, https://www.animayo.com/
noticias/NP_animayo_222.pdf; Jonathan Turley, "Happy
Birthday, Adam Smith: The Invisible Hand Just Slapped Disney,"
The Hill, November 25, 2023, https://thehill.com/opinion/fi-
nance/4326247-happy-birthday-adam-smith-the-invisible-hand-
just-slapped-disney.

81   "The Walt Disney Company Reports Third Quarter and Nine
Months and Earnings for Fiscal 2023," The Walt Disney Company, August 9, 2023, 5, https://thewaltdisneycompany.com/app/
uploads/2023/08/q3-fy23-earnings.pdf.

82   The Walt Disney Company, "United States Securities and
Exchange Commission Form 10-K: Annual Report 'Pursuant
to Section 13 or 15(d) and the Securities Exchange Act of 1934,"
October 18, 2023, https://www.sec.gov/ix?doc=/Archives/edgar/
data/0001744489/000174448923000216/dis-20230930.htm.

83   Jacob Passy, "Disney World Hasn't Felt This Empty in Years,"
Wall Street Journal, July 10, 2023, https://www.wsj.com/
articles/disney-world-crowds-universal-studios-florida-
36b0a579?mod=business_lead_pos5.

84   "Nationwide Issues Survey," The Trafalgar Group, Partnered with
Convention of States Action, 2022, https://www.thetrafalgar-
group.org/wp-content/uploads/2022/04/COSA-DisneyBusiness-
Full-Report-0410.pdf.

85   Aislinn Murphy, "Round 3 of Disney Job Cuts Starting," Fox
Business, May 23, 2023, https://www.foxbusiness.com/markets/
round-three-disney-job-cuts-starting?utm_campaign=Fidu-
ciary%20Focus&utm_source=hs_email&utm_medium=e-

mail&_hsenc=p2ANqtz-9bSoyAR7km4BtA6WW4Zy4p_Z8wBK-
SpqW6apoyL9n6UlOvYeHzGso6VWIL41uEQddi510cZ.

86 "Market Capitalization of Walt Disney (DIS)," Largest Companies by Market Cap, May 2024, https://companiesmarketcap.
com/walt-disney/marketcap.

87 Sarah Whitten, "Disney CEO Says Company Opposes 'Don't Say
Gay' Bill in Florida," CNBC, March 9, 2022, https://www.cnbc.
com/2022/03/09/disney-ceo-says-company-opposes-dont-say-
gay-law-in-florida.html.

88 "S&P 500®," S&P Dow Jones Indices, accessed June 5, 2024,
https://www.spglobal.com/spdji/en/indices/equity/sp-
500/#overview.

89 "Market Capitalization of Walt Disney."

90 The Walt Disney Company, "United States Securities and Exchange Commission Form 10-K."

91 Ibid.

92 "The Walt Disney Company (DIS)," MSN, accessed May 7,
2024, https://www.msn.com/en-us/money/watchlist?tab=Relat-
ed&id=a1r2z2&ocid=ansMSNMoney11&duration=1D&src=b_
fingraph&relatedQuoteId=a1r2z2&relatedSource=MlAl.

93 Harriet Agnew, "Investor Nelson Peltz: 'I'm Not Trying to Fire
Bob Iger, I Want to Help Him,'" *Financial Times*, March 22,
2024, https://www.ft.com/content/0a182c97-6af7-42a6-ad9f-
ae980562bb45.

94 Cara Lombardo and Lauren Thomas, "Nelson Peltz Got Crushed
by Disney. Can He Recover?," *Wall Street Journal*, April 17, 2024,
https://www.wsj.com/finance/investing/nelson-peltz-disney-
proxy-fight-586e1c5f.

95 Yael Halon, "Target CEO Says Woke Capitalism 'Great' for
Their Brand and 'the Right Thing for Society,'" Fox News, May
23, 2023, https://www.foxnews.com/media/target-ceo-woke-
capitalism-great-brand-right-thing-society.

96 Ibid; Paul du Quenoy, "Target Is the Latest Proof—Going Woke
Means Going Broke—Opinion," *Newsweek*, June 1, 2023, https://
www.newsweek.com/target-latest-proofgoing-woke-means-
going-broke-opinion-1803675.

97   Brian Flood, "Target Holds 'Emergency' Meeting over LGBTQ
      Merchandise in Some Stores to Avoid 'Bud Light Situation,'" Fox
      News, May 23, 2023, https://www.foxnews.com/media/target-
      holds-emergency-meeting-lgbtq-pride-merchandise-stores-
      avoid-bud-light-situation.

98   Halon, "Target CEO Says Woke Capitalism 'Great'"; du Quenoy,
      "Target Is the Latest Proof."

99   "Market Capitalization of Target (TGT)," CompaniesMarketCap,
      May 2024, https://companiesmarketcap.com/target/marketcap.

100   "Target Corporation (TGT)," MSN, accessed May 7, 2024,
      https://www.msn.com/en-us/money/stockdetails/fi-a246z2?ocid
      =ansMSNMoney11&id=a246z2.

101   Breck Dumas, "Modelo Topples Bud Light to Become America's
      Best-Selling Beer for the Year," Fox Business, August 23, 2023,
      https://www.foxbusiness.com/markets/modelo-topples-bud-
      light-americas-best-selling-beer-year.

102   "Market Capitalization of Anheuser-Busch Inbev (BUD)" Largest
      Companies by Market Capitalization, May 2024, https://compa-
      niesmarketcap.com/anheuser-busch-inbev/marketcap.

103   "S&P 500®."

104   Taylor Telford and Julian Mark, "DEI Is Getting a New Name.
      Can It Dump the Political Baggage?," *Washington Post*, May 5,
      2024, https://www.washingtonpost.com/business/2024/05/05/
      dei-affirmative-action-rebrand-evolution.

105   Ibid.

Chapter 4: The Environment, as a Tool

1   "Climate Change," PRI (Principles for Responsible Investment),
      accessed May 7, 2024, https://www.unpri.org/climate-change.

2   Roy Spencer, "Global Warming: Observations vs. Climate Mod-
      els," The Heritage Foundation, January 24, 2024, https://www.
      heritage.org/environment/report/global-warming-observations-
      vs-climate-models; Hannah Devlin, Ben Webster, and Phillipe
      Naughton, "Inconvenient Truth for Al Gore as His North Pole
      Sums Don't Add Up," *Times* (London), December 15, 2009,

https://www.thetimes.com/article/inconvenient-truth-for-al-gore-as-his-north-pole-sums-dont-add-up-bkt66olh5ls; James Freeman, "What Else Did Al Gore Get Wrong?," *Wall Street Journal*, July 25, 2017, https://www.wsj.com/articles/what-else-did-al-gore-get-wrong-1501021804; Samantha Chang, "John Kerry Humiliated as Climate Change Prediction Turns Out to Be Totally Wrong," *Western Journal*, April 9, 2021, https://www.westernjournal.com/john-kerry-humiliated-climate-change-prediction-turns-totally-wrong/; Jack Birle, "Birthday Blunders: Four Times 80-Year-Old John Kerry's Climate Warnings Have Fallen Flat, *Washington Examiner*, December 11, 2023, https://www.washingtonexaminer.com/news/2436361/birthday-blunders-four-times-80-year-old-john-kerrys-climate-warnings-have-fallen-flat.

3   "There Is No Climate Emergency," Global Climate Intelligence Group, August 14, 2023, https://clintel.org/wp-content/uploads/2023/08/WCD-version-081423.pdf.

4   Jonathan Weisman and Jazmine Ulloa, "As the Planet Cooks, Climate Stalls as a Political Issue," *New York Times*, July 17, 2022, https://www.nytimes.com/2022/07/17/us/politics/climate-change-manchin-biden.html.

5   Ibid; "849 United States Registered Voters," *New York Times/ Siena College Research Institute*, July 5–7, 2022, 3, https://scri.siena.edu/wp-content/uploads/2022/07/US0722-Crosstabs-SCRI071222.pdf.

6   "Nearly Half of Voters Would Consider a Third-Party Presidential Candidate In 2024," Quinnipiac University National Poll Finds; Majority Expect Climate Change to Negatively Affect World in Their Lifetime," Quinnipiac University Poll, July 19, 2023, https://poll.qu.edu/poll-release?releaseid=3876; "New Survey, Same Results: Americans Reject Carbon Dioxide Taxes in Favor of Affordable and Reliable Energy," American Energy Alliance, January 9, 2024, https://www.americanenergyalliance.org/2024/01/new-survey-same-results-americans-reject-carbon-dioxide-taxes-in-favor-of-affordable-and-reliable-energy.

7   Ibid.

8   "849 United States Registered Voters," 3.

9   Larry Fink, "Larry Fink's 2020 Letter to CEOs: A Fundamental Reshaping of Finance," BlackRock, 2020, https://www.blackrock.com/corporate/investor-relations/2020-larry-fink-ceo-letter.

10   Ibid.

11   Ibid.

12   Ibid.

13   Ibid.

14   BlackRock Reports First Quarter 2020 Diluted EPS of $5.15, or $6.60 as Adjusted," BlackRock, April 16, 2020, 4, https://s24.q4cdn.com/856567660/files/doc_financials/2020/Q1/BLK-1Q20-Earnings-Release.pdf.

15   "Larry Fink's 2020 Letter to CEOs."

16   "About the PRI," PRI (Principles for Responsible Investment), 2023, https://www.unpri.org/about-us/about-the-pri.

17   "Principles for Responsible Investment," BlackRock, September 9, 2022, https://www.blackrock.com/corporate/sustainability/pri-report.

18   "What Are the Principles of Responsible Investing?," PRI (Principles for Responsible Investment," accessed May 27, 2024, https://www.unpri.org/about-us/what-are-the-principles-for-responsible-investment?.

19   "Climate Change," PRI (Principles for Responsible Investment), accessed May 27, 2024, https://www.unpri.org/sustainability-issues/climate-change.

20   "Leading International Agencies Form Taskforce on Net Zero Policy to Further HLEG Recommendations," PRI (Principles for Responsible Investment), December 3, 2023, https://www.unpri.org/news-and-press/leading-international-agencies-form-taskforce-on-net-zero-policy-to-further-hleg-recommendations/11967.article.

21   "What are the Principles for Responsible Investment?"

22   "Fiduciary Duty in the 21st Century Final Report," PRI (Principles for Responsible Investment), October 22, 2019, https://www.unpri.org/fiduciary-duty/fiduciary-duty-in-the-21st-century-final-report/4998.article.

23   "Larry Fink's 2020 Letter to CEOs."

24   Larry Fink, "Larry Fink's 2018 Letter to CEOs: A Sense of Purpose," BlackRock, 2018, https://www.blackrock.com/corporate/investor-relations/2018-larry-fink-ceo-letter.

25   Mark O'Connell, "'Fire the Bastards!': The Great Defender of William Gaddis," *New Yorker*, February 17, 2012, https://www.newyorker.com/books/page-turner/fire-the-bastards-the-great-defender-of-william-gaddis.

26   "Larry Fink's 2020 Letter to CEOs."

27   Ibid.

28   Ibid.

29   This document has since been taken down, but it is referenced and quoted in Leon Kaye, "BlackRock Bluntly Tells Companies They're 'On Watch,'" Triple Pundit, July 16, 2020, https://www.triplepundit.com/story/2020/blackrock-ESG-watch/120916 and Declan Harty, "BlackRock Voted against Management at 53 Companies over Climate Concerns," S&P Global Market Intelligence, July 14, 2020, https://www.spglobal.com/marketintelligence/en/news-insights/latest-news-headlines/blackrock-voted-against-management-at-53-companies-over-climate-concerns-59426142.

30   Larry Fink, "Larry Fink's 2021 Letter to CEOs," BlackRock, 2021, https://www.blackrock.com/corporate/investor-relations/2021-larry-fink-ceo-letter.

31   Ibid.

32   Ibid.

33   Ibid.

34   Ibid.

35   Ibid.

36   Ibid.

37   Ibid.

38   Ibid.

39   "Larry Fink's 2020 Letter to CEOs."

40   "Larry Fink's 2021 Letter to CEOs."

41   End Wokeness (@EndWokeness), "Why has everything gone woke these days? ESG scores. Here is BlackRock CEO Larry Fink along with the CEO of AmEx explaining his desire to 'force behaviors' (2017)," X, June 4, 2023, 1:46 p.m., https://twitter.com/

EndWokeness/status/1665414711188287489.

42   Alastair Marsh and Jess Shankleman, "Vanguard, BlackRock Join Investors Pledging to Hit Net Zero," Bloomberg, March 29, 2021, https://www.bloomberg.com/news/articles/2021-03-29/vanguard-blackrock-join-investors-pledging-net-zero-emissions.

43   "The Net Zero Asset Managers Initiative," Net Zero Asset Managers (NZAM), accessed May 7, 2024, https://www.netzeroassetmanagers.org.

44   Mark Segal, "State Street Global Advisors Joins Net Zero Asset Managers Initiative," ESG Today, April 21, 2021, https://www.esgtoday.com/state-street-global-advisors-joins-net-zero-asset-managers-initiative.

45   "The Net Zero Asset Managers Commitment," Net Zero Asset Managers (NZAM), December 2021 https://www.netzeroassetmanagers.org/media/2021/12/NZAM-Commitment.pdf.

46   Justin Baer and Dawn Lim, "The Hedge-Fund Manager Who Did Battle with Exxon—and Won," *Wall Street Journal*, June 12, 2021, https://www.wsj.com/articles/the-hedge-fund-manager-who-did-battle-with-exxonand-won-11623470420.

47   "Profile: Jennifer Grancio: CEO, Engine No. 1," *Forbes*, 2022, https://www.forbes.com/profile/jennifer-grancio/?sh=4f74f3f45209.

48   "Engine No. 1 Releases White Paper Detailing Changing Energy Landscape in Response to ExxonMobil Investor Day Presentation," Business Wire, March 3, 2021, https://www.businesswire.com/news/home/20210303005822/en/Engine-No.-1-Releases-White-Paper-Detailing-Changing-Energy-Landscape-in-Response-to-ExxonMobil-Investor-Day-Presentation.

49   David G. Victor (in association with Engine No. 1), "Energy Transformations: Technology, Policy, Capital and the Murky Future of Oil and Gas," Reenergize Exxon, March 3, 2021, 4, https://reenergizexom.com/documents/Energy-Transformations-Technology-Policy-Capital-and-the-Murky-Future-of-Oil-and-Gas-March-3-2021.pdf.

50   "Letter to the Board of Directors," Reenergize Exxon, December 7, 2020, https://reenergizexom.com/materials/

letter-to-the-board-of-directors.

51   "Sustainability Report," ExxonMobil, 2021, 9, https://corporate. exxonmobil.com/-/media/Global/Files/sustainability-report/ publication/Sustainability-Report.pdf.

52   ExxonMobil, "ExxonMobil Reports Results for Fourth Quarter 2022 and Provides Perspective on Forward Plans," press release, February 2, 2021, https://corporate.exxonmobil.com/news/ news-releases/2021/0202_exxonmobil-reports-results-for-fourth-quarter-2020-and-provides-perspective-on-forward-plans.

53   "Engine No. 1 Releases White Paper."

54   "Letter to the Board of Directors."

55   Ibid.

56   "Letter to Shareholders," Reenergize Exxon, 2021, https://reenergizexom.com/materials/letter-to-shareholders.

57   "ExxonMobil 2121 Energy & Carbon Summary," ExxonMobil, 2021, 3. This document is not available online, but the pdf is in the possession of the author.

58   Matthew Johnston, "Top ExxonMobil Shareholders," Investopedia, updated September 13, 2022, https://www.investopedia. com/articles/insights/052416/top-3-exxon-mobil-shareholders-xom.asp.

59   ExxonMobil, "ExxonMobil Presentation Details Strategy to Grow Shareholder Value, Protect Dividend and Transition to Lower-Carbon Future," press release, April 27, 2021, https://corporate. exxonmobil.com/news/news-releases/2021/0427_exxonmobil-details-strategy-to-grow-shareholder-value-and-transition-to-lower-carbon-future.

60   Matt Phillips, "Exxon's Board Defeat Signals the Rise of Social-Good Activists," *New York Times*, June 9, 2021, https://www. nytimes.com/2021/06/09/business/exxon-mobil-engine-no1-activist.html.

61   Ibid.

62   BlackRock, "Investment Stewardship Vote Bulletin ExxonMobil Corporation," press release, May 26, 2021, https://www.blackrock.com/corporate/literature/press-release/blk-vote-bulletin-exxon-may-2021.pdf.

63 Ibid.

64 Phillips, "Exxon's Board Defeat Signals the Rise of Social-Good Activists."

65 Debbie Carlson, "Engine No. 1 Says Its New Representation on ExxonMobil's Board Has Already Scored a Win," MarketWatch, September 24, 2021, https://www.marketwatch.com/story/engine-no-1-says-its-new-representation-on-exxonmobils-board-has-already-scored-a-win-11632508131.

66 ExxonMobil, "ExxonMobil Announces Ambition for New Zero Greenhouse Gas Emissions by 2050," press release, January 18, 2022, https://corporate.exxonmobil.com/news/news-releases/2022/0118_exxonmobil-announces-ambition-for-net-zero-greenhouse-gas-emissions-by-2050.

67 Katrina Ang, "WTI Crude Oil Price Analysis for Feb. 23, 2022," FX Daily Report, February 23, 2022, https://fxdailyreport.com/wti-crude-oil-price-analysis-for-feb-23-2022.

68 "Crude Oil Prices Increased in First-Half 2022 and Declined in Second-Half 2022," EIA (U.S. Energy Information Administration), January 4, 2023, https://www.eia.gov/todayinenergy/detail.php?id=55079.

69 "WTI Crude Oil Prices—10 Year Daily Chart," MacroTrends, 2024, https://www.macrotrends.net/2516/wti-crude-oil-prices-10-year-daily-chart.

70 "Historical Price Lookup," ExxonMobil Corporation, November 5, 2021, https://ir.exxonmobil.com/historical-price-lookup?8c7bdd83-a726-4a84-b969-494be2477e47%5BXOM%5D%5Bdate_month%5D=11&8c7bdd83-a726-4a84-b969-494be2477e47%5BXOM%5D%5Bdate_day%5D=1&8c7bdd83-a726-4a84-b969-494be2477e47%5BX-OM%5D%5Bdate_year%5D=2021&url=.

71 "WTI Crude Oil Prices."

72 "Historical Price Lookup."

73 WTI Crude Oil Prices."

74 "Historical Price Lookup."

75 Zacks Equity Research, "Here's Why ExxonMobil (XOM) Stock Surges 74.3% in a Year," Yahoo!Finance, September 5, 2022,

https://finance.yahoo.com/news/heres-why-exxonmobil-xom-stock-125012416.html.

76   Kevin Crowley, "Exxon Sees $2.1 Billion Earnings Lift from Oil Prices, Refining," Bloomberg, October 4, 2023, https://www.bloomberg.com/news/articles/2023-10-04/exxon-sees-2-1-billion-earnings-lift-from-oil-prices-refining.

77   Kevin Crowley and Saijel Kishan, "Why One-Time Exxon Adversary's Board Picks Backed Mega Deal," Bloomberg, October 12, 2023, https://www.bloomberg.com/news/articles/2023-10-12/exxon-s-one-time-adversary-engine-no-1-unanimously-backed-deal.

78   "WTI Crude Oil Prices."

79   "Historical Price Lookup."

80   Philip van Doorn, "These 20 Stocks Were the Biggest Winners of 2022," MarketWatch, December 30, 2022, https://www.marketwatch.com/story/these-20-stocks-were-the-biggest-winners-of-2022-11672360388.

81   Larry Fink, "Larry Fink's 2022 Letter to CEOs: The Power of Capitalism," Blackrock, 2022, https://www.blackrock.com/corporate/investor-relations/larry-fink-ceo-letter.

Chapter 5: The War on Profit

1   Larry Fink, "Larry Fink's 2021 Letter to CEOs," BlackRock, 2021, https://www.blackrock.com/corporate/investor-relations/2021-larry-fink-ceo-letter.

2   Larry Fink, "Larry Fink's 2018 Letter to CEOs: A Sense of Purpose," BlackRock, 2018, https://www.blackrock.com/corporate/investor-relations/2018-larry-fink-ceo-letter.

3   Larry Fink, "Larry Fink's 2019 Letter to CEOs: Purpose & Profit," BlackRock, 2019, https://www.blackrock.com/corporate/investor-relations/2019-larry-fink-ceo-letter.

4   "Larry Fink's 2019 Letter to CEOs."

5   Ibid.

6   "Larry Fink's 2021 Letter to CEOs."

7   "Larry Fink's 2019 Letter to CEOs."

8   Ibid.

9   Ibid.

10   Ibid.

11   Larry Fink, "Larry Fink's 2022 Letter to CEOs: The Power of Capitalism," Blackrock, 2022, https://www.blackrock.com/corporate/investor-relations/larry-fink-ceo-letter.

12   Ibid.

13   Ibid.

14   "Oil Left in the World," Worldometer, accessed May 7, 2024, https://www.worldometers.info/oil/#:~:text=World%20Oil%20Consumption%201%20The%20world%20consumes%2035%2C442%2C913%2C090,people%29%20or%200.5%20gallons%20per%20capita%20per%20day.

15   "Larry Fink's 2018 Letter to CEOs."

16   "Larry Fink's 2019 Letter to CEOs."

17   "Larry Fink's 2021 Letter to CEOs."

18   "Larry Fink's 2019 Letter to CEOs."

19   Larry Fink, "Larry Fink's 2020 Letter to CEOs: A Fundamental Reshaping of Finance," Blackrock, 2020, https://www.blackrock.com/corporate/investor-relations/2020-larry-fink-ceo-letter.

20   "Larry Fink's 2021 Letter to CEOs."

21   "Thomas Jefferson Quotes," AZ Quotes, accessed May 6, 2024, https://www.azquotes.com/quote/559886#google_vignette; "Thomas Jefferson," Wikiquotes, accessed May 6, 2024, https://simple.wikiquote.org/wiki/Thomas_Jefferson.

Chapter 6: An Economic Miracle

1   Barack Obama, "Remarks by the President in Conversation on Poverty at Georgetown University," White House, May 12, 2015, https://obamawhitehouse.archives.gov/the-press-office/2015/05/12/remarks-president-conversation-poverty-georgetown-university.

2   "Angus Maddison 1926–2010," University of Groningen, November 25, 2021, https://www.rug.nl/ggdc/historicaldevelopment/maddison/original-maddison?lang=en.

NOTES

3   "Global GDP over the Long Run," Our World in Data, updated January 4, 2024, https://ourworldindata.org/grapher/global-gdp-over-the-long-run. "Data adapted from World Bank, Bolt and van Zanden, Angus Madison."

4   Max Roser et al., "Economic Growth," Our World in Data, 2023, https://ourworldindata.org/economic-growth.

5   Jeff Desjardins, "Over 2,000 Years of Economic History in One Chart," Visual Capitalist, September 8, 2017, https://www.visual-capitalist.com/2000-years-economic-history-one-chart.

6   Derek Thompson, "The Economic History of the Last 2000 Years: Part II," *The Atlantic*, June 20, 2012, https://www.theatlan-tic.com/business/archive/2012/06/the-economic-history-of-the-last-2000-years-part-ii/258762.

7   "Jonathan Haidt—Thomas Cooley Professor of Ethical Leader-ship," NYU/Stern, accessed May 7, 2024, https://www.stern.nyu.edu/faculty/bio/jonathan-haidt.

8   Jonathan Haidt, "How Capitalism Changes Conscience," Center for Humans & Nature, September 28, 2015, https://humansand-nature.org/how-capitalism-changes-conscience.

9   Ibid.

10 Thomas Jefferson to Thomas Mann Randolph, May 30, 1790, https://www.adamsmithworks.org/documents/1776-and-all-that-thomas-jefferson-on-adam-smith-1.

11 "GDP per Capita, 1898," Our World in Data, accessed May 7, 2024, https://ourworldindata.org/grapher/gdp-per-capita-maddi son?tab=chart&country=~NLD#explore-the-data

12 "GDP per Capita, 1000 to 2018," Our World in Data, accessed May 7, 2024, https://ourworldindata.org/grapher/gdp-per-capita-maddison?tab=chart&country=GBR~Western+Europe+%28MP D%29~USA#explore-the-data.

13 "Western Europe's Post–WWII Economies," Statista, accessed May 7, 2024, https://www.statista.com/study/72513/western-europe-s-post-wwii-economies.

14 Gregory Gethard, "The German Economic Miracle Post WWII," Investopedia, updated August 30, 2023, https://www.investope-dia.com/articles/economics/09/german-economic-miracle.asp.

15   "Ludwig Erhard," Ludwig Erhard Zentrum, accessed May 7, 2024, https://www.ludwig-erhard-zentrum.de/en/ludwig-erhard.

16   Robert A. Peterson, "Origins of the German Economic Miracle," FEE (Foundation for Economic Education)," December 1, 1988, https://fee.org/articles/origins-of-the-german-economic-miracle.

17   "Golden Age of Capitalism," United Nations Department for Economic and Social Affairs Economic Analysis, August 23, 2017, https://www.un.org/development/desa/dpad/tag/golden-age-of-capitalism.

18   Lucien Ellington, "Learning from the Japanese Economy," SPICE (Stanford Program on International and Cross-Cultural Education)," updated and revised September 2004, https://spice.fsi.stanford.edu/docs/learning_from_the_japanese_economy.

19   Ibid.

20   "Average Annual GDP Growth in the U.S., Japan and Europe in the Periods 1950–73 and 1973–87," Statista, accessed May 7, 2024, https://www.statista.com/statistics/1234645/gdp-growth-us-japan-europe-1950-1987.

21   Angus Maddison, "Development Center Studies: The World Economy," OECD (Organization for Economic Co-operation and Development) Publishing, accessed June 5, 2024, 185, https://www.stat.berkeley.edu/~aldous/157/Papers/world_economy.pdf.

22   Ibid., 264.

23   Ibid., 279.

24   Ibid., 185.

25   Ibid., 278.

26   Ibid, 185.

27   David M. Levy and Sandra J. Peart, "Soviet Growth and American Textbooks: An Endogenous Past," *Journal of Economic Behavior & Organization* 78, nos. 1–2 (April 2011), https://www.sciencedirect.com/science/article/abs/pii/S0167268111000114?via%3Dihub.

28   Ian Harvey, "The Nobel Economist Who Predicted the Soviet Economy Would Overtake the U.S.," The Vintage News, August 23, 2018, https://www.thevintagenews.com/2018/08/23/

soviet-gnp.

29   "Paul A. Samuelson," MIT Press, accessed May 7, 2024, https://
     mitpress.mit.edu/author/paul-a-samuelson-2381.

30   Phillip W. Magness, "The Soviet Economy Was Not Growing; It
     Was Dying," AIER (American Institute for Economic Research),
     January 10, 2020, https://www.aier.org/article/the-soviet-
     economy-was-not-growing-it-was-dying.

31   Gary North, "Paul Samuelson on the Soviet Economy (1989),"
     Gary North's Specific Answers, July 29, 2015, https://www.
     garynorth.com/public/14098.cfm.

32   Margaret Thatcher (@realmrsthatcher), "Countries are not rich
     in proportion to their natural resources. If they were Russia
     would now be the richest country in the world . . . but they
     have not had an enterprise economy," X, May 2, 2022, 1:30 p.m.,
     https://twitter.com/realmrsthatcher/status/1521180216978067456.

33   "2018 Index of Economic Freedom," Heritage Foundation,
     February 2, 2018, 26, http://www.iberglobal.com/files/2018/heri-
     tage_2018.pdf.

34   "2018 Index of Economic Freedom," 21.

35   "GDP per Capita (Constant 2015 US$)," World Bank, accessed
     May 7, 2024, https://data.worldbank.org/indicator/NY.GDP.
     PCAP.KD?most_recent_value_desc=false.

36   "Gross Domestic Product 2022," World Bank, accessed May 7,
     2024, 1, https://databankfiles.worldbank.org/public/ddpext_
     download/GDP.pdf.

37   Andrew Szamosszegi and Cole Kyle, "An Analysis of State-
     Owned Enterprises and State Capitalism in China," U.S.-China
     Economic and Security Review Commission, October 26, 2011,
     1, https://static1.squarespace.com/static/5e41c6f5227c7b05e81b-
     b87a/t/5ebc4f41cb51d10a41c54989/1589399365069/AZS-CK-
     China-SOE.pdf.

38   "China's Economic Rise: History, Trends, Challenges, and Impli-
     cations for the United States," Congressional Research Service,
     updated June 25, 2019, https://crsreports.congress.gov/product/
     pdf/RL/RL33534.

39   "China GDP Per Capita 1960–2024," MacroTrends, 2024, https://

www.macrotrends.net/global-metrics/countries/CHN/china/
gdp-per-capita.

[40] Szamosszegi and Kyle, "An Analysis."

[41] "GDP per Capita (Current US$)—United States," World Bank, accessed May 7, 2024, https://data.worldbank.org/indicator/ NY.GDP.PCAP.CD?locations=US.

[42] "GDP per Capita (Current US$)—China," World Bank, accessed May 7, 2024, https://data.worldbank.org/indicator/NY.GDP. PCAP.CD?locations=CN.

[43] "GDP per Capita (Current US$)—United States."

[44] "GDP per Capita (Current US$)—European Union," World Bank, accessed May 7, 2024, https://data.worldbank.org/indica-tor/NY.GDP.PCAP.CD?locations=EU.

[45] "GDP per Capita (Current US$)—Japan," World Bank, accessed May 7, 2024, https://data.worldbank.org/indicator/NY.GDP. PCAP.CD?locations=JP.

[46] Barry Nielsen, "The Lost Decade: Lessons from Japan's Real Estate Crisis," Investopedia, updated January 14, 2022, https://www. investopedia.com/articles/economics/08/japan-1990s-credit-crunch-liquidity-trap.asp.

[47] Adam Smith, *The Theory of Moral Sentiments* (London and Edinburgh: Andrew Millar, Alexander Kincaid, and J. Bell, 1759), https://oll.libertyfund.org/quotes/adam-smith-on-social-change-and-the-man-of-system-1759.

[48] Tanner Greer, "Xi Jinping in Translation: China's Guiding Ideology," Palladium, May 31, 2019, https://www.palladiummag. com/2019/05/31/xi-jinping-in-translation-chinas-guiding-ideology.

[49] Ibid. Emphasis in the original.

[50] "Reassessing the Role of State Ownership in China's Economy," SCCEI (Stanford Center on China's Economy and Institutions), updated January 15, 2024, https://sccei.fsi.stanford.edu/china-briefs/reassessing-role-state-ownership-chinas-economy.

[51] Hony Yu, "Reform of State-Owned Enterprises in China: The Chinese Communist Party Strikes Back," *Asian Studies Review* 43, no. 1 (May 2019), https://www.tandfonline.com/doi/full/10.10

80/10357823.2019.1590313.

52   "Xi Vows 'No Mercy' as He Deepens Graft Fight in Key Sectors," Bloomberg, January 8, 2024, https://www.bloomberg.com/news/articles/2024-01-08/xi-vows-to-deepen-china-s-sweeping-anti-corruption-crackdown.

53   Chad de Guzman, "China Appears to Choose National Security over Foreign Investment," *Time*, July 7, 2023, https://time.com/6292785/china-foreign-investment-national-security-revised-espionage-business-consultants.

54   Laura He, "Detained, Missing, or under Investigation: Business Leaders in China Face an 'Aggressive' Crackdown," CNN, November 10, 2023, https://www.cnn.com/2023/11/10/business/china-business-leaders-crackdown-intl-hnk/index.html.

55   Ibid.

56   Cheng Leng, "Foreign Direct Investment in China Falls to Lowest Level in Decades," *Financial Times*, February 19, 2024, https://www.ft.com/content/bcb1d331-5d8e-4cac-811e-eac7d9448486.

57   George Calhoun, "What Really Happened to Jack Ma?," *Forbes*, June 24, 2021, https://www.forbes.com/sites/georgecalhoun/2021/06/24/what-really-happened-to-jack-ma/?sh=789d69037c7e.

58   Sneha Saha, "Where Is Jack Ma? Not in China Anymore, He Is Out of the Country," *India Today*, November 30, 2022, https://www.indiatoday.in/technology/news/story/where-is-jack-ma-not-in-china-anymore-he-is-out-of-the-country-2303663-2022-11-30.

59   Calhoun, "What Really Happened?"

60   Laura He, "China Is Trying to End Its 'Epic' Property Crisis. The Hard Work Is Just Beginning," CNN, May 21, 2024, https://www.cnn.com/2024/05/21/economy/china-property-crisis-stimulus-challenges-intl-hnk/index.html.

61   Robyn Mak, "China's Overcapacity Is Here to Stay," Reuters, April 9, 2024, https://www.reuters.com/breakingviews/chinas-overcapacity-is-here-stay-2024-04-09.

62   "China's High-Stakes Struggle to Defy Demographic Disaster,"

The Economist, April 9, 2024, https://www.economist.com/
china/2024/04/09/chinas-high-stakes-struggle-to-defy-
demographic-disaster.

63 Charlie Campbell, "China's Ageing Population Is a Major Concern. But Its Youth May Be an Even Bigger Problem," *Time*, June
6, 2023, https://time.com/6284994/china-youth-unemployment-
aging-demographics.

64 Evelyn Chang, "China's Consumer Spending Isn't Roaring Back
to Pre-pandemic Levels Yet," CNBC, October 11, 2023, https://
www.cnbc.com/2023/10/11/chinas-consumer-spending-isnt-
growing-as-fast-as-it-did-pre-pandemic.html.

65 Engen Tham, Xie Yu, and Ziyi Tang, "China's Debt-Laden Local
Governments Pose Challenges to Economic Growth, Financial Situation," Reuters, March 10, 2023, https://www.reuters.
com/world/china/debt-laden-local-governments-pose-fresh-
challenges-chinas-growth-financial-2023-03-10.

66 Joe Cash, "China's Trade Slumps, Threatening Recovery Prospects," Reuters, August 8, 2023, https://www.reuters.com/world/
china/chinas-july-exports-imports-fall-much-faster-than-
expected-2023-08-08.

67 Eugenio Cerutti, Gita Gopinath, and Adil Mohommad, "The
Impact of US-China Trade Tensions," *IMF Blog*, May 23, 2019,
https://www.imf.org/en/Blogs/Articles/2019/05/23/blog-the-
impact-of-us-china-trade-tensions.

68 Sun Yu, "Chinese Economists Told Not to Be Negative as Rebound Falters," *Financial Times*, August 5, 2023, https://www.
ft.com/content/b2e0ad77-3521-4da9-8120-1f0c1fdd98f8.

69 Eswar S. Prasad, "China Stumbles but Is Unlikely to Fall," International Monetary Fund, December 2023, https://www.imf.
org/en/Publications/fandd/issues/2023/12/China-bumpy-path-
Eswar-Prasad.

70 William Pesek, "China's $7 Trillion Crash Masks the Really Bad
News," *Forbes*, February 9, 2024, https://www.forbes.com/sites/
williampesek/2024/02/09/chinas-7-trillion-crash-masks-the-
really-bad-news/?sh=4403028c5359.

71 Edward White, "Chinese Companies Revive Mao Zedong-Era

Militias," *Financial Times*, February 19, 2024, https://www.
ft.com/content/d6b2e4d6-2f84-4ef9-bf99-10d76d92d045.

72   "CNBC Transcript: JPMorgan Chase Chairman & CEO Jamie
Dimon Speaks with CNBC's 'Squawk Box' from the World
Economic Forum in Davos, Switzerland Today," CNBC, January
17, 2024, https://www.cnbc.com/2024/01/17/cnbc-transcript-
jpmorgan-chase-chairman-ceo-jamie-dimon-speaks-with-
cnbcs-squawk-box-from-the-world-economic-forum-in-davos-
switzerland-today.html.

73   Obama, "Remarks by the President in Conversation on Poverty."

74   Max Roser, "The Short History of Global Living Conditions and
Why It Matters That We Know It," Our World in Data, December
14, 2016, https://ourworldindata.org/a-history-of-global-liv-
ing-conditions.

75   Ibid.

76   Ibid.

77   Ibid.

78   Global Stats, "World Population—History & Projection
(1820–2100)," YouTube, January 16, 2021, https://www.bing.com/
videos/riverview/relatedvideo?q=what+was+the+world+pop-
ulation+in+1820&mid=7D02979117D1A09EB3887D-
02979117D1A09EB388&FORM=VIRE.

79   Michail Moatsos, "Long-Run Trends and Confidence Intervals in
the Cost of Basic Needs and Global Poverty: A Ballpark Approach," Munich Personal RePEc Archive, May 10, 2022, https://
mpra.ub.uni-muenchen.de/113035/1/MPRA_paper_113035.pdf.

80   Global Stats, "World Population."

81   Roser, "The Short History of Global Living Conditions."

82   "Understanding Poverty," World Bank, accessed May 7, 2024,
https://www.worldbank.org/en/understanding-poverty.

83   Roser, "The Short History of Global Living Conditions."

84   Thanks to Jeff Chasney, the former Chief Information Officer for
CKE Restaurants, Inc., and a good friend, for his help compiling
and preparing the charts in this chapter.

85   Roser, "The Short History of Global Living Conditions."

86   "Origin of "a Rising Tide Lifts All Boats," English Language

& Usage, updated July 12, 2020, https://english.stackex-change.com/questions/230520/origin-of-a-rising-tide-lifts-all-boats#:~:text=The%20aphorism%20%22a%20rising%20tide%20lifts%20all%20boats%22,he%20was%20inaugurating%20was%20a%20pork%20barrel%20project.

87   Roser, "The Short History of Global Living Conditions."

88   Ibid.

89   Ibid.

90   Ibid.

91   Adam Smith, *An Inquiry into the Nature and Causes of the Wealth of Nations* (London: W. Strahan and T. Cadell, 1776), https://fee.org/articles/adam-smith-on-what-it-means-to-flourish.

Chapter 7: The Resistance

1   Michel Foucault, *The History of Sexuality, Volume 1: An Introduction*, trans. Robert Hurley (New York: Pantheon, 1978), 125–26, https://www.goodreads.com/quotes/337405-where-there-is-power-there-is-resistance.

2   Klaus Schwab, "Shaping the Fourth Industrial Revolution," Project Syndicate, January 11, 2016, https://www.project-syndicate.org/commentary/fourth-industrial-revolution-human-development-by-klaus-schwab-2016-01.

3   BBC Monitoring and BBC Reality Check, "What Is the Great Reset—and How Did It Get Hijacked by Conspiracy Theories?," BBC, June 23, 2021, https://www.bbc.com/news/blogs-trending-57532368?_hsenc=p2AN-qtz-8zETogFHmCE4bSQjdlV7lepwBVX4THN2mVdZjC-CDm7SXY6Z9W-F6mdt-CnvQnGSqaKfSj9.

4   Klaus Schwab, "What Kind of Capitalism Do We Want?," Project Syndicate, December 2, 2019, https://www.project-syndicate.org/commentary/stakeholder-capitalism-new-metrics-by-klaus-schwab-2019-11.

5   Schwab, "What Kind of Capitalism?"

6   "Business Roundtable Redefines the Purpose of a Corporation to Promote 'An Economy That Serves All Americans,'" Business

Roundtable, August 19, 2019, https://www.businessround-table.org/business-roundtable-redefines-the-purpose-of-a-corporation-to-promote-an-economy-that-serves-all-americans.

7   Ibid.

8   David Gelles and David Yaffe-Bellany, "Shareholder Value Is No Longer Everything, Top C.E.O.s Say," *New York Times*, August 19, 2019, https://www.nytimes.com/2019/08/19/business/business-roundtable-ceos-corporations.html.

9   Ibid.

10   Council of Institutional Investors, "Council of Institutional Investors Responds to Business Roundtable Statement on Corporate Purpose," press release, August 19, 2019, https://www.cii.org/files/about_us/press_releases/2019/08_19_19%20BRT%20response_finalx.pdf.

11   Ibid.

12   Ibid.

13   Ibid.

14   Ibid.

15   Larry Fink, "Larry Fink's 2020 Letter to CEOs: A Fundamental Reshaping of Finance," BlackRock, 2020, https://www.blackrock.com/corporate/investor-relations/2020-larry-fink-ceo-letter.

16   Ibid.

17   "Johnson & Johnson (J&J): Major Holders," Yahoo!Finance, accessed May 30, 2024, https://finance.yahoo.com/quote/JNJ/holders.

18   Justin Danhoff, "Business Roundtable Becomes One Bloated Bullseye," *The Hill*, August 28, 2019, https://thehill.com/opinion/finance/458841-business-roundtable-becomes-one-bloated-bullseye.

19   "Our Mission: To Restore an Economic Consensus That Emphasizes the Importance of Family, Community, and Industry to the Nation's Liberty and Prosperity," American Compass, accessed May 30, 2024, https://americancompass.org/about.

20   Patrick Deneen and Andy Puzder, "The Corporate Obligations Debate," American Compass, July 8, 2020, https://americancompass.org/corporate-obligations-debate.

21 "Joe Biden Speech Transcript on Economic Recovery Plan July 9," *Rev* (blog), July 9, 2020, https://www.rev.com/blog/transcripts/joe-biden-speech-transcript-on-economic-recovery-plan-july-9.

22 Andy Puzder, "Biden's Assault on 'Shareholder Capitalism,'" *Wall Street Journal*, August 17, 2020, https://www.wsj.com/articles/bidens-assault-on-shareholder-capitalism-11597705153.

23 Karl Marx, *Das Kapital. Kritik der politischen Oekonomie*, vol. 1, book 1 (Hamburg: Verlag von Otto Meissner and New York: L. W. Schmidt, 1867).

24 Stephen R. Soukup, *The Dictatorship of Woke Capital: How Political Correctness Captured Big Business* (New York: Encounter Books, 2021).

25 Barton Swaim, "The Best Books of 2021: Politics," *Wall Street Journal*, December 10, 2021, https://www.wsj.com/articles/the-best-books-of-2021-politics-political-history-founding-fathers-supreme-court-woke-corporations-11639155591.

26 Fiduciary Duties, 29 U.S. Code § 1104, 1974, https://www.law.cornell.edu/uscode/text/29/1104.

27 History of EBSA and ERISA," U.S. Department of Labor, accessed May 7, 2024, https://www.dol.gov/agencies/ebsa/about-ebsa/about-us/history-of-ebsa-and-erisa.

28 "Fiduciary Responsibilities," U.S. Department of Labor, accessed May 7, 2024, https://www.dol.gov/general/topic/retirement/fiduciaryresp.

29 Eugene Scalia, "Retirees' Security Trumps Other Social Goals," *Wall Street Journal*, June 23, 2020, https://www.wsj.com/articles/retirees-security-trumps-other-social-goals-11592953329?mod=article_inline.

30 Larry Fink, "Larry Fink's 2018 Letter to CEOs: A Sense of Purpose," BlackRock, 2018, https://www.blackrock.com/corporate/investor-relations/2018-larry-fink-ceo-letter.

31 Scalia, "Retirees' Security."

32 Ibid.

33 Ibid.

34 Ibid.

35   "Larry Fink's 2018 Letter to CEOs."

36   Scalia, "Retirees' Security."

37   "Financial Factors in Selecting Plan Investments: A Rule by the Employee Benefits Security Administration," *Federal Register*, November 13, 2020, https://www.federalregister.gov/documents/2020/11/13/2020-24515/financial-factors-in-selecting-plan-investments.

38   Ibid.

39   Ibid.

40   Ibid.

41   "The Ties That Bind: BlackRock and Biden," Nicollet Invest Management, Inc., July 21, 2021, https://www.nicolletinvest.com/navigator/the-ties-that-bind-blackrock-and-biden.

42   "Prudence and Loyalty in Selecting Plan Investments and Exercising Shareholder Rights: A Rule by the Employee Benefits Security Administration," *Federal Register*, December 1, 2022, https://www.federalregister.gov/documents/2022/12/01/2022-25783/prudence-and-loyalty-in-selecting-plan-investments-and-exercising-shareholder-rights.

43   U.S. Department of Labor, "US Department of Labor Announces Final Rule to Remove Barriers to Considering Environmental, Social, Governance Factors in Plan Investments," press release, November 22, 2022, https://www.dol.gov/newsroom/releases/ebsa/ebsa20221122.

44   Joe Manchin, "Manchin Votes for Bipartisan Challenge to Biden Rule Politicizing Americans' 401Ks," press release, March 1, 2023, https://www.manchin.senate.gov/newsroom/press-releases/manchin-votes-for-bipartisan-challenge-to-biden-rule-politicizing-americans-401ks.

45   Ibid.

46   "Biden Uses First Veto to Defend Rule on ESG Investing," Reuters, March 20, 2023, https://www.reuters.com/business/sustainable-business/biden-vetoes-resolution-block-labor-dept-rule-esg-investing-2023-03-20.

47   "Prudence and Loyalty in Selecting Plan Investments."

48   Texas Senate Bill 13, 87th Legislature, September 1, 2021, https://

legiscan.com/TX/bill/SB13/2021.

49   "TPPF: Bill to End Energy Discrimination Sent to Governor's Desk," Texas Public Policy Foundation, May 30, 2021, https://www.texaspolicy.com/press/tppf-bill-to-end-energy-discrimination-sent-to-governors-desk.

50   Definitions, Tex. Gov't Code § 809.001, 87th Legislature, September 1, 2021, https://casetext.com/statute/texas-codes/government-code/title-8-public-retirement-systems/subtitle-a-provisions-generally-applicable-to-public-retirement-systems/chapter-809-prohibition-on-investment-in-financial-companies-that-boycott-certain-energy-companies/subchapter-a-general-provisions/section-809001-definitions.

51   Ibid.

52   Ken Paxton, "Advisory on Texas Law Prohibiting Contracts and Investments with Entities That Discriminate against Firearm Entities or Boycott Energy Companies or Israel," Texas Attorney General, October 18, 2023, 5, https://www.texasattorneygeneral.gov/sites/default/files/images/executive-management/OAG%20advisory%20on%20SB%2013%20and%2019%2010.18.23.pdf.

53   Texas Comptroller of Public Accounts, "Texas Comptroller Glenn Hegar Announces List of Financial Companies that Boycott Energy Companies," press release, August 24, 2022, https://comptroller.texas.gov/about/media-center/news/20220824-texas-comptroller-glenn-hegar-announces-list-of-financial-companies-that-boycott-energy-companies-1661267815099.

54   "Purchasing: Divestment Statute Lists," Texas Comptroller of Public Accounts, June–December 2023, https://comptroller.texas.gov/purchasing/publications/divestment.php.

55   "Texas Comptroller Glenn Hegar Announces List of Financial Companies."

56   Ibid.

57   Texas Comptroller of Public Accounts, "Texas Comptroller Glenn Hegar Announces Update to List of Financial Companies that Boycott Energy Companies," press release, November 1, 2023, https://comptroller.texas.gov/about/media-center/news/20231101-texas-comptroller-glenn-hegar-announces-up-

date-to-list-of-financial-companies-that-boycott-energy-compa-
nies-1698777763111.

58   "Purchasing: Divestment Statute Lists."

59   Silla Bush and Shelly Hagan, "BlackRock Tells Texas It Supports
Investments in Oil and Gas (2)," Bloomberg, May 19, 2022,
https://news.bloomberglaw.com/esg/blackrock-tells-texas-it-
supports-investments-in-oil-and-gas-1.

60   Catherine Clifford, "Texas Accuses 10 Financial Companies,
including BlackRock, of 'Boycotting' Energy Companies and
Orders State Pension Funds to Divest from Holdings," CNBC,
August 25, 2022, https://www.cnbc.com/2022/08/25/texas-says-
10-companies-including-blackrock-boycotting-energy-.html.

61   BlackRock, "BlackRock Investment Stewardship: Vote Bulletin:
ExxonMobil Corporation," press release, May 26, 2021, https://
www.blackrock.com/corporate/literature/press-release/blk-vote-
bulletin-exxon-may-2021.pdf.

62   Allie Morris, "Texas' Teacher Pension Fund Shed $500M in
BlackRock Investments over Fossil Fuel Law," *Dallas Morning
News*, March 10, 2023, https://www.dallasnews.com/news/
politics/2023/03/10/texas-teacher-pension-fund-shed-500m-in-
blackrock-investments-over-fossil-fuel-law.

63   Aaron Kinsey (@AaronKinseyTX), "Today, Texas Permanent School Fund leadership delivered an official notice to
global asset manager BlackRock terminating its financial
management of approximately $8.5 billion. . . .," X, March 19,
2024, 10:10 a.m., https://twitter.com/AaronKinseyTX/sta-
tus/1770090460935020835.

64   "City Shuts Once-Envied Muni Business," InvestmentNews,
December 15, 2023, https://www.investmentnews.com/industry-
news/news/citi-shuts-once-envied-muni-business-247173.

65   "Navigating State Regulation of ESG," Ropes & Gray, February
28, 2024, https://www.ropesgray.com/en/sites/navigating-state-
regulation-of-esg.

66   Andy Puzder and Diane Black, "Who Really Pays for ESG Investing?," *Wall Street Journal*, May 12, 2021, https://www.wsj.com/
articles/who-really-pays-for-esg-investing-11620858462?st=fougg

oy87a4wayx&reflink=article_email_share.

67   "Larry Fink's 2018 Letter to CEOs."

68   Jonathan Williams et al., "Unaccountable and Unaffordable, 7th
      Edition," American Legislative Exchange Council, September
      30, 2023, https://alec.org/publication/unaccountable-and-
      unaffordable-7th-edition.

69   Scalia, "Retirees' Security."

70   Ashley K. Dunning, "Fiduciary Duties of Public Retirement
      System Trustees: Presentation to the CalPERS Board of Admin-
      istrators," Nossaman, January 17, 2023, 8, https://www.calpers.
      ca.gov/docs/board-agendas/202301/full/CalPERS-Fiduciary-
      Principles-to-Guide-Public-Retirement-Fund-Trustees_a.
      pdf#:~:text=%E2%97%BC%20Under%20the%20California%20
      Constitution%20%28Article%20XVI%2C%20Section,of%20
      providing%20benefits%20to%2C%20participants%20and%20
      their%20beneficiaries.

71   Mitzner v. Jarcho, 44 N.Y.2d 39 (1978), 3, https://casetext.com/
      case/mitzner-v-jarcho-1.

72   "Comment Letters & Issues," SFOF (State Financial Officers
      Foundation), May 25, 2021–April 18, 2024, https://sfof.com/
      issues.

73   "State Government Employee Retirement Protection Act,"
      American Legislative Exchange Council, August 28, 2023, https://
      alec.org/model-policy/state-government-employee-retirement-
      protection-act.

74   "State Pension Fiduciary Duty Act," Heritage Foundation,
      accessed May 7, 2024, https://www.heritage.org/article/state-
      pension-fiduciary-duty-act.

75   "State Government Employee Retirement Protection Act"; "State
      Pension Fiduciary Duty Act."

76   "State Government Employee Retirement Protection Act."

77   "State Pension Fiduciary Duty Act."

78   Larry Fink, "Larry Fink's 2020 Letter to CEOs: A Fundamental
      Reshaping of Finance," BlackRock, 2020, https://www.blackrock.
      com/corporate/investor-relations/2020-larry-fink-ceo-letter.

79   "Navigating State Regulation of ESG."

Chapter 8: The Pressure Intensifies

1 Thomas Jefferson to Dupont de Nemours, April 24, 1816, https://founders.archives.gov/documents/Jefferson/03-09-02-0471.

2 Ernest Hemingway, *The Sun Also Rises* (New York: Charles Scribner's Sons, 1926), 141, https://www.google.com/books/edition/The_Sun_Also_Rises/BUtLkp3VPUC?hl=en&gbpv=1&bsq=gradually,%20then.

3 "Depoliticizing Corporate America: Strive Asset Management Launches to Advance Excellence Capitalism over 'Stakeholder Capitalism,'" Business Wire, May 9, 2022, https://www.businesswire.com/news/home/20220509006251/en/Depoliticizing-Corporate-America-Strive-Asset-Management-Launches-To-Advance-Excellence-Capitalism-Over-%E2%80%98Stakeholder-Capitalism%E2%80%99.

4 Ibid.

5 "The Net Zero Asset Managers Initiative," Net Zero Asset Managers (NZAM), accessed May 7, 2024, https://www.netzeroassetmanagers.org.

6 "The Net Zero Asset Managers Commitment," Net Zero Asset Managers (NZAM), December 2021, https://www.netzeroassetmanagers.org/media/2021/12/NZAM-Commitment.pdf.

7 Giulia Christianson, Ariel Pinchot, and Yili Wu, "How BlackRock and Vanguard Can Advance the Net-Zero Emissions Movement," World Resources Institute, April 16, 2021, https://www.wri.org/insights/how-blackrock-and-vanguard-can-advance-net-zero-emissions-movement.

8 "Net Zero Asset Managers Initiative Publishes Initial Targets for 43 Signatories as the Number of Asset Managers Committing to Net Zero Grows to 273," Net Zero Asset Managers, May 31, 2022, https://www.netzeroassetmanagers.org/net-zero-asset-managers-initiative-publishes-initial-targets-for-43-signatories-as-the-number-of-asset-managers-committing-to-net-zero-grows-to-273.

9 Christianson, Pinchot, and Wu, "How BlackRock and Vanguard Can Advance."

10   Ron DeSantis: 46th Governor of Florida, "Governor Ron DeSantis Takes Action against Communist China and Woke Corporations," press release, December 20, 2021, https://www.flgov.com/2021/12/20/governor-ron-desantis-takes-action-against-communist-china-and-woke-corporations.

11   Ron DeSantis: 46th Governor of Florida, "Governor Ron DeSantis Announces Initiatives to Protect Floridians from ESG Financial Fraud," press release, July 27, 2022, https://www.flgov.com/2022/07/27/governor-ron-desantis-announces-initiatives-to-protect-floridians-from-esg-financial-fraud.

12   Patrick Temple-West and Brooke Masters, "Florida to Pull $2bn from BlackRock in Spreading ESG Backlash," *Financial Times*, December 1, 2022, https://www.ft.com/content/38f87ec9-41c6-441d-a6c2-314ff0435166.

13   Ross Kerber, "Florida Pulls $2 Bln from BlackRock in Largest Anti-ESG Divestment," Reuters, December 1, 2022, https://www.reuters.com/business/finance/florida-pulls-2-bln-blackrock-largest-anti-esg-divestment-2022-12-01.

14   Mike Pence, "Republicans Can Stop ESG Political Bias," *Wall Street Journal*, December 1, 2022, https://www.wsj.com/articles/only-republicans-can-stop-the-esg-madness-woke-musk-consumer-demand-free-speech-corporate-america-11653574189.

15   Riley Moore to John Kerry, May 25, 2021, https://www.documentcloud.org/documents/23599730-west-virginia-treasurer-riley-moores-letter-to-john-kerry-on-fossil-fuel-lending-52521.

16   Ibid, 1.

17   Ibid, 2.

18   Riley Moore to "To Whom It May Concern in the U.S. Banking Industry," State of West Virginia, Office of the Treasurer, November 22, 2012, 1, https://www.documentcloud.org/documents/23599684-west-virginia-treasurer-riley-moores-letter-fossil-banking-letter-to-whom-it-may-concern-in-the-us-banking-industry-112221.

19   Alicia McElhaney, "West Virginia Treasury Drops BlackRock over Stance on Climate Risk," Institutional Investor, January 18, 2022, https://www.institutionalinvestor.com/

article/2bstlkf8328cq1951648w/corner-office/west-virginia-treasury-drops-blackrock-over-stance-on-climate-risk.

20 Mark Brnovich et al. to Laurence D. Fink, August 4, 2022, https://mcusercontent.com/cc1fad182b6d6f8b1e352e206/files/5b-cd9811-ee15-e7a3-0a00-923a9b327aa7/BlackRock_Letter.pdf.

21 Ibid.

22 "ESG Practices Conflicting with Law, Jeff Landry Issues Guidance to State Retirement Systems," Jeff Landry, accessed June 6, 2024, https://jefflandry.com/esg-practices-conflicting-with-louisiana-law-attorney-general-jeff-landry-issues-legal-guidance-to-state-retirement-systems.

23 Todd Rokita, Attorney General of Indiana, to the Honorable Eric Koch, September 1, 2022, https://content.govdelivery.com/attachments/INAG/2022/09/01/file_attachments/2259125/Official%20Opinion%202022-3.pdf.

24 Julie Bycowicz and Angel Au-Yeung, "Conservatives Have a New Rallying Cry: Down With ESG," *Wall Street Journal*, February 26, 2023, https://www.wsj.com/articles/conservatives-have-a-new-rallying-cry-down-with-esg-2ef98725?st=5uidkpaofr84lvu.

25 Ibid.

26 Ibid.

27 "Who Is Larry Fink?," WhoIsLarryFink, accessed May 7, 2024, https://whoislarryfink.com.

28 "About BlackRock: Consumer Warning," About BlackRock, accessed May 7, 2024, https://aboutblackrock.com.

29 Ibid.

30 Kerber, "Florida Pulls $2 Bln."

31 Louisiana State Treasurer John M. Shroder, "Shroder Protects Treasury Funds from ESG," press release, October 5, 2022, https://www.treasury.la.gov/_files/ugd/a4de8b_588fa93a5a9242009b177e54f556f4ce.pdf.

32 Office of the Arizona Treasurer Kimberly Lee, Treasurer, "Arizona Treasurer Kimberly Yee Statement on BlackRock Divestments," press release, December 8, 2022, https://www.aztreasury.gov/_files/ugd/8bb536_a5f39955155343c5a9f0b71d6027bd83.pdf.

33 Allie Morris, "Texas' Teacher Pension Fund Shed $500M in

BlackRock Investments over Fossil Fuel Law," *Dallas Morning News*, March 10, 2023, https://www.dallasnews.com/news/politics/2023/03/10/texas-teacher-pension-fund-shed-500m-in-blackrock-investments-over-fossil-fuel-law.

34 Vivek Malek, "Treasurer Fitzpatrick Announces MOSER Has Pulled $500 Million in State Pension Funds from BlackRock" press release, October 18, 2022, https://treasurer.mo.gov/news-room/news-and-events-item?pr=80669a5f-5c6b-491f-a0f0-6abe4c012604.

35 Brian Croce, "South Carolina Treasurer to Pull $200 Million from BlackRock over ESG Concerns," Pensions&Investments, October 11, 2022, https://www.pionline.com/esg/south-carolina-latest-red-state-divest-blackrock-funds-over-esg-concerns.

36 Michael R. Wickline, "Arkansas State Treasurer Yanks about $125M Out of Accounts Managed by BlackRock," *Arkansas Democrat-Gazette*, March 17, 2022, https://www.arkansasonline.com/news/2022/mar/17/arkansas-state-treasurer-yanks-about-125m-out-of.

37 Tom Fitzpatrick, "Utah's State Treasurer Pulls Millions from Investment Firm over Its Climate and Social Agenda," *Salt Lake Tribune*, September 18, 2022, https://www.sltrib.com/news/politics/2022/09/18/utah-state-treasurer-pulls.

38 Karin Rives, "West Virginia Fires BlackRock over Asset Manager's Climate and China Stance," S&P Global Market Intelligence, January 18, 2022, https://www.spglobal.com/marketintelligence/en/news-insights/latest-news-headlines/west-virginia-fires-blackrock-over-asset-manager-s-climate-and-china-stance-68468375.

39 Bryan Bashur, "BlackRock Divestment Tracker," Americans for Tax Reform, April 5, 2024, https://www.atr.org/esgradar.

40 "Charting the Course for Economic Freedom: 2023 Annual Report," SFOF (State Financial Officers' Foundation), 2023, https://www.dropbox.com/scl/fi/r1updvs8c9iq4iil3yh1q/SFOF-2023AnnualReportOptimized.pdf?rlkey=dyrvby1sjrzw3ztpywj8x-ej6b&e=2&dl=0.

41 Aaron Kinsey (@AaronKinseyTX), "Today, Texas Permanent

School Fund leadership delivered an official notice to global asset manager BlackRock terminating its financial management of approximately $8.5 billion. . . .," X, March 19, 2024, 10:10 a.m., https://twitter.com/AaronKinseyTX/status/1770090460935020835.

42   DeSantis War Room (@DeSantisWar Room), "WATCH: BlackRock CEO Larry Fink now says he's 'ashamed' of ESG, admits @RonDeSantis 'hurt' his firm by pulling $2 billion in assets. This is a win . . . but DeSantis is just getting started," X, June 27, 2023, 10:09 a.m., https://twitter.com/DeSantisWarRoom/status/1673695148193067010.

43   Larry Fink, "Larry Fink's 2018 Letter to CEOs: A Sense of Purpose," 2018, BlackRock, https://www.blackrock.com/corporate/investor-relations/2018-larry-fink-ceo-letter.

44   Larry Fink, "Larry Fink's 2020 Letter to CEOs: A Fundamental Reshaping of Finance," BlackRock, 2020, https://www.blackrock.com/corporate/investor-relations/2020-larry-fink-ceo-letter.

45   Ibid.

46   Larry Fink, "Larry Fink's 2021 Letter to CEOs," BlackRock, 2021, https://www.blackrock.com/corporate/investor-relations/2021-larry-fink-ceo-letter.

47   Sanjai Bhagat, "An Inconvenient Truth about ESG Investing," *Harvard Business Review*, March 31, 2022, https://hbr.org/2022/03/an-inconvenient-truth-about-esg-investing.

48   Aneesh Raghunandan and Shiva Rajgopal, "Do ESG Funds Make Stakeholder-Friendly Investments?," *Review of Accounting Studies* 27, June 27, 2022, https://link.springer.com/article/10.1007/s11142-022-09693-1.

49   Tim Quinson, "Big ESG Funds Are Doing Worse than the S&P 500: Green Insight," Bloomberg, December 7, 2022, https://www.bloomberg.com/news/articles/2022-12-07/big-esg-funds-are-doing-worse-than-the-s-p-500-green-insight.

50   Rupert Darwell, "2022: The Year ESG Fell to Earth," RealClearEnergy, December 27, 2022, https://www.realclearenergy.org/articles/2022/12/27/2022_the_year_esg_fell_to_earth_872040.html.

51   Tommy Wilkes and Patturaja Murugaboopathy, "ESG Funds

Set for First Annual Outflows in a Decade after Bruising Year," Reuters, December 19, 2022, https://www.reuters.com/business/ sustainable-business/esg-funds-set-first-annual-outflows-decade-after-bruising-year-2022-12-19.

52   Mike Edleson and Andy Puzder, "Is ESG Profitable? The Numbers Don't Lie," *Wall Street Journal*, March 10, 2023, https:// www.wsj.com/articles/is-esg-profitable-the-numbers-dont-lie-benchmarks-analytics-politics-neutral-fiduciary-duty-market-woke-5da4a533.

53   "Motion to Intervene and Protest by Consumers' Research, Inc." in United States of America before the Federal Energy Regulatory Commission, accessed May 7, 2024, 2, https://consumersresearch.org/wp-content/uploads/2023/01/FERC-Protest_Consumers-Research58.pdf.

54   Will Hild, "End Vanguard's ESG Meddling with Utilities," *Wall Street Journal*, December 1, 2022, https://www.wsj. com/articles/end-vanguards-esg-meddling-with-utilities-11669938471?st=d2fua915xqfjbzy&reflink=share_mobilewebshare.

55   "An Update on Vanguard's Engagement with the Net Zero Asset Managers Initiative (NZAM)," Vanguard, December 7, 2022, https://corporate.vanguard.com/content/corporatesite/us/en/ corp/articles/update-on-nzam-engagement.html.

56   Ibid.

57   Ibid.

58   Ibid.

59   Ibid.

60   Chris Flood et al., "Vanguard Chief Defends Decision to Pull Asset Manager Out of Climate Alliance," *Financial Times*, February 20, 2023, https://www.ft.com/content/9dab65dd-64c8-40c0-ae6e-fac4689dcc77.

61   End Wokeness (@EndWokeness), "Why has everything gone woke these days? ESG scores. Here is BlackRock CEO Larry Fink along with the CEO of AmEx explaining his desire to 'force behaviors' (2017)," X, June 4, 2023, 1:46 p.m. https://twitter.com/ EndWokeness/status/1665414711188287489.

62   Flood et al., "Vanguard Chief."

63 Terrence Keeley, "Vanguard's CEO Bucks the ESG Orthodoxy: Tim Buckley Pulls Out of the Net Zero Managers Initiative and Affirms His Fiduciary Duty to Clients," *Wall Street Journal*, February 23, 2023, https://www.wsj.com/articles/vanguards-ceo-bucks-the-esg-orthodoxy-tim-buckley-net-zero-emissions-united-nations-initiative-nzam-f6ae910d.

64 Flood et al., "Vanguard Chief."

65 Leo Almazora, "Vanguard Announces CEO Tim Buckley to Retire," Industry News, February 29, 2024, https://www.investmentnews.com/industry-news/news/vanguard-announces-ceo-tim-buckley-to-retire-250203#:~:text=It%E2%80%99s%20the%20end%20of%20an%20era%20as%20Vanguard%2C,including%20more%20than%20six%20years%20at%20the%20helm.

66 Vanguard, "Vanguard Announces Appointment of Salim Ramji as New CEO," press release, May 14, 2024, https://corporate.vanguard.com/content/corporatesite/us/en/corp/who-we-are/pressroom/press-release-vanguard-announces-appointment-salim-ramji-new-ceo-05142024.html.

67 Ibid.

68 Celia Huber, "Ron O'Hanley of State Street on Corporate Resilience and ESG," McKinsey & Company, July 13, 2021, https://www.mckinsey.com/capabilities/strategy-and-corporate-finance/our-insights/ron-ohanley-of-state-street-on-corporate-resilience-and-esg.

69 Ibid.

70 Ibid.

71 Ibid.

72 Ibid.

73 Ibid.

74 Will Hild (@WillHild), ".[sic]@StateStreet Global Chief Investment Officer Lori Heinel sends a shot across the bow at @BlackRock and CEO Larry Fink: 'We are actually quite concerned. . . .,'" X, December 15, 2022, 1:10 p.m., https://twitter.com/WillHild/status/1603452522680795156.

75 Ibid.

76 Will Hild (@WillHild), "@StateStreet Global Chief Investment

Officer Lori Heinel admits ESG is *NOT* a performance en-hancer. . . .," X, December 15, 2022, 3:49 p.m., https://twitter.com/WillHild/status/1603492415410692111.

77 DeSantis War Room (@DeSantisWar Room), "WATCH."

78 Charles Gasparino, "BlackRock's 'No. 1' Goal in 'Woke' Investing: Huge ESG-Funds Haul," *New York Post*, June 5, 2021, https://nypost.com/2021/06/05/blackrocks-no-1-goal-in-woke-investing-huge-esg-funds-haul.

79 DeSantis War Room (@DeSantisWar Room), "WATCH."

80 Jack Pitcher, "Step Aside, ESG. BlackRock Is Doing 'Transition Investing' Now," *Wall Street Journal*, March 3, 2024, https://www.wsj.com/finance/investing/step-aside-esg-blackrock-is-doing-transition-investing-now-59df3908.

81 Alyssa Stankiewicz, "U.S. Sustainable Funds Register First Annu-al Outflows in 2023," Morningstar, January 17, 2024, https://www.morningstar.com/sustainable-investing/us-sustainable-funds-register-first-annual-outflows-2023.

82 Ibid.

83 *A Bad Day at Black Rock*, directed by John Sturges, written by Millard Kaufman, Don McGuire, and Howard Breslin (Metro-Goldwyn-Mayer, 1955).

84 Berhard Warner, "Investors Pull Billions from Sustainable Funds amid Political Heat: A New Report Showed That $13 Billion Was Withdrawn Last Year from Funds that Invest in Companies with Environmental, Social and Governance Principles," *New York Times*, January 19, 2024, https://www.nytimes.com/2024/01/19/business/esg-funds-withdrawals.html#:~:text=Investors%20pulled%20%245%20billion%20out,funds.

85 Frances Schwartzkopff, "US Investor Exodus Deals Historic Blow to Global ESG Fund Market," Bloomberg, January 25, 2024, https://www.bloomberg.com/news/articles/2024-01-25/sustainable-funds-see-first-ever-global-quarterly-net-outflows.

86 Ibid.

87 About Climate Action 100+," Climate Action 100+, accessed May 7, 2024, https://www.climateaction100.org/about.

88 "Climate Action 100+ Signatory Handbook, Climate Action,

June 2023, 18, https://www.climateaction100.org/wp-content/
uploads/2023/06/Signatory-Handbook-2023-Climate-
Action-100.pdf.

89   About Climate Action 100+."

90   Emma Simon, "US Asset Management Giants Quit Climate Coalition," Corporate Adviser, February 20, 2024, https://corporate-
adviser.com/us-asset-management-giants-quit-climate-coalition.

91   "An ESG Asset Manager Exodus," editorial, *Wall Street Journal*,
February 15, 2024, https://www.wsj.com/articles/climate-action-
100-exodus-j-p-morgan-state-street-blackrock-esg-investing-
b78d2a06.

92   Mark Brnovich, "ESG May Be an Antitrust Violation," *Wall
Street Journal*, March 6, 2022, https://www.wsj.com/articles/
esg-may-be-an-antitrust-violation-climate-activism-energy-
prices-401k-retirement-investment-political-agenda-coordinated-
influence-11646594807.

93   Ibid.

94   Austen Knudsen et al., "Dear Asset Manager," March 30,
2023, 3, https://content.govdelivery.com/attachments/
MTAG/2023/03/30/file_attachments/2453301/2023-03-30%20
Asset%20Manager%20letter%20Press%20FINAL.pdf.

95   Ibid, omitting internal citation.

96   "An ESG Asset Manager Exodus."

97   Patrick Temple-West and Brooke Masters, "JPMorgan and State
Street Quit Climate Group as BlackRock Scales Back," *Financial
Times*, February 15, 2024, https://www.ft.com/content/3ce06a6f-
f0e3-4f70-a078-82a6c265ddc2.

98   Ibid.

99   Alastair Marsh, "Climate Investors Warn the Right Is Winning
the War on ESG," Bloomberg, February 28, 2024, https://www.
bloomberg.com/news/articles/2024-02-28/climate-investors-
warn-the-right-is-winning-the-war-on-esg.

100   C. S. Lewis, *God in the Dock: Essays on Theology*, ed. Walter
Hooper (Wm. B. Eerdmans Publishing Co., 2014), https://www.
goodreads.com/quotes/526469-of-all-tyrannies-a-tyranny-sin-
cerely-exercised-for-the-good.

101   Pete Townshend, "Won't Get Fooled Again," *Who's Next*, Rolling Stones Marble , 1971.

Chapter 9: Their Words May Change, Their Policies Do Not

1   Megan Conner, "Interview: Cate Blanchett: 'You Know You're a Pessimist When You Win an Oscar and Think, 'Oh God, I've Peaked,'" *The Guardian*, November 30, 2013, https://www.theguardian.com/film/2013/nov/30/cate-blanchett-actor-pessimist-oscar.

2   John Frank, "Black Rock CEO Larry Fink 'Ashamed' to Be Part of ESG Political Debate," Axios, June 25, 2023, https://www.axios.com/2023/06/26/larry-fink-ashamed-esg-weaponized-desantis.

3   Ibid.

4   "Conscientious Capitalism Initiative: Inspire and Teach," Leavey School of Business, Santa Clara University, accessed June 1, 2024, https://www.scu.edu/business/about/strategic-priorities/conscientious-capitalism.

5   David Henzel, "How and Why to Apply 'Conscious Capitalism' to Your Business," *Forbes*, August 4, 2023, https://www.forbes.com/sites/theyec/2023/08/04/how-and-why-to-apply-conscious-capitalism-to-your-business/?sh=1cb168ef2856.

6   DeSantis War Room (@DeSantisWar Room), "WATCH: Black-Rock CEO Larry Fink now says he's 'ashamed' of ESG, admits @RonDeSantis 'hurt' his firm by pulling $2 billion in assets. This is a win . . . but DeSantis is just getting started," X, June 27, 2023, 10:09 a.m., https://twitter.com/DeSantisWarRoom/status/1673695148193067010.

7   Larry Fink, "Larry Fink's 2024 Annual Chairman's Letter to Investors," BlackRock, 2024, https://www.blackrock.com/corporate/investor-relations/larry-fink-annual-chairmans-letter.

8   Ibid.

9   "Investor Signatories," Climate Action 100+, accessed May 7, 2024, https://www.climateaction100.org/whos-involved/investors.

10 "Moving from Words to Action on Climate: ESG Currents," Bloomberg, March 20, 2024, https://www.bloomberg.com/news/audio/2024-03-20/climate-action-100-on-moving-from-words-to-action-esg-currents.

11 "The Net Zero Asset Managers Initiative," Net Zero Assets Managers (NZAM), accessed May 7, 2024, https://www.netzeroassetmanagers.org.

12 "S&P 500® ESG Index: Integrating ESG Values into the Core," S&P Dow Jones Indices: A Division of S&P Global, accessed May 7, 2024, https://www.spglobal.com/spdji/en/documents/additional-material/brochure-sp-500-esg-index.pdf.

13 "BlackRock Investing Stewardship: Proxy Voting Guidelines for U.S. Securities," Blackrock, January 2024, 8, https://www.blackrock.com/corporate/literature/fact-sheet/blk-responsible-investment-guidelines-us.pdf.

14 Ibid, 9.

15 Ibid.

16 "Global Proxy Voting and Engagement Policy," State Street Global Advisors, March 25, 2024, 9, https://www.ssga.com/library-content/assets/pdf/global/asset-stewardship/proxy-voting-and-engagement-policy.pdf.

17 Ibid.

18 Ibid, 10.

19 Ibid.

20 "Vanguard-Advised Funds: Proxy Voting Policy for U.S. Portfolio Companies," Vanguard, February 2024, 4, https://corporate.vanguard.com/content/dam/corp/advocate/investment-stewardship/pdf/policies-and-reports/us_proxy_voting_policy_2024.pdf.

21 Ibid., 6.

22 Ibid.

23 "BlackRock Investing Stewardship: Proxy Voting Guidelines," 20.

24 Ibid.

25 "Our Approach to Engagement on Human Capital Management: Investment Stewardship," BlackRock, 2024, 1, https://www.blackrock.com/corporate/literature/publication/

blk-commentary-engagement-on-human-capital.pdf.

26   "Global Proxy Voting and Engagement Policy," 16.

27   "EEO Data Collections," U.S. Equal Employment Opportunity Commission, accessed May 7, 2024, https://www.eeoc.gov/data/eeo-data-collections#:~:text=The%20EEO-1%20Component%201%20report%20is%20a%20mandatory,sex%20and%20race%20or%20ethnicity%2C%20to%20the%20EEOC.

28   "Global Proxy Voting and Engagement Policy," 28.

29   "Vanguard-Advised Funds: Proxy Voting Policy," 11.

30   Ibid.

31   Ibid.

32   Students for Fair Admissions, Inc. v. President and Fellows of Harvard College, 600 U.S. 81 (2023), at 29, https://www.supreme-court.gov/opinions/22pdf/20-1199_hgdj.pdf.

33   Title VII of the Civil Rights Act of 1964, U.S. Equal Employment Opportunity Commission, accessed May 7, 2024, https://www.eeoc.gov/statutes/title-vii-civil-rights-act-1964.

34   Michael Toff, "Is Your Company's DEI Program Lawful?," *Wall Street Journal*, July 2, 2023, https://www.wsj.com/articles/is-your-companys-dei-program-lawful-business-title-vii-race-affirmative-action-harvard-cd4d9582.

35   Corporate America Promised to Hire a Lot More People of Color. It Actually Did.," Bloomberg, September 25, 2023, https://www.bloomberg.com/graphics/2023-black-lives-matter-equal-opportunity-corporate-diversity.

36   Ibid, 17.

37   Ibid.

38   Chris Flood et al., "Vanguard Chief Defends Decision to Pull Asset Manager Out of Climate Alliance," *Financial Times*, February 20, 2023, https://www.ft.com/content/9dab65dd-64c8-40c0-ae6e-fac4689dcc77.

39   "BlackRock Investing Stewardship: Proxy Voting Guidelines," 17–18.

40   "International Sustainability Standards Board," IFRS (International Financial Reporting Standards Foundation), 2024, https://www.ifrs.org/groups/

international-sustainability-standards-board.

41   "IFRS S1 General Requirements for Disclosure of Sustainability-Related Financial Information," IFRS (International Financial Reporting Standards Foundation), June 2023, https://www.ifrs.org/issued-standards/ifrs-sustainability-standards-navigator/ifrs-s1-general-requirements.

42   "IFRS S2 Climate-related Disclosures," IFRS (International Financial Reporting Standards Foundation), June 2023, https://www.ifrs.org/issued-standards/ifrs-sustainability-standards-navigator/ifrs-s2-climate-related-disclosures.

43   "BlackRock Investing Stewardship: Proxy Voting Guidelines," 18.

44   Ibid.

45   Ibid.

46   Ibid.

47   "Climate-Related Risks and the Low-Carbon Transition: Investment Stewardship," Blackrock, 2024, 1, https://www.blackrock.com/corporate/literature/publication/blk-commentary-climate-risk-and-energy-transition.pdf.

48   Ibid., 2.

49   Ibid., 3.

50   Ibid., 1.

51   Ibid.

52   "Global Proxy Voting and Engagement Policy," 24.

53   Ibid., 26.

54   Ibid., 24.

55   Ibid, 15.

56   "BlackRock Investing Stewardship: Proxy Voting Guidelines," 18–19.

57   "Vanguard-Advised Funds: Proxy Voting Policy," 11.

58   Ibid.

59   Ibid.

60   Julie Hyman, "Fossil Fuels Aren't Going Anywhere Anytime Soon, Big Energy Says," Yahoo!Finance, March 20, 2024, https://finance.yahoo.com/news/fossil-fuels-arent-going-anywhere-anytime-soon-big-energy-says-100046288.html.

61   Ibid.

62 Brad Plumer and Nadja Popovich, "A New Surge in Power Use Is Threatening U.S. Climate Goals," *New York Times*, March 14, 2024, https://www.nytimes.com/interactive/2024/03/13/climate/electric-power-climate-change.html?action=click&pgtype=Article&state=default&module=styln-climate&variant=show&region=MAIN_CONTENT_1&block=storyline_levelup_swipe_recirc.

63 Ibid.

64 Spencer Kimball, "Saudi Aramco CEO Says Energy Transition Is Failing, World Should Abandon 'Fantasy' of Phasing Out Oil," CNBC, March 18, 2024, https://www.cnbc.com/2024/03/18/saudi-aramco-ceo-says-energy-transition-is-failing-give-up-fantasy-of-phasing-out-oil.html.

65 Max Bearak and Brad Plumer, "At CERAWeek, Saudi Aramco C.E.O. Says Energy Transition 'Visibly Failing,'" *New York Times*, March 19, 2024, https://www.nytimes.com/2024/03/19/climate/ceraweek-saudi-fantasy-energy-transition.html.

66 Kimball, "Saudi Aramco CEO Says Energy Transition is Failing."

67 "World Energy Outlook 2023," IEA (International Energy Agency), 2023, https://origin.iea.org/reports/world-energy-outlook-2023.

68 Bearak and Plumer, "At CERAWeek."

69 Kate Aronoff, "Oil Executives Are Getting Refreshingly Honest These Days," *New Republic*, March 20, 2024, https://newrepublic.com/article/179949/exxon-conocophillips-oil-climate-change.

70 Chevron, "Chevron Announces Agreement to Acquire Hess," press release, October 23, 2023, https://www.chevron.com/newsroom/2023/q4/chevron-announces-agreement-to-acquire-hess.

71 ExxonMobil, "ExxonMobil Announces Merger with Pioneer Natural Resources in an All-Stock Transaction," press release, October 11, 2023, https://corporate.exxonmobil.com/news/news-releases/2023/1011_exxonmobil-announces-merger-with-pioneer-natural-resources-in-an-all-stock-transaction.

72 "Why One-Time Exxon's Exxon Adversary's Board Picks Backed Mega Deal," Bloomberg, October 12, 2023, https://www.bloomberg.com/news/articles/2023-10-12/

exxon-s-one-time-adversary-engine-no-1-unanimously-backed-deal.

73   Catherine Clifford, "Why Exxon and Chevron Are Doubling Down on Fossil Fuel Energy with Big Acquisitions," NBC News, October 25, 2023, https://www.nbcnews.com/science/environment/exxon-chevron-are-doubling-fossil-fuel-energy-big-acquisitions-rcna122094.

74   Ibid.

75   Troy Segal, "Understanding Private Equity (PE)," Investopedia, updated February 9, 2024, https://www.investopedia.com/articles/financial-careers/09/private-equity.asp.

76   "S&P_500_130/30_Strategy_Index Methodology," S&P Dow Jones Indices, March 2011, 5, https://www.spglobal.com/spdji/en/documents/methodologies/methodology-sp-500-130-30-strategy-index.pdf.

77   Kevin McVeigh "Why the S&P 500 Isn't What You Think It Is," *Engage Capital Management Blog*, September 25, 2018, https://www.exchangecapital.com/blog/why-the-sp-500-isnt-what-you-think-it-is#:~:text=Although%20the%20S%26P%20500%20overseers%20stated%20belief%20is,percent%20annually%2C%20or%20approximately%2022%20changes%20each%20year.

Chapter 10: This Is Not Over—but There Is Hope

1   Winston Churchill, speech at the Lord Mayor's Luncheon, Mansion House, London, November 10, 1942, https://www.iwm.org.uk/collections/item/object/1030031903.

2   Lindsey Stewart, "Big U.S. Fund Companies Retreat on Support for ESG Proxy Votes," Morningstar, January 11, 2024, https://www.morningstar.com/sustainable-investing/big-us-fund-companies-retreat-support-esg-proxy-votes.

3   "Investor Stewardship_2023," Diligent Market Intelligence, 2023, 6, https://learn.diligent.com/rs/946-AVX-095/images/Investor_Stewardship_2023.pdf?version=0.

4   Alan Murray and Nicholas Gordon, "Vanguard, BlackRock, State Street Vote Down ESG Proposals," *Fortune*, October 31, 2023,

https://fortune.com/2023/10/31/blackrock-vanguard-state-street-esg-proposals-voting.

5   "Our Mission," Committee to Unleash Prosperity, May 7, 2024, https://committeetounleashprosperity.com/our-mission.

6   Staff of the Committee to Unleash Prosperity, "Politics over Pensions: The First Annual Report Card on Investment Fund Managers and Proxy Voting Behavior," Committee to Unleash Prosperity, May 2023, 9, https://committeetounleashprosperity.com/wp-content/uploads/2023/05/PensionPolitics_Report-1.pdf.

7   Ibid., 6.

8   Ibid., 3.

9   Jerry Bowyer, Stephen Moore, and the Staff of the Committee to Unleash Prosperity, "Putting Politics over Pensions: The 2024 Committee to Unleash Prosperity Report Card on Investment Fund Managers and Proxy Voting Behavior," Committee to Unleash Prosperity, April 2024, 8, https://www.pensionpolitics.com/wp-content/uploads/2024/04/PensionPolitics-2024-Report.pdf.

10 Ibid., 4.

11 Ibid., 7.

12 1792 Exchange, "1792 Launches New Database Tracking Political Bias of Executives and Board Members of Fortune 250 Companies," press release, April 2, 2024, https://1792exchange.com/press-releases/1792-exchange-launches-new-database-tracking-political-bias-of-executives-and-board-members-at-fortune-250-companies.

13 1792 Exchange, "New Proxy Voting Database Shows Asset Managers' ESG Agenda Abuses Taxpayer Funds," press release, September 14, 2023, https://1792exchange.com/press-releases/new-proxy-voting-database-shows-asset-managersesg-agenda-abuses-taxpayer-funds.

14 Ibid.

15 "Empowering Investors through BlackRock Voting Choice," BlackRock, 2024, https://www.blackrock.com/corporate/about-us/investment-stewardship/blackrock-voting-choice.

16 "Proxy Voting Choice Empowers Investors," State Street Global Advisors, 2024, https://www.ssga.com/us/en/intermediary/etfs/

about-us/what-we-do/asset-stewardship/proxy-voting-choice.

17   "Vanguard to Expand Proxy Voting Choice to Additional Funds in 2024," Vanguard, December 5, 2023, https://corpo-rate.vanguard.com/content/corporatesite/us/en/corp/articles/expanding-proxy-voting-choice.html.

18   "Empowering Investors through BlackRock Voting Choice."

19   "BlackRock to Expand Proxy Voting Choice to Its Largest ETF," Business Wire, July 17, 2023, https://www.businesswire.com/news/home/20230717296297/en/BlackRock-to-Expand-Proxy-Voting-Choice-to-Its-Largest-ETF.

20   "Proxy Voting Choice Empowers Investors"; Ross Gerber, "State Street to Offer Proxy Voting Choices to Retail Investors," Reuters, May 22, 2023, https://www.reuters.com/business/finance/state-street-offer-proxy-voting-choices-retail-investors-2023-05-22/; State Street Global Advisors, "State Street Global Advisors to Extend Proxy Voting Choice to ETFs and Mutual Funds," press release, May 22, 2023, https://investors.statestreet.com/investor-news-events/press-releases/news-details/2023/State-Street-Global-Advisors-to-Extend-Proxy-Voting-Choice-to-ETFs-and-Mutual-Funds/default.aspx; Vanguard, "Vanguard Launches Proxy Voting Choice Pilot," press release, February 1, 2023, https://corporate.vanguard.com/content/corporatesite/us/en/corp/who-we-are/pressroom/press-release-vanguard-launches-proxy-voting-choice-pilot-020123.html?mod=article_inline; "Vanguard to Expand Proxy Voting Choice to Additional Funds in 2024."

21   "Our Approach to Engagement on Incentives Aligned with Financial Value Creation," BlackRock, January 2024, 1, https://www.blackrock.com/corporate/literature/publication/blk-commentary-engagement-on-incentives-aligned-with-value-creation.pdf.

22   "About ISS," ISS (Institutional Shareholder Services), May 7, 2024, https://www.issgovernance.com/about/about-iss.

23   "Glass Lewis," Glass Lewis, accessed May 7, 2024, https://www.glasslewis.com.

24   "Voting Policies 2024," ISS (Institutional Shareholder Services),

2024, https://www.issgovernance.com/policy-gateway/voting-policies; "2024 Glass Lewis Proxy Voting Policies," Glass Lewis, 2024, https://www.glasslewis.com/voting-policies-2024.

25   "Cracking the Proxy Advisory Duopoly," editorial, *Wall Street Journal*, July 12, 2023, https://www.wsj.com/articles/proxy-advisory-firms-glass-lewis-institutional-shareholder-services-esg-investing-761e044f.

26   "United States Proxy Voting Guidelines: Benchmark Policy Recommendations," ISS (Institutional Shareholder Services, January 2024, https://www.issgovernance.com/file/policy/active/americas/US-Voting-Guidelines.pdf?v=1; "United States 2024 Benchmark Policy Guidelines," Glass Lewis, November 2023, https://www.glasslewis.com/wp-content/uploads/2023/11/2024-US-Benchmark-Policy-Guidelines-Glass-Lewis.pdf.

27   Sean D. Reyes et al. to Gary Retelny and Kevin Cameron, January 17, 2023, 7, https://ag.ks.gov/docs/default-source/documents/2023-01-17-utah-texas-letter-to-glass-lewis-iss.pdf?sfvrsn=372cbd1a_2.

28   Ibid., 3.

29   Ibid., 4.

30   J. Andrew Sorrell et al. to Gary Retelny, October 24, 2023, https://sfof.com/wp-content/uploads/2023/10/Letter-from-SFOF-to-ISS-Regarding-Debanking-1.pdf; J. Andrew Sorrell et al. to Kevin Cameron, October 24, 2023, https://sfof.com/wp-content/uploads/2023/10/Letter-from-SFOF-to-Glass-Lewis-Regarding-Debanking-1.pdf.

31   "Hooray! JP Morgan's Jamie Dimon Fires Leftist Proxy Vote Advisers," Committee to Unleash Prosperity, April 10, 2024, https://committeetounleashprosperity.com/hotlines/hooray-jp-morgans-jamie-dimon-fires-leftist-proxy-vote-advisers.

32   The Staff of the Committee to Unleash Prosperity, "Politics over Pensions," May 2023, 7.

33   Bowyer, Moore, and the Staff of the Committee to Unleash Prosperity, "Politics over Pensions," April 2023, 4.

34   Jamie Dimon, "Annual Report 2023: Chairman & CEO Letter

to Shareholders," JP Morgan Chase & Co., 2024, https://reports. jpmorganchase.com/investor-relations/2023/ar-ceo-letters.htm.

35   Ibid.

36   Lindsey Stewart, "New Proxy-Voting Options for IVV and Other Index Funds from BlackRock, State Street, and Vanguard," Morningstar, December 13, 2023, https://www.morningstar. com/funds/new-proxy-voting-options-ivv-other-index-funds-blackrock-state-street-vanguard.

37   "Voting Choice—Voting Policy Comparison," BlackRock, May 2023, 2, https://www.blackrock.com/corporate/literature/brochure/voting-choice-voting-policy-comparison.pdf.

38   Stewart, "New Proxy-Voting Options."

39   Ibid.

40   "Voting Choice—Voting Policy Comparison," 2.

41   "Summary of Bowyer Research Proxy Voting Guidelines for States," Bowyer Research, accessed May 7, 2024, https://bowyer-research.com/proxy.html.

42   Ibid.

43   "S&P 500® ESG Index: Integrating ESG Values into the Core," S&P Dow Jones Indices: A Division of S&P Global, accessed May 7, 2024, https://www.spglobal.com/spdji/en/documents/additional-material/brochure-sp-500-esg-index.pdf.

44   J. Andrew Sorrell et al. to Ronald O'Hanley, March 14, 2024, https://cdn01.dailycaller.com/wp-content/uploads/2024/03/SFOF-SS-Letter.pdf?utm_campaign=Fiduciary%20Focus&utm_medium=email&_hsmi=298874177&_hsenc=p2ANqtz--BiQWW-mTolioArw2FBVVsjJUabuga9TZ_PpEhtM_549qrRlohcnGxok-bvuYZp6f7n4b7P6O95Zj2uAapoj62agawByRQ&utm_content=298874177&utm_source=hs_email to SFOF-SS-Letter.pdf.

45   Ibid.

46   "Voting Choice—Voting Policy Comparison," 2; "Proxy Voting Choice Empowers Investors."

47   "Voting Choice—Voting Policy Comparison," 2.

48   Ibid.; "Proxy Voting Choice Empowers Investors."

49   "Voting Choice—Voting Policy Comparison," 2.

50   "Your Money, Your Voice: How Vanguard Is Piloting Proxy

Voting Options for Everyday Investors," Vanguard, 2022, https://institutional.vanguard.com/content/dam/inst/iig-transformation/insights/pdf/2023/your-money-your-voice.pdf.

51   Lindsey Stewart, "How BlackRock, State Street and Vanguard ESG Proxy Votes Were Cast," Morningstar, June 12, 2023, https://www.morningstar.com/sustainable-investing/how-blackrock-state-street-vanguard-cast-their-esg-proxy-votes.

52   "Empowering Investors through BlackRock Voting Choice."

53   Ibid.

54   BlackRock, "BlackRock Expands Voting Choice through New Egan-Jones Voting Guidelines and Customization," press release, June 11, 2024, https://www.blackrock.com/corporate/newsroom/press-releases/article/corporate-one/press-releases/blackrock-expands-voting-choice.

55   Ibid.

56   Ibid.

57   "Egan-Jones Proxy Services Standard Proxy Voting Principles and Guidelines," Egan-Jones Proxy Services, 2024, 26, 29, https://irp.cdn-website.com/283ddce3/files/uploaded/Egan-JonesSTANDARDProxyVotingPrinciplesandGuidelines_2024-9e0014f8.pdf.

58   Egan-Jones Proxy Services Wealth Focused Proxy Voting Principles and Guidelines," Egan-Jones Proxy Services, 2024, 27, https://irp.cdn-website.com/283ddce3/files/uploaded/Egan-JonesWEALTHFOCUSEDProxyVotingPrinciplesAndGuidelines_2024-7cd44b58.pdf.

59   Bowyer Research, "Bowyer Research Proxy Voting Guidelines to Be Available through ISS," press release, March 4, 2024, https://www.bowyerresearch.com/docs/Press%20Release%20-%20Voting%20Guidelines.pdf.

60   Ibid.

61   Ross Kerber, "Exclusive: Proxy Adviser ISS Expands Offerings for 'ESG Skeptic' Clients," Reuters, March 4, 2024, https://www.reuters.com/sustainability/boards-policy-regulation/proxy-adviser-iss-expands-offerings-esg-skeptic-clients-2024-03-04.

62   Ibid.

63   Bowyer Research, "Bowyer Research Proxy Voting Guidelines."

64   Ibid.

65   "Bowyer Research Guidelines Product Overview," Bowyer
      Research, February 2024, 4, https://bowyerresearch.com/docs/
      policy_overview.pdf.

66   Bowyer Research, "Bowyer Research Proxy Voting Guidelines."

67   "Summary of Bowyer Research Proxy Voting Guidelines for
      States."

68   Bowyer Research, "Bowyer Research Proxy Voting Guidelines."

69   "Summary of Bowyer Research Proxy Voting Guidelines for
      States."

70   Bowyer Research, "Bowyer Research Proxy Voting Guidelines."

71   Ibid.

Conclusion

1   John Adams to Thomas Jefferson, February 2, 1816, https://
      founders.archives.gov/documents/Jefferson/03-09-02-0285.

2   Larry Fink, "Larry Fink's 2018 Letter to CEOs: A Sense of Pur-
      pose," BlackRock, 2018, https://www.blackrock.com/corporate/
      investor-relations/2018-larry-fink-ceo-letter.

3   "Item 1A. Risk Factors" in BlackRock, "United States Securities
      and Exchange Commission Form 10-K: Annual Report Pursuant
      to Section 13 or 15(d) and the Securities Exchange Act of 1934,"
      February 23, 2024, 32, https://www.sec.gov/Archives/edgar/
      data/1364742/000095017024019271/blk-20231231.htm#item_1a_
      risk_factors.

4   Ibid.

5   Definitions, Tex. Gov't Code § 809.001, 87th Legislature,
      September 1, 2021, https://casetext.com/statute/texas-codes/
      government-code/title-8-public-retirement-systems/subtitle-a-
      provisions-generally-applicable-to-public-retirement-systems/
      chapter-809-prohibition-on-investment-in-financial-companies-
      that-boycott-certain-energy-companies/subchapter-a-general-
      provisions/section-809001-definitions.

6   "Item 1A. Risk Factors," 32.

7   "State Government Employee Retirement Protection Act,"

American Legislative Exchange Council, 2024, https://alec.
org/model-policy/state-government-employee-retirement-
protection-act/; "State Pension Fiduciary Duty Act," accessed
May 7, 2024, Heritage Foundation, https://www.heritage.org/
article/state-pension-fiduciary-duty-act.

8   Ibid; "State Government Employee Retirement Protection Act."

9   "Larry Fink's 2018 Letter to CEOs."

10   Eugene Scalia, "Retirees' Security Trumps Other Social
     Goals," *Wall Street Journal*, June 23, 2020, https://www.wsj.
     com/articles/retirees-security-trumps-other-social-goals-
     11592953329?mod=article_inline.

11   Aaron Kinsey (@AaronKinseyTX), "Today, Texas Perma-
     nent School Fund leadership delivered an official notice to
     global asset manager BlackRock terminating its financial
     management of approximately $8.5 billion. . . .," X, March 19,
     2024, 10:10 a.m., https://twitter.com/AaronKinseyTX/sta-
     tus/1770090460935020835.

12   Ibid.

13   BlackRock (@BlackRock), "Read BlackRock's response to
     @AaronKinseyTX, Chairman of the State Board of Education in
     Texas," X, March 21, 2024, 3:36 p.m., https://twitter.com/Black-
     Rock/status/1770897379195064762.

14   Ibid.

15   Kinsey (@AaronKinseyTX), "Today, Texas."

16   "Larry Fink's 2018 Letter to CEOs."

17   Larry Fink, "Larry Fink's 2024 Annual Chairman's Letter to
     Investors," BlackRock, 2024, https://www.blackrock.com/corpo-
     rate/investor-relations/larry-fink-annual-chairmans-letter.

18   BlackRock (@BlackRock), "Read BlackRock's response."

19   "Civil Enforcement Complaint" in State of Tennessee *ex rel.*
     Jonathan Skrmetti, Attorney General and Reporter v. BlackRock,
     Inc., December 18, 2023, 1, https://www.tn.gov/content/dam/
     tn/attorneygeneral/documents/pr/2023/pr23-59-complaint.
     pdf?utm_campaign=Fiduciary%20Focus&utm_source=hs_
     email&utm_medium=email&_hsenc=p2ANqtz-8n_r32QwN-
     BuWXEw45nlSSBMOMGx-soanoE2xtO066KCg3v3tg-

gVe3sNGEABlaT3tThrpXv.

20   "Summary Cease and Desist Order and Notice of Intent to
     Impose Administrative Penalty," In the Matter of: BlackRock,
     Inc.; BlackRock Investments, LLC; BlackRock Advisors, LLC;
     BlackRock Fund Advisors; and iShares Trust, March 26,
     2024, https://www.sos.ms.gov/content/enforcementactions-
     search/EnforcementActions/BlackRock%20Inc.,%20et%20
     al..pdf?utm_campaign=Fiduciary%20Focus&utm_medi-
     um=email&_hsenc=p2ANqtz-89u2vehB5eLUmR7lA3XsBKxb-
     bZ5ihkMjxObq3UNPy7XZ-Ap71II8conV7Z6YPy7OztdW7t-
     8gAIk18ChlkjwbPE7gXr3g&_hsmi=300850752&utm_con-
     tent=300850752&utm_source=hs_email.
21   "Index Funds Need to Be Passive, Not Political," editorial,
     Bloomberg, May 2, 2024, https://www.bloomberg.com/opinion/
     articles/2024-05-02/big-three-index-funds-need-to-be-passive-
     not-political.
22   Ibid.
23   Ibid.
24   Chris Flood et al., "Vanguard Chief Defends Decision to Pull
     Asset Manager Out of Climate Alliance, *Financial Times*, Febru-
     ary 20, 2024, https://www.ft.com/content/9dab65dd-64c8-40c0-
     ae6e-fac4689dcc77.
25   Staff of the Committee to Unleash Prosperity, "Politics over
     Pensions: The First Annual Report Card on Investment Fund
     Managers and Proxy Voting Behavior," Committee to Unleash
     Prosperity, May 2023, 3, https://committeetounleashprosperity.
     com/wp-content/uploads/2023/05/PensionPolitics_Report-1.pdf.
26   Will Hild (@WillHild), ".[sic]@StateStreet Global Chief Invest-
     ment Officer Lori Heinel sends a shot across the bow at @Black-
     Rock and CEO Larry Fink: 'We are actually quite concerned.
     . . .,'" X, December 15, 2022, 1:10 p.m., https://twitter.com/will-
     hild/status/1603452522680795156?s=12&t=VMUxsgV5QJ2aFb-
     0sYSWdsA.
27   Will Hild (@WillHild), "@StateStreet Global Chief Investment
     Officer Lori Heinel admits ESG is *NOT* a performance en-
     hancer. . . .," X, December 15, 2022, 3:49 p.m., https://twitter.com/

WillHild/status/1603492415410692111.

28   The Staff of the Committee to Unleash Prosperity, "Politics over Pensions," 3.

29   Jerry Bowyer, Stephen Moore, and the Staff of the Committee to Unleash Prosperity, "Putting Politics over Pensions: The 2024 Committee to Unleash Prosperity Report Card on Investment Fund Managers and Proxy Voting Behavior," Committee to Unleash Prosperity, April 2024, 3, https://www.pensionpolitics.com/report.

30   Abraham Lincoln, address to the Young Men's Lyceum, Springfield, Illinois, January 27, 1838, https://www.abrahamlincolnonline.org/lincoln/speeches/lyceum.htm.

Acknowledgements

1   "Remarks at a Meeting of the White House Conference for a Drug Free America," Ronald Reagan Presidential Library & Museum, February 29, 1988, https://www.reaganlibrary.gov/archives/speech/remarks-meeting-white-house-conference-drug-free-america.

INDEX